The EDUCATION OF GEORGE WASHINGTON

The

EDUCATION OF GEORGE WASHINGTON

**HOW A FORGOTTEN BOOK SHAPED
THE CHARACTER OF A HERO**

AUSTIN WASHINGTON

REGNERY
HISTORY

Cataloging-in-Publication data on file with the Library of Congress

ISBN 978-1-62157-205-3

Published in the United States by
Regnery History
An imprint of Regnery Publishing, Inc.
One Massachusetts Avenue NW
Washington, DC 20001
www.RegneryHistory.com

Manufactured in the United States of America

10 9 8 7 6 5 4 3 2 1

Books are available in quantity for promotional or premium use. Write to Director of Special Sales, Regnery Publishing, Inc., One Massachusetts Avenue NW, Washington, DC 20001, for information on discounts and terms, or call (202) 216-0600.

Distributed to the trade by
Perseus Distribution
250 West 57th Street
New York, NY 10107

For you

Contents

Prologue

I grew up with a lock of George Washington's hair on the shelf of my father's closet.

Burglars, take note: I've put it on semi-permanent loan to Mount Vernon. I just like knowing it's still, technically, in the family.

Perhaps more interestingly, I grew up spending my weekends in George Washington's brother's house, which is also still in the family. It's used occasionally for charity events, but the rest of the time, actually lived in. We even built a swimming pool there. An eighteenth-century mud hole might have been more picturesque, but my mother had this thing about germs, so we opted for the modern, blue, and highly chlorinated kind. Some people are no fun.

In the dining room hangs a large portrait of one of two of George Washington's brothers who are great (etc.) grandfathers of mine. In the kitchen there was a much smaller, dirtier, and decrepit-looking picture of a childless great-uncle, whose name, I learned, was George.

It never crossed my mind 'til much later that this George guy was anything but the less important brother—being, as he was, in the kitchen, not the dining room, and having a smaller, dirtier picture.

Since then I've learned that not everyone sees the world the way I did when I was four years old. But, anyway, that's how I first got to know my great (etc.) uncle. It was only much later I began to learn, hype and cherry trees aside, that he actually was an amazing man. A great man, a good man, and a great-uncle.

Most people still don't know that about George Washington. They just see the image, the guy on the dollar bill—like a cartoon character, almost. Mickey Mouse is happy, George Washington is honest. That's about as deep as it goes for most people. Some people admire what he did. But no one in over two centuries has really understood how he did it.

Until now.

This book will reveal the key—a genuine secret, hidden in plain sight for two centuries, that explains how my great-uncle became a great man. This secret might help you do what he did, at least a bit. Be good and great, that is.

George Washington was a poor kid with limited education whose father died when he was only eleven, yet he turned himself—

he consciously and deliberately turned himself—first into one of the richest and most influential men in the country, and then into a man so good that he risked his life, for the second half of his life, fighting for an ideal and winning for us all. (What ideal? The one that a small part of the world still benefits from today—and the rest of the world dreams of. Freedom, liberty, and all that.)

Who does that? Who not only does something amazing for himself—but then turns around and does something even more incredible for other people?

Maybe you, after reading this book.

Some years after discovering the dingy picture of George Washington in the kitchen of our family house, I was studying colonial American history.

One day I was looking at an electronic archive of George Washington's papers when I saw a notice indicating that the archivists were indefinitely postponing putting up his childhood writings. Presumably no one thought these were important.

Well, one person would have disagreed with this decision—George Washington. He strongly believed that "the first transactions…of an individual upon his first entrance into life, make the deepest impression, and are to form the leading traits in [his] character."

Unfortunately, great men, who know how to be great, aren't normally the ones making the decisions about which of their documents are published—with all due respect to archivists and librarians. In fact, if it hadn't been for a bit of providential luck, the decision not to make those childhood writings public might have kept the key to George Washington's character from being known to me. And to you, too.

George Washington didn't become George Washington by accident. He followed a deliberate plan. That plan had disappeared from his papers long ago, but the key to it was there, in plain view, like the purloined letter, hiding in plain sight, taunting biographers and historians for over two centuries.

They had all missed it. The decision of an archivist in a dusty cellar (or, more likely, a climate-controlled, dust-free room, with ten fifty-thousand-dollar air cleaners) might have kept this key from us for another two hundred years—but for the insight of one man.

I first met the man who discovered the secret to George Washington's success in the restaurant of the Army Navy Club in Washington, D.C., just two blocks from the White House. Dr. X doesn't seek publicity, so I'll allow him to remain hidden discreetly behind this devilishly clever alias. He had a big white beard but still carried himself with a military bearing.

Dr. X wanted me to help him raise $60 million for a project he was working on. He figured I could tap my rich friends.

I don't have the heart to tell people—and why would I, it would only spoil the fun—that we Washingtons lost whatever money we once had during the Civil War. Still, through some twists of fate, I *do* know a few counts and billionaires. I mean, c'mon, who doesn't? It's not like I've led a totally sheltered life.

So I vaguely promised to hook Dr. X up and invite my chimerical friends to his fundraising events.

Dr. X had spent part of his career doing something associated with cryptography (precisely what will forever remain a secret—because his info about Uncle George was so cool I forgot to ask him about that. Hey, maybe it really was top secret. I like to think so.)

His skills in cryptography had helped him. He clearly had developed an eye for seeing patterns where others don't see them. Being, at the same time, an historian of American history, he had spent a lot of time with George Washington's papers. Trained to look where other people didn't, Dr. X had carefully examined the papers from George's childhood, overlooked for centuries. Examining these rarely handled documents—writing exercises, two love poems, and George's earliest accounting records—Dr. X had noticed something that no one had ever paid attention to before.

Skeptical of his claim that no one had ever paid attention to this secret hiding in plain sight before, I wrote its name down on a scrap of paper so that I could look it up. Later that day, I couldn't find it mentioned on Google. (By way of contrast, "flying camels" has over twelve million hits. "Two-headed dogs who like lollipops" has over nine hundred thousand. My search, therefore, was really, really, really, really, really, really, really, really rare.)

I searched the online catalogue for the Library of Congress. Nothing.

Dr. X had made a discovery that would change my life...evidence that an object historians and biographers—and librarians and archivisits—had overlooked for two hundred years was the key that George Washington used to turn himself into—well, into George Washington.

A few days later, I was actually looking at the thing he had discovered. A thing from George Washington's school days.

George Washington, you see, had intended to go to the same school his father and older half-brothers had gone to—Appleby, in England. The inflexible and unpragmatic education at Appleby was the sort of education expected of English gentlemen then and, to an extent, to this day. George's older half-brothers read Latin and Greek. (They were as familiar with the ancient world as you may be with Brad and Angelina.)

However, there wasn't enough money left after George's father died for him to follow in their footsteps. George was forced to make do with a local school in the Virginia woods, near the home of his half-brother, Austin Washington.

At that school George learned the kind of pragmatic things that his "better educated" half-brothers would never understand—most notably, surveying and bookkeeping, which were to be vital in George's future life. At Austin's home, however, through conversation, formal tutorials, and reading the books Austin kept in his library, George got at least a smattering of the sorts of ideas and knowledge he would have been immersed in at Appleby.

Ultimately, though, it is only because George was deprived of a "good education" that he got a great education, the one that changed his life.

George is not alone in this.

Churchill read a lot, and even read a lot aloud, both to compensate for what he saw as a defective education and to improve what he saw as a lack of talent as an orator. It seems to have worked. In World War II, Churchill's words were thought to be as powerful as any weapon the Allies possessed. People really can transform themselves.

George, too, read to learn about the world, as well as to implant in his mind a vision of the kind of person he wanted to become. He didn't skim books to prepare for an exam. He read fewer books than his brothers had read, but he read them more deeply—just as Churchill did. A "well-educated" student might see reading as a chore, or a memorization exercise for an exam. For George, reading was a privilege, a key he used to understand the world and expand his mind and horizons. George Washington and Winston Churchill both read to turn themselves into the men—and gentlemen—they seem to have been born to become.

A "better educated" George Washington would surely have been a smoother operator, more facile with ideas, able to incorporate a wider range of references into his conversations, letters, and thinking. Instead, because he was largely an autodidact, George was more deeply educated, ending up with more wisdom than wit. His unusual education affected the core of his being, not just the surface

Left more to his own devices than he would have been at Appleby, George perused his relatives' bookshelves with perhaps the same motivations that we surf the net—to learn, for entertainment, but also to keep boredom at bay. After all, there wasn't much else that could engage your mind in the woods of colonial Virginia. Fortunately, these bookshelves contained a slightly more elevated content than Brad and Angelina's Twitter feed.

We have the evidence in George's own writing that there was a secret key that changed his life. Despite this, several centuries later, I seemed to have been only the second person to realize its significance.

The thing I was looking at was, on a superficial level, a mere book. But that word, somehow, diminishes it. It was a vessel in which the brightest part of a great spirit had lived, undisturbed, since a great man had died, biding its time, waiting to light a spark in whoever came upon it with a receptive and open mind.

The book was not a mere record of a hero's life—it was a record of a hero's character. The character that inspired George Washington to turn himself from a disadvantaged country kid into the George Washington who changed the world. The spirit of this heroic model, the essence of what made him extraordinary, had been captured in the pages of a book written by his friend after his death. That book served as George's guide in his own act of self-creation.

A Panegyrick to the Memory of His Grace Frederick, Late Duke of Schonberg by a certain H. de Luzancy (chaplain and friend to the Duke) is a somewhat effusive recounting of the talents and accomplishments of a seventeenth-century nobleman, a military commander under William of Orange (of "William and Mary" fame) in his successful invasion of England, which culminated in the Glorious Revolution of 1688.

Looks can be deceiving, though. When I first flipped through it, the *Panegyrick* didn't seem special to me. It seemed—well, irrational and effusive in a kind of hagiographic way. That this book has been forgotten seemed no great mystery. The *Panegyrick*, which inspired the fifteen-year-old George Washington to dreams of knights fighting for truth and justice, seemed alien to me, seeing it, for the first time, in a world largely devoid of either truth or justice.

The subject and hero of the book, Frederick, the Duke of Schonberg, was a soldier and leader in a day when you didn't get ahead by slogging through an exam or trading collateralised debt obligations, or—literally or figuratively—jumping (or throwing balls) through hoops. Not that everyone had an ideal character then, any more than now. But the ideals, if not the reality, were more ideal. More noble. More refined. More beautiful.

The King of France, for example, was both head of government and a ballet dancer. You don't tend to see that sort of thing today. Frederick, Duke of Schonberg, went beyond superficial virtues, though. He clearly was honorable, affable, humble, and yet heroic. He was also—superficially—the Marquess of Harwich, Earl of Brentford, Count of the Holy Roman Empire, Estate-holder of Prussia, Grandee of Spain, General of All His Majesty's Land Forces, and Knight of the Most Noble Order of the Garter.

Despite all these honors, it seems that character, not honors, was what concerned the Duke of Schonberg. He was a military officer who eschewed vanity, putting duty first. He had the kind of taste that, when it was transferred to George Washington, can be seen in, for example, Mount Vernon—not humble, exactly, but not flashy either. Noble. Schonberg lived his life with what was, at the time, still unironically called "honor." He displayed the virtues of a "Christian gentleman." We'll explore what that meant to the Duke, and George Washington, a bit later, but, in essence, think of the values of King Arthur, in a slightly more modern context.

Why is the *Panegyrick* important to me and perhaps to you, too? For years Mount Vernon, Williamsburg, and other places that commemorate colonial America have done a brisk business unloading forests of the famous—infamous, to me—*Rules of Civility*, largely sold to grandmothers who think their grandchildren might like to follow in George Washington's footsteps. Grandchildren, generally, prefer computer games, but even for those few who are interested in George Washington, this book is of zero value, or worse.

It makes them lose interest.

The *Rules* is touted as the guide that the youthful, cherry-cheeked George used to rise to the magnificent heights of manhood that he eventually attained.

The fact is, however, that this is simply not true. No one actually believes this who knows even a little about George Washington. We all know that this is a tourist gimmick. Like an inflatable Mickey Mouse.

The *Rules of Civility* was a writing exercise, possibly assigned to the students in George's school. (People used to do a lot of copying and reciting in those days.) It's filled with such priceless drops of wisdom as "if you See any filth or thick Spittle put your foot Dexterously upon it."

Does anyone seriously think George Washington turned himself into George Washington as a result of a decorous habit of serenely stepping on spit?

Not even grandmothers, I'd warrant, believe that once they get *Rules of Civility* home. But by then it's too late—they've been fooled by the cover and advertising copy. (Can't a judge a book by its cover, I've always been told.) The grandmothers find their grandkids' *Rules of Civility* being used to prop up their Wii console, if it is seen at all. If a grandkid ever opened the book, he might find the spit part fascinating but would probably appreciate it more if George had become great by learning to spit especially well, rather than hiding spit. That none of it is true, and it is obviously useless information, is the final nail.

The *Panegyrick*, on the other hand, contains the principles George Washington *chose* to follow in order to *transform* his life. (And they can change yours, too.)

The *Panegyrick* is one of only three items in the first purchase George Washington kept a record of, using the bookkeeping skills he was learning in school.

He bought three books from his cousin, Baily Washington. The note "Schonberg" by the entry for the third book led Dr. X to deduce that his purchase was the Schonberg *Panegyrick*.

Why would George Washington buy the *Panegyrick*—and make a special note of it? He had plenty of books to read. After all, he was living in his brother Austin's house and had access to every book in Austin's library. Apparently, though, when George took a cursory look at his cousin Baily's copy of the *Panegyrick*, he couldn't give it back—George had to own it. This book was special, at least for George.

When I first read the *Panegyrick*, I was not gobsmacked the way George had been, but I did stick with it because, the evidence shows, this is what my great-uncle George did.

The wisdom of the *Panegyrick* is not immediately obvious—at least, it wasn't to my reflexively modern, rational way of thinking. For example, one of the main things de Luzancy conveys is the Duke's chivalry, something that the mass media and the modern world have brainwashed me into seeing as irrational, unquantifiable, and silly. However, as I read, I began to realize that this was my problem and our modern society's and media's problem, not the problem of the *Panegyrick*.

Why was George open to these visions of what must have seemed, from the rural woods of Virginia, a fairyland? Why didn't this book about a knight of the Round Table–sort of European hero seem to him, as it initially did to me, otherworldly and, therefore, pointless? Did something happen to George as a child that made him receptive to the magic he found in the *Panegyrick*?

Yes. But no one has believed this story for two hundred years, either.

"I Cannot Tell a Lie"— the Cherry Tree Story Is True (but Different from How You Heard It)

"What shall I say of the Nobleness of his Mind; and of that Character of Honor, Truth and Justice, which was so Natural to him... incapable of the Dissimulation, and other sordid Arts of Court. He could not promise what he did not intend to perform."
—H. de Luzancy, *A Panegyrick to the Memory of His Grace Frederick, Late Duke of Schonberg*

Parson Weems was married to the wife of a cousin of George Washington's close friend, Dr. James Craik. Parson Weems knew George Washington. Parson Weems preached at George Washington's church.

So why all the hating?

The tale of George Washington and the cherry tree has been mistold for two hundred years—and thus mistakenly criticized, as people have been criticizing a story that Parson Weems never told. Still, despite all the debunking, the story of George Washington and the cherry tree is almost as iconic in America as Santa Claus and his elves.

It therefore seems worthwhile to spend a little time explaining how we can say with certainty that yes, Virginia, the story of George and the cherry tree is true (but no, it's not the story you've heard).

For those non-Americans out there, the story, in essence, is this: George Washington, when he was a small child, chopped down a cherry tree with a hatchet. When confronted by his father, he confessed, "I cannot tell a lie. I did it with my little hatchet."

That's the story. (Not much of a story, is it? But the story *of* the story could change your life.)

No one in America believes it any more. We've all been told *ad nauseam* that the whole story is a pious fable—a confabulation invented by Parson Weems.

What's wrong with the story? Why can't we trust Parson Weems?

We obviously can't trust him because he admired George Washington. No, honestly, that's a *big* part of the argument. Parson Weems is a fanboy and therefore can't be trusted. The generally accepted idea, expressed by *Wikipedia*, is this: "Weems also called Washington the 'greatest man that ever lived.' This degree of adulation, combined with the circumstance that his anecdotes cannot be independently verified, demonstrates clearly that they are confabulations and parables."

But wait just a minute.

1. I'd always thought *ad hominem* attacks were a logical fallacy.

2. If something that cannot be independently verified is, *ipso facto*, not true, then all trees falling in all forests are always silent. That's just silly.

3. Actually, the story *can* be independently verified.
Beyond that, it passes the sniff test. Pretty clearly.

The more fundamental problem is that these sorts of arguments would fit perfectly in the mouths of people at a Star Wars convention arguing about whether Obi-Wan Kenobi secretly likes ice cream cones.

That's entertainment. This is real. And it matters. The purpose of history should not be entertainment or the "gee-whiz" factor. The purpose is to impart wisdom.

To miss the "first transactions" of George Washington's life—the kind of experiences that he himself believed made "the deepest impression" and formed the "leading traits" of a man's character—is to help create a society like...well, just look around you. Like what you see? Then throw this book out the window. It's not for you.

Think about it. The *Panegyrick* to the Duke of Schonberg appealed to the teenaged George Washington for a reason. By the time he first saw it in his cousin Baily's possession, he was already primed to admire someone like the Duke and appreciate the qualities that made him great.

Invaluable insights into how George had already attained this level of character by the time he found the *Panegyrick* were, fortunately, captured for posterity by a clergyman with a keen eye and careful ear, who happened to live near Mount Vernon.

Parson Weems *retold* the tales of George Washington's boyhood in the form of stories aimed at children. He didn't make them up. His goal was to make these small histories of George Washington's childhood part of the "first transactions" of all Americans' lives and thus define generations of Americans to come. However, because Weems's motives were overt and his language aimed primarily at children, the histories he conveyed are doubted by cynics who don't bother to learn the truth.

⁓

Parson Mason Weems was a warmhearted man who intended to do with George Washington's reputation exactly what George Washington himself wanted to do with it—use it for good. This may not have made Weems as great as George Washington—or as erudite an academic historian (a concept that didn't really exist at that time anyway).

However, there's no evidence it made him a liar. He simply wanted the example of George Washington's best attributes to make a deep impression, so that they would form the "leading traits" of the characters of the emergent nation's children—and thus of the nation.

⁓

Parson Weems can, if we let him, take us in a time machine back to George Washington's childhood—that is, to a time and place completely different from ours. When we get there, we'll find that our brief trip through this weirdly different world can actually change us.

We may see, in dramas of the past, people dressing differently and facing different problems, but they're basically like us (or, at least like Jude Law). In fact, the hardest thing to get our minds around about the past is that people *thought* differently then. They didn't just believe different "facts" (bleeding sick people with leeches is a powerful cure, for example). It is their unquestioned fundamental assumptions that truly made their world different from ours.

You might assume that when George Washington was a child, people saw children as children. In fact it seems like a tautology, not even worth saying. A child is a child as a brick is a brick.

But, in fact, the average person today doesn't see what an eighteenth-century Virginian saw when observing an immature human being.

In the Virginia of George Washington's childhood, children were not cut off from "real life" the way they are now. Fathers didn't "go to work." And boys "went to school" at a much later age. School, work, friends—it was all there in the home. "Children" in colonial Virginia—rather than spending their days, as in our world, confined to the children's ghetto of school—were part of a busy household and inevitably taken more seriously as individuals, often appreciated for their unique and valuable merit.

There were very few hard-and-fast age restrictions on anything. "Children" rode horses in ways and at ages that today would lead to horse breeders being sued (lawyers would find a way, surely). Child Protective Services would rip the kids off their saddles and put them in foster homes as their parents were hauled off to jail for child endangerment.

Childhood itself, some historians believe, is a kind of modern invention. This strange idea is brought into relief when you look at art from the era. Into the eighteenth century, some artists portrayed children as miniature adults—not only in dress, but also in bodily proportions. Of course, it is arguable that this was because of a lack of skill. There may be more to it than that, though.

Just think about what children who weren't held back by modern conventions used to accomplish at ages when we would still infantilize them. Lafayette was a military cadet at twelve and a captain in the army at sixteen. (Today, the UN would probably impose sanctions on your country and try your president at The Hague if you had twelve-year-old cadets.) Although not quite as precocious, George Washington was a major in the Virginia militia when he was only nineteen.

Is it so incredible, therefore, that George acted like a miniature adult and did what honor dictated at the age of six when, having behaved irresponsibly with his hatchet, he was confronted by his father? He did much more incredible things later on. No one doubts that he led a scrag-gly band of semi-shoeless soldiers through the icy cold to beat the great-est army in the world. If we accept that (and I think everyone does, unless they're the sort who doubt men walked on the moon), why should anyone doubt that, once upon a time, George Washington told the truth? Mozart was writing music at six. And George Washington can't tell the truth?

George Washington, quite late in his life, said, "I hope I shall possess firmness and virtue enough to maintain (what I consider the most envi-able of all titles) the character of an honest man." He believed this when he was fifty-six years old. What is the evidence that he didn't believe it when he was six? None.

Here's another question: Why did anyone care enough to remember this incident? Was there something we don't know that made honesty particularly important in colonial Virginia?

Why, yes (forehead smack), there was.

In fact, there was something astonishing about George Washington's Virginia in the 1700s that sheds light on why the story of George, his hatchet, and the cherry tree is remembered (or, to be perfectly accurate, misremembered, but more on that in a moment).

There were no credit cards in colonial Virginia. But, then, you knew that. There were also no banks to speak of—at least, banks as we under-stand them. Did you know that?

How about this? There was no cash to speak of either. Did you know that?

There were, of course, people dealing with large amounts of wealth in colonial Virginia, but they weren't accumulating what we think of as cash—there wasn't even much gold and silver in circulation.

Let's jump forward for a moment (we already have the time machine all oiled up). Do you know what happened when Franklin Roosevelt declared a "bank holiday" in the middle of the Great Depression—obviously, with no advance notice, as that would have ruined the primary purpose, which was to stop runs on banks? That very same afternoon, people were trading IOUs as they had been trading currency that morning.

Money is a creation of the human mind, and it will exist wherever human beings exist in any great numbers. Aside from certain very primitive human societies that don't seem to have anything resembling money, it is, basically, universal. In prisons they use cigarettes or cans of tuna fish. We don't need the government to make money for us. Nor, in fact, do we need gold or silver.

In George Washington's Virginia, the economy was conducted as it was in many parts of America during the Great Depression's bank holiday. Documents and accounting books kept track of who owed what to whom.

Do you detect a potential fly in the ointment?

Dishonesty would destroy the whole system.

Therefore, honesty in eighteenth-century Virginia was as important as your credit score is today. If someone didn't believe you would keep your word, you were out of luck.

Even when no overt "lending" took place, it was customary to keep about 80 percent of most purchases "on the book." In other words, at the time of the deal, 80 percent was paid in honor. And even the 20 percent paid at the time of a transaction was not generally paid in cash. (If you're really curious about how it worked in Virginia, in 1727 Virginia formally adopted a system of "tobacco notes," a kind of quasi-currency based on the colony's major crop, to systematize a nearly universal mode of exchange that had originally been more informal. It wasn't physical possession of tobacco you normally took, just a receipt.)

In this kind of economy, your reputation for honesty was paramount. Sterling or fourteen-karat-gold integrity got you as far as a perfect credit score might today. It was vital. The practical importance of honesty for making deals in colonial Virginia inevitably bolstered the kind of culture in which the young George would imbibe the ideal of honesty. This same culture would have led his parents—not necessarily in a cynical way—to make sure everyone knew the story of George and the cherry tree.

Which is not to say that a carrot—or a karat—hanging in front of a Virginian's nose was necessary to impel him down the path of honesty. Still, a society in which people's very livelihood depended on being able to trust each other was a society in which the virtue of truth-telling might well be publicized. It was recognized as the mark of a good character, the attribute of a man other men could rely on without hesitation.

Honesty would also be an important characteristic for a commander that soldiers would follow through horrific conditions to hard-won victory. This would hold equally true for a leader that a nation would choose to oversee the creation of its Constitution and elect, almost unanimously, as its first president.

No wonder the story of young George's honesty was passed on in George Washington's circle of friends and acquaintances. It's strange to think, though, isn't it, that the story has just kept going. It has been passed on, through the ages, from George Washington's parents, all the way to…you. Can you even remember where you first heard it?

Are you, knowing all this, still content to belong to the vast majority of modern Americans who—for no very good reason—snidely reject the cherry tree story as naive and pointless? Or, will you be one of the elite, willing to listen to the evidence for the story—and thereby to allow George to be to you what the Duke of the *Panegyrick* was to George Washington?

Probably the former. Statistically speaking, at least. But it's up to you.

⁓

I just had a little coffee break and spoke to my accountant. He agreed on the plan I concocted as the coffee steamed and sizzled (okay, it dripped, but I'm trying to be dramatic here; this is one of the ways I intend to sell more books). I am now authorized to make the following offer. One million dollars in cold, hard cash if you can spot the point in Parson Weems's cherry tree story at which George Washington chops it down.

Can't be that hard, can it? I mean, if you're like most Americans, you've heard the story—and heard it wasn't true—practically your whole life. Here's the story (and then the debunking of the story) on Mount Vernon's own website:

Did George Washington chop down a cherry tree?

Probably not. The story was invented by Parson Mason Weems who wrote a biography of George Washington shortly after Washington's death. Since so little is known about Washington's childhood, Weems invented several anecdotes about Washington's early life to illustrate the origins of the heroic qualities Washington exhibited as an adult. Introduced to countless schoolchildren as a moral tale in the McGuffey Reader textbook, the parable has become a persistent part of American mythology.

Let's be clear. Mount Vernon just spent $60 million on an—I have to say—extraordinarily cool visitors' center. It really is amazing, and I suggest any and all of you go. (I find many museums boring and find Disneyland too…Disney. Mount Vernon, though, is the perfect balance of cool and informative. It really is worth seeing, I'm not kidding about that.) Having said that, though—they didn't debunk the actual story. They debunked the mythical story, which has grown to be absurd enough to be easily debunked.

The actual story Parson Weems wrote, even without supporting evidence (and I have gathered plenty of supporting evidence below), is almost impossible to debunk. Anyway, I realize the purse is just $1 million, not even enough to buy your own Falcon jet, but the offer is good. One million dollars to the first one of you who spots the moment in the cherry tree story when George Washington chops it down.

Ready? Go!

> When George was about six years old, he was made the wealthy master of a *hatchet!* of which, like most little boys, he was immoderately fond, and was constantly going about chopping every thing that came in his way. One day, in the garden, where he often amused himself hacking his mother's pea-sticks, he unluckily tried the edge of his hatchet on the body of a beautiful young English cherry-tree, which he barked so terribly, that I don't believe the tree ever got the better of it. The next morning the old gentleman finding out what had befallen his tree, which, by the by, was a great favorite, came into the house, and with much warmth asked for the mischievous author, declaring at the same time, that he would not have taken five guineas for his tree. Nobody could tell him any thing about it. Presently George and his hatchet made their appearance. *George,* said his father, *do you know who killed that beautiful little cherry-tree yonder in the garden?*

This was a *tough question*; and George staggered under it for a moment; but quickly recovered himself: and looking at his father, with the sweet face of youth brightened with the inexpressible charm of all-conquering truth, he bravely cried out, *"I can't tell a lie, Pa; you know I can't tell a lie. I did cut it with my hatchet."*—*"Run to my arms, you dearest boy,"* cried his father in transports, *"run to my arms; glad am I, George, that you killed my tree; for you have paid me for it a thousand fold. Such an act of heroism in my son, is more worth than a thousand trees, though blossomed with silver, and their fruits of purest gold."*

Didn't see it, did you?

George didn't chop the tree down. That is kind of hard to imagine a six-year-old doing. He just, kind of…chipped away at the bark. Which inadvertently killed the tree. If the debunkers are wrong about what the cherry tree story actually *is*, maybe they're wrong about whether it's true or not, too.

⟨∽⟩

In Weems's actual story, the young George Washington never chopped the cherry tree down. He only "barked" it.

If you were inventing the story of George and the cherry tree, do you know what you'd probably have him do? You'd probably have him chop the cherry tree down, not just take some of its bark off. Wouldn't that be more dramatic?

On the other hand—isn't that precisely and exactly what a six-year-old would do? Experimentally chip away at the bark of a tree? I can, as I think about it, recall doing that myself when I was a kid. Not all the way around the trunk. But I can recall peeling bark off of a tree. It's sort of softer than wood but harder than leaves or twigs. A bit spongy. Do you remember doing that? Not enough to kill a tree, maybe, but just a little bit?

And if you'd had a brand-new, shiny hatchet as a present—and no Nintendo to occupy your time—can you imagine shaving the bark all around the trunk of a small tree to reveal the shiny, smooth wood underneath? Thinking about it, I want to go and try it myself.

On the other hand, it's not *that* amazing, but it *is* kind of extreme, to imagine a little boy actually *chopping down a tree*, even a small one. But "barking"? That's *exactly* what a six-year-old would do. It's exactly what I would do. Where's a tree? Where's my hatchet?!

On this clear and compelling evidence alone, I submit, you ought to accept the tale as true. My client is guilty! He did it with his little hatchet. And Parson Weems is innocent of fabricating the story.

But we're just getting started with the evidence. Here comes a defense not just of the cherry tree story, but of Parson Weems and all his tales. Hold on to your tri-cornered hats.

THE CASE FOR THE PROSECUTION
(of Parson Weems, not George Washington)

Narrator: We've already seen the Mount Vernon website claim that Parson Weems "invented" his stories. Arthur Schlesinger Jr. summarizes the prevailing assessment of Weems, saying he "drowned the historical Washington in a bath of amiable fable."

Besides that bald assertion, what do Weems's accusers have to say?

The Prosecuting Attorney: If it may please the court, the accused is a liar. His claim to have preached at "Mount Vernon Parish" must have been fictitious. Why, no such place exists! Here is a map. Can you, Parson Weems, please point to Mount Vernon Church?

The Ghost of Parson Mason Locke Weems: First, just call me Mason. Second, let me see that map. May I have my glasses, please? Thank you. There. See, that's Mount Vernon. And that, there—right next to George Washington's property—that is Mount Vernon's Church.

Prosecutor: The map, sir, says Pohick Episcopal Church.

The Ghost of Weems: Yes, that is its official name. But I've preached there. We used to call it Mount Vernon Parish because everyone knows where Mount Vernon is. Do you know where Pohik is?

[A Pinter-length pause fills the courtroom.]

No one who can tell a hatchet from a cherry tree disputes that Parson Weems preached at this church, where George Washington had a private pew and both he and his father were members of the vestry.

THE CASE FOR THE DEFENSE

Narrator: Presented for your approval—nineteenth-century genealogist Horace Edwin Hayden, an authority exceptional for not dismissing Weems out of hand. "Whatever may have been the character of Weems," Hayden points out, "his pretty and natural anecdotes of the boyhood of Washington are much more easily ridiculed than disproved."

The Attorney for the Defense: Your honor, Mr. Hayden is correct. These *ad hominem* attacks against my client are unfounded. But even if these petty complaints were true, ridicule of someone, or even the fact that someone *is* ridiculous (if I were to concede my client's ridiculousness, purely for the sake of argument), does not make what he says untrue.

We have already shown the prosecution's case has no substance. But, rather than merely debarking—er, debunking—these substanceless attacks (it is such child's play to do so, after all, even without a "little hatchet"), we can prove beyond a reasonable doubt that my client's stories are accurate. Let's look at the evidence in my client's book, *A History of the Life and Death, Virtues and Exploits of General George Washington.*

Ladies and gentlemen of the jury, the written sources back Weems up. It is true he recounts a smattering of events from those years before George Washington's own meticulous records begin. But where what my client wrote *can* be compared with George Washington's papers, George Washington's own papers corroborate my client's stories—even in the minutest details.

These written sources, which Weems couldn't have consulted when he wrote his book, back Weems up.

In other words, where Parson Weems can be checked, he checks out. Isn't that reason enough to trust Weems where by the very nature of the case he *can't* be checked—where he's the only source for a few valuable anecdotes of George Washington's childhood?

A prime example of the deadly accuracy of Weems's biography where it *can* be checked against the paper record is this: my client debunks the popular belief "that Washington was a *Latin scholar*! But 'tis an error. He never learned a syllable of Latin."

How could my client say that with such confidence, if he was not intimately acquainted with the Washingtons? Most members of George Washington's background and class studied Latin. But Weems's sources were accurate on this anomalous fact.

Beyond this, my client managed to ferret out the specific curriculum of Washington's education. Weems did not have access to Washington's schoolwork, which, at the time he wrote his book, was not yet public. Yet Weems found out—through his interviews of Washington's family and friends—that it consisted of "reading, spelling, English grammar, arithmetic, surveying, book-keeping, and geography."

Precisely and exactly right. Washington's surviving schoolwork reflects this list. But my client, you see, could only have *heard* this fact from the relations and friends of George Washington, who were also his own friends and neighbors, who were also the source of the cherry tree story.

If it please the court, allow me to submit a final, conclusive example in support of my client's veracity. Parson Weems reported that George Washington had a close relationship with a family he boarded with in his youth. Weems says that although their family name was "Stevenson," it was "generally pronounced *Stinson*." How would Weems have known, without accurate knowledge of George Washington's life from *firsthand* sources, that the Stevensons pronounced their name in as idiosyncratic a way as, say, the singer Sade (pronounced Shah Day) does in more recent times? Another lucky guess?

Listen to George Washington himself on the subject. Not only does he mention Mrs. Stevenson and all seven of her sons in his diaries (confirming their friendship), but he confirms my client's report of the un-guessable pronunciation of the Stevenson name, instructing Tobias Lear to visit "Colo. John Stephenson (commonly called Stinson)."

Yet another coincidence, ladies and gentlemen of the jury? The prosecution's case against Parson Weems falls apart because it rests on too many unbelievable coincidences.

My client may be in spirit form now, but he was a mere mortal when he wrote his book—devoid of psychic powers both by nature and by virtue of his position as parson in a church that would have condemned psychic powers as works of the devil. Ladies and gentlemen of the jury, Parson Mason Locke Weems was no devil, but a mere man when he wrote his *Life* of Washington. The trumped-up case against Parson Weems falls in the light of the corroborating evidence supporting my client's noble and accurate work of history.

Prejudice against Parson Weems is the only reason to reject the anecdotes he tells of Washington's life.

The defense rests.

Thank goodness we have these small histories of George Washington's early life. As the defense has shown, George Washington's papers confirm these small histories where both they and George's own records cover the same ground. But Parson Weems's sources were *not* George

Washington's papers, but instead contemporaneous witnesses—including perhaps even George Washington himself and certainly his friends and relatives. There is no reason to doubt the few small histories that Weems recounts that predate George's own records.

So what if Weems "drowned" his reporting in superlatives?

The facts that Weems recorded, from the memories of those who actually knew George Washington, are more reliable in some ways than mere paper records. Think about it. Did *your* parents keep official written records of the things you did and said at age six? Okay, they have videos—but was the camera always on at the most impressive moments? Probably not.

You've only got their word to rely on. Yet what you were like at that age has a lot to do with how you turned out in the long run—you're the same person you were then, plus the choices and influences that set your direction in later years. Your innate character, your original self, is revealed in the stories that your parents will always tell about you as a child.

Beyond this, of course, by telling these stories within earshot of you, they are reinforcing certain innate aspects of your character, making them stronger. Even as a kid you were naturally attracted to some things and not to others. When George was a child, the same thing was true of him.

Nature, nurture. Nothing new here.

Just like George Washington, whether you were aware of it or not, you were pushed in certain directions by your parents, the books you read, the television shows you watched, and even the shining example of Britney Spears (or whoever dominated the cultural landscape of your youth). Or, as the *Panegyrick* puts it, slightly more lyrically, "Education makes us truly what we are; and if Nature prepares Men to, it is that that lays the Foundation of Great Actions."

George's father pushed him in a direction that seems to have suited George's nature. George kept right on going in that same direction after his father died. This made the slightly older George susceptible to the appeal of the *Panegyrick*. He then did his best to imitate the virtues of the Duke of Schonberg—at the same age you, because of your childhood influences, were trying to shake your chest Britney-style as you walked down the school hallway.

Or was that just me?

Now do you see how much work we have to do?

Hit me baby, one more time.

The six-year-old George Washington we see in the cherry tree story skates on the fine edge of first class dorkdom. But he doesn't fall over the edge. Instead—well, he's magnificent. He's not a momma's little boy. How many boys carrying hatchets would you call a momma's boy?

Exactly.

More to the point, he is not obeying a *person*, not his mother or his father, but an ideal.

He is obeying his ideal at the risk of his personal safety.

Maybe his father would respond by taking out a belt and whipping him? Or, perhaps six-year-old George would simply suffer his father's disapproval. Do you remember being six? All you want is your father's praise, respect. You want him to watch you kick a ball or jump in a pool and make a splash. George, though, was willing to risk all of that. For honesty. For honor. He was determined to do what was right.

In exactly the same way, later, he would stand up to the King of England, looking down on that monarch from a platform built higher than a mere monarchy, on the principles of honor and liberty. He would do so at the very real risk of losing everything that he had, and being forced to stand on a different platform—the gallows. At the age of six, this fierce and fearless sense of honor was already beating in his heart.

But it didn't get there by magic. His father helped put it there.

Would George Washington have had the guts to stand up to King George—would he have been strong enough to stick to his guns and do what his honor dictated, at the risk of the ultimate humiliation of being hanged as a traitor, if his father had not instilled this lesson in George when he was six?

No, he wouldn't. America would not be here without George Washington, George Washington would not be George Washington without honor, and honor would not have been instilled in him without that early lesson from his father: *"I can't tell a lie, Pa; you know I can't tell a lie."*

Honesty was obviously the most important lesson his father expected young George to learn. The lesson really took. That early and ingrained lesson goes a long way toward explaining why the *Panegyrick* appealed to George so much: honesty was more than a vital business necessity in colonial Virginia. It was a core value.

In a great Virginia family like George Washington's, you were supposed to be a Christian gentleman—another way of getting at that elusive concept of "honor." This is the ideal that the *Panegyrick to the Memory of His Grace Frederick, Late Duke of Schonberg* holds up to its readers. This is the reason the *Panegyrick* was so appealing to George. It embodied an ideal that meant everything to him, emotionally (and an ideal that also was the perfect passport to financial and social success in colonial Virginia).

Perhaps that ideal seems alien and possibly even ridiculous today. Maybe the touching scene at the end of the cherry tree story—with George's father rejoicing that his son has acted with honor, like a miniature Christian gentleman—seems completely over the top. (I'll grant you, it's not what Honey Boo Boo would do. What would Honey Boo Boo do? Think of that when you go to sleep tonight. It will inspire you to read the next chapter of this book tomorrow.)

The sense of nobility that young George had was expected in his day. It was the universal ideal that everyone, at least everyone of his background, from families like his, aspired to. Not everyone made it, but everyone wanted it.

❧

Perhaps they knew something we've forgotten. History doesn't only move forward, after all. It also rises and falls. We live in a more fractured time, with multiple competing ideals. Maybe we want to be a jock or a nerd—maybe a rich one, like Bill Gates. Maybe Snoop Dogg is our ideal.

Colonial Virginians weren't pulled in so many different directions. They pretty much all saw this one thing as the thing most worth having—the nobility, the honesty, the honor that George Washington was aiming for, even as a boy of six. The fact that we find his honesty and nobility so difficult to believe that we have invented a myth that the cherry tree story is a mere myth says everything about us and nothing about George Washington.

❧

Where did the ideal that George learned from his father come from? It had its precursors in the qualities of the heroes of ancient Greece and Rome—characters as popular in colonial Virginia as rock stars are today. These ancient heroes tended to have one thing in common: they stuck to their principles. In ancient times, of course, people who stuck to their guns (which of course didn't yet exist) might do so for principles that would seem barbaric to a Christian gentleman. The "Christian" element of "Christian gentleman" added to this ancient strength of character the principles of kindness, gentleness, and respect for all people, principles that were not fundamental in the ancient world. These more modern Christian ideals are associated with the Knights of the Round Table rather than with ancient Rome, and were, in George Washington's day, leading the Western world in the direction of "all men are created equal."

Beyond honesty, what exactly did it mean to be a Christian gentleman? It can't be boiled down to a list of instructions. It's not just about putting your foot over spit. Or even just always telling the truth.

A Christian gentleman was humble yet a leader. "He would not presume to Command," says the *Panegyrick* about the Duke, "before he knew perfectly how to Obey." (This is not as contradictory as it sounds; to lead, you have to understand the minds of those who will follow you.)

A Christian gentleman aspired to be great (think Genghis Khan) and also good (think a saint). As the *Panegyrick* says of the Duke of Schonberg, "Greatness and Goodness, so seldom united in others, have been in him inseparably link'd." This is a particularly rare and hard-to-achieve combination, as the *Panegyrick*'s author also points out: "To be Great and Good is extraordinary and difficult. To live in the Noise and Violence of Wars, and yet preserve a Religious Temper, and a Conscience Tender of the least Evil, is infinitely rare."

The Christian gentleman's taste was grand—and yet modest. The Duke of Schonberg "was of a Frugal, and yet a magnificent Disposition. Nothing so noble as his Houshold, his Equipage, his way of Living: And yet nothing of Luxury, Pride, Ostentation, and a certain desire to look Great by Color and Noise."

This is the very definition of the house George Washington created for himself at Mount Vernon.

How do these things fit together? You could ape and parrot all the outward manifestation and still never "get it"—never really understand what it means to be the kind of person George Washington was aiming to be from the age of six, the kind of person George's book about the Duke of Schonberg helped him become.

The purpose of the book you now have in your hands, which is structured to reflect those aspects of George Washington's life that, in turn, reflect the Duke of Schonberg's life, is to help you "get it," just the way you eventually "got" driving a car. Just the way George Washington clearly "got" the *Panegyrick*. (And to entertain you along the way. We must bow to the gods of our times, there is no getting around that.)

Unfortunately, though, there is no list of instructions. No 7 EZ Steps 2B GW. If you'd buy that, and expect it to work, you can't yet "get" the secret of the *Panegyrick*—or understand George Washington.

I'm certainly not claiming to have absolutely "got" it myself. I do think at times, though, that I've at least seen a reflected glimmer, somewhere on the horizon.

In my defense, after all, even George Washington had to start somewhere, as we all do. If we imitate him, as he imitated the Duke of Schonberg, we might just end up with some of his integrity, his honor, even his nobility.

What did George Washington actually *do* to reflect all this, other than tell the truth?

Well, here's an example:

George Washington did not take Communion. He was not, no matter what anyone may wish, a "Christian" in anything like the way that word is typically used today. Like the Duke of Schonberg, George Washington was "free from Affectation, Bigotry, and a sort of intemperate Zeal, which is rather a Scandal than a furtherance to Christianity." (Says a man of the cloth, let's not forget!)

Leaving definitions of "Christian" to the side, George Washington certainly *was* a Christian gentleman of the sort the *Panegyrick*'s author— a Christian minister himself, so I'll defer to his expertise—was talking about. Without getting too deeply into theology yet (a bit more about that in the next chapter), George Washington did not see much difference between the various denominations of Christianity as practiced in America in the 1700s.

In fact, he famously even prayed, at least once, to the Indians' Great Spirit.

When it was pointed out to George Washington, when he was president, that it set a bad example for him not to take Communion, he didn't start taking Communion. He stopped coming to church on the Sundays when it was given.

Here George Washington displayed "the Resolution of a settled Mind," as the *Panegyrick* puts it. He was following out to its logical conclusion the same Protestant principle that impelled the Duke of Schonberg to refuse the great honors and responsibilities that had been offered to him by the King of France, on the one small condition that he accept the Catholic faith. George Washington took his public responsibilities very seriously. Yet, like the Duke, he would not act against his conscience. He would choose integrity above political expediency.

Finally, I mentioned that great Virginia families tended to share a common ideal of the way men should be—the ideal the *Panegyrick* refers to as a "Christian gentleman." But who exactly were these families?

Well, the Washingtons were large landowners, members of the higher of the two distinct classes in Virginia at the time. Only a few generations after arriving in the "new world," the Washingtons were doing well but were still enterprising and industrious—though this wasn't universally the case amongst members of their class. (George Washington once complained that many of his compatriots were given a horse and a servant at a very young age and didn't strive much after that. George Washington's family still seems to have been aware that they were wealthy in a country in which wealth and effort were related.)

Virginians of this class, at this time, believed they were civilizing an untamed wilderness (something disputed to this day by the original inhabitants of Virginia, but that's another book). In their own eyes they were something like a cross between Thurston Howell III—they did bibs and bobs of luxury, when they could afford them—and Robinson Crusoe. (The Washingtons had in fact ended up in Virginia as the result of a shipwreck, albeit not as dramatic a wreck as Robinson Crusoe's, yet they tried to maintain a civilized air in the wilderness.)

They were not cushioned in any way. They had to fight their own battles, earn their own way, and pay for everything themselves. Having to work hard for everything else, working for his own character perhaps seemed natural to a Washington. Therefore, for somebody like George Washington, deciding to be a Christian gentleman wasn't what we think of as an individual lifestyle choice. To decide to be a Christian gentleman was to decide to help your civilization grow and prosper. (It is easily arguable that the exact same option still exists today—it is just easier to instead follow a more indulgent path, as there are many more such alternate paths to follow.)

Think about what someone's character meant back then: neither the word "police," nor even the concept, was a part of the consciousness of any Virginian at this time. If you were a member of the upper class, you'd be in charge. If something against the social order happened—anything from an armed rebellion to a private crime—you and your social equals got together to quell it.

There was no concept of anyone interfering in your life on your own property. As an extreme example, you wouldn't rape your wife, but you could. You wouldn't beat your children, but you could. You could do anything you damned well pleased, but you wouldn't—because you were a Christian gentleman, you were raised to have standards, and you cared about your honor.

At the same time, education was neither imposed nor provided by the state. It was a privilege that, as a member of the upper class, you acquired for yourself and your children. George Washington spent his early years, at least until the age of eleven when his father died, at his home. His mother likely taught him his earliest lessons, along with his siblings. George is also recorded as saying he had a tutor, though we don't know the details. As his father's ironworks were nearby, George would have understood, from his earliest memories, about business and work, and the wider world. Some of his father's business meetings inevitably took place in his home, while there was no distant and remote office his father regularly "commuted" to.

George played games with his younger brothers and sisters, and, as the oldest of his mother's children, and also an unusually large child, the role of leader was ingrained in his earliest experiences and memories.

Children today dream of fabulous futures—the girls are going to be ballerinas, perhaps, and the boys superheroes—yet somehow most end up accountants, or brand managers for Kraft International. In George Washington's day, though, imagine this—the most viable job opportunity was, in fact, hero. (At least for boys. Girls were kind of stuck.)

It was not only realistic but expected that one day you would be a dashing man on a horse. You'd ride to battle or chase foxes, bounding on horseback over fences and through the woods. You'd lead your community and its government (which was only a minute part of life in those days). You'd be a fabulous dancer who imported a few luxury goods from Europe to at least simulate the refined life of a European in the midst of what was, largely, still the malarial swamp of Virginia.

These quite realistic visions of their future were shared by George Washington and his contemporaries from their earliest childhoods. There was no television or other media to deflect them. The zeitgeist and the literature popular at the time celebrated the heroes of the ancient world—strong men on horses, not weak men in offices. Everyone aspired to be what George Washington, in fact, became.

Don't get put off, though, by the superficial differences between our circumstances and George Washington's. Be glad you live today. Be glad you have hot running water. The visions that George Washington had of his future were ennobled by his emulation of a deeper kind of heroism—the ideal of "Honor and Vertue" that he found in the *Panegyrick*. That's an ideal that even those of us who will never hunt foxes or build a mansion at Mount Vernon can still aspire to.

Chapter Two

George Washington's Religion—"the Miraculous Care of Providence"

"[His] accomplishments flow'd from a religious temper. Piety,
that admirable Discipline, which Divinifies man and raises him
above himself, was his continual application."
—H. de Luzancy, *A Panegyrick to the Memory of*
His Grace Frederick, Late Duke of Schonberg

One of the things George Washington talked about a lot—and I mean a lot—was God. But he didn't call God "God."

That's because, perhaps, he wasn't talking about the God you're thinking of.

This isn't a theological lesson, or argument, or dissertation. I'm just reporting the facts.

The most common name by which George Washington called this thing—whatever it was—was "Providence."

Here, as it happens, is yet another reason to give poor, maligned Parson Weems credence. An incident he recounts of Gus Washington, George's father, teaching the young George a lesson about a helpful, divine intelligence, is completely in keeping with George Washington's thoughts about Providence that he mentions throughout his life.

Parson Mason Weems, let us remember, was a clergyman of the established Church of England. If Weems had his own ax to grind—rather than letting George wield his own "little hatchet"—he would have made George talk about Jesus.

But he didn't.

Here, then, is an authentic early lesson George got about God—Providence—from his father, whether or not George Washington's "Providence" fits in with your understanding of God.

⁕

One day when George was six or seven, his father secretly planted some cabbage seeds in the pattern of George's name. When, ten days later, George discovered his name spelled out in baby plants, he was stunned. Later on that day, when six- or seven-year-old George saw his father, he breathlessly told him what he had found.

Gus Washington told his son it must have happened by chance.

George couldn't believe it. After a bit more teasing, his father admitted that he had planted the seeds himself, in the pattern of George's name.

Then his father made his point: Although George hadn't seen his father plant the seeds, it couldn't be denied. Anyone could easily see "George Washington" spelled out in cabbage. The pattern of plants left by Gus Washington's hand showed that he had been there even though George had not seen his father's hand spell his name.

In other words, random chance does not create "George Washington" out of nothing.

"You did not see me when ten days ago I made this little plant bed, where you see your name in such beautiful green letters; but though you did not see me here, yet you know I was here!!" said Gus, to which young George replied, "Yes, Pa, that I do—I know you was here."

George's father used that seed of an idea, about seeds, to make a larger point about Providence:

> Well then, and as my son could not believe that chance had made and put together so exactly the letters of his name, (though only sixteen) then how can he believe that chance could have made and put together all those millions and millions of things that are now so exactly fitted to his good.... ten thousand other good things more than my son can ever think of, and all so exactly fitted to his use and delight?…

George responded, "Oh, Pa, that's enough! That's enough! It can't be chance, indeed—it can't be chance, that gave me all these things."

Why is this story important?

"I mean, it is kind of cool," you might think, "to know the lessons George Washington learned as a kid. But I went to Sunday School, too. I learned a bunch of sappy lessons at that age, too. But then I got older, wiser, and saw that it was all lies."

Or, perhaps, you believe something entirely different.

Different people believe different things.

But what can we know? What does the evidence show us?

Whatever you think, we'll start with a simple premise almost everyone can agree with. You are not (*are* you?) one of the most influential people of the last half millennium. (Not yet, at least.) Have you become one of the most powerful and loved people in your country yet? No? Yes?

Before dismissing this lesson as childish pabulum, wait and see how clearly and specifically this lesson was to influence George's entire life. It is arguably a lesson that *saved* his life. It is inarguable that George *believed* Providence saved his life, on multiple occasions.

So how did Providence save George's life?

Just barely.

Skipping ahead for a moment to the next great American war after the Revolution, the Civil War, some do-gooders got together and gave away pocket-sized Bibles. Later on, much was made of the supposedly miraculous incidents in which someone's life was saved by a bullet hitting a Bible, often in a breast pocket covering a soldier's heart.

Nothing at all was made of those incidents, which surely must also have occurred, when someone's head was blown from here to Kentucky by a cannonball, along with scraps of his jacket and bits of his pocket Bible.

People naturally see patterns in events, although often the patterns are only in the beholder's mind. Gamblers rely on the patterns they think they see, but the long-term odds prove them wrong. It seems obvious that if you sorted through the half million or so deaths in the Civil War, you'd find that Bibles did not offer any statistically measurable protection. It seems obvious, and my intuition is that it is probably true.

And yet…and yet…there is a kind of belief in being protected in dangerous times that seems to have some truth to it. Sometimes, as the author of the *Panegyrick* explains, "Heaven seem[s] to have prepar'd a concourse of Causes" that somehow mysteriously make things turn out just right.

If you tabulated the soldiers who died in the American Revolution and somehow had access to their thoughts and beliefs, you'd think you would find men who felt invulnerable and were blown to smithereens and men who were sure they'd be shot who nonetheless went on to have grandchildren bouncing happily on their knees.

It seems obvious that that would be the case. But until someone does a scientific study—and I'm not sure that one *could* be done—we are forced to admit our presumption may be wrong.

Whether the Providence he believed in is real or not, George certainly had more opportunities than we do to feel that he had been providentially saved from death. Don't forget that before the germ theory of disease, antibiotics, and inoculations (new in George Washington's day, and often fatal themselves), death was as much a part of life as the common cold is today. The course of George's whole life was determined by premature deaths (which were even more common in swampy, malarial Virginia than generally in the eighteenth century).

If George's father's first wife had lived to old age, he never would have existed at all. If George's half-brother Lawrence had not died of tuberculosis (more on this tragedy in the next chapter), George would never have inherited Mount Vernon.

I once met a recording engineer who had been in the Vietnam War. He had been some kind of an assistant—a sergeant, I think—to a colonel. He said he always stuck as close to the colonel as possible, as the colonel seemed to have a sixth sense—"he always *was* where the bullets *weren't*" was the way he put it.

Without double-blind, controlled, replicable studies, no one will be able to fully test such beliefs. So we have to look at the evidence we do have.

CASE STUDY #1: GEORGE WASHINGTON

Demographic: white male

Occupation: soldier

Time and place: July 9, 1755, Braddock's Field, Pennsylvania (the Battle of the Monongahela, at the beginning of the French and Indian War)

The subject engaged in numerous behaviors that by all reasonable expectation should have led to his death. He put himself in situations of extreme danger. He was an officer, and therefore a prime target for enemy soldiers, to begin with. During at least one battle, expert marksmen were specifically assigned to shoot and kill officers. One marksman shot at our subject seventeen times during that battle, to no effect. By the end of the battle, the subject's commanding officer and every other officer serving under him had been shot off his horse, and most of the soldiers were dead—but our subject was unscratched.

Bullets were known to go through George Washington's coat, his hat—but no bullet ever grazed George Washington's skin nor touched a hair on his head. Bullets aimed at him could never find their mark. The Indian marksman who had shot at George seventeen times outside Fort Duquesne concluded that George Washington was protected by "the Great Spirit."

George shared this belief with his erstwhile assassin, only substituting his word, "Providence," for the Indian's "Great Spirit." That George saw no substantive difference between different views of God is made clear by the multiple ways he described the "Governor of the Universe" and also by his seeing only "slight shades of difference" between the various denominations of his countrymen.

Writing to Virginia governor Robert Dinwiddie about the aforementioned incident, Washington attributed his good fortune to luck, saying he "luckily escap'd with't a wound tho' I had four Bullets through my Coat and two Horses shot under me."

George allegedly had a difficult relationship with his mother, which some say lacked the closeness and warmth these relationships often have. Perhaps that would explain why he did the eighteenth-century equivalent of copying and pasting, using precisely the same phrase when he wrote to his mother about this same series of near-misses, saying that he "luckily escap'd with't a wound…."

However, no one doubts that George was close to his younger brother John. This was his favorite brother, to whom he gave the keys, so to speak, of Mount Vernon when he was away battling the French—entrusting him with his fortune and future. If the crops and farm had deteriorated, George would not have had the money to become the George Washington he became. Beyond all this, George also entrusted his brother, at this time, with his real feelings on the near misses: "I now exist and appear in the land of the living by the miraculous care of Providence, that protected me beyond all human expectation; I had 4 Bullets through my Coat, and two Horses shot under me, and yet escaped unhurt."

The use of the word "Providence" was not merely a turn of phrase. It was the way he spoke to people he felt he could be open and honest with. It expressed his genuine view, the way he thought the world actually ticked.

George continued to go ungrazed by a bullet his entire life, despite spending half that life on various battlefields. He continued to believe that life in general, and his own life specifically, were guided by

Providence. This, in George's mind, accounted for his bullet-free existence, the formation of the United States, and much else—if not everything in the world.

George's father first introduced his son to the concept of a guiding intelligence responsible for the universe—and also responsible for his own life. Then in the *Panegyrick*, George encountered the notion of piety as the mark and the inspiration of a great man. "His accomplishments," de Luzancy asserted of the Duke of Schonberg, "flowed from a religious temper. Piety divinifies man and raises him above himself."

The Duke believed in Providential escapes from near-certain death, too. As the *Panegyrick* explains, the Duke was driven out of France by religious persecution, only to run into a terrible storm at sea. In the midst of the tempest, "There was no calm but in the duke's looks.… He caus'd continual prayers in the ship, to be made to him who commands the Waves to be still. That Piety which had supported him in so many dangers, was their Preservation. God seem'd to have given him the Souls of these Men. There is none of them that perish'd, or suffer'd injury."

But was George really *pious*? It seems like such a wimpy, unheroic thing to be.

Piety literally means (at least according to the Oxford Online Dictionary) "the quality of being religious or reverent."

But the way the word is normally used today is better conveyed by the next definition: "a belief or point of view that is accepted with unthinking conventional reverence: *the accepted pieties of our time*."

But George's "piety" was not about irrationally clinging to conventions. His belief in Providence was very much akin to the Duke of Schonberg's Protestantism, a real inward personal conviction, supported by evidence. As the *Panegyrick* says of the Duke, "He was Bred in the Protestant Religion: But he did not owe the Zeal he had for it, to the first Impressions of Education, or the examples of his Ancestors, but to the inward Conviction of his Mind. One of the strongest Arguments to embrace it, is, that it is highly Rational in it self, and free from those Impositions, which other Opinions force on our Reason."

In any case, the way "piety" was used in George Washington's day was somewhat different from either of my computer dictionary's definitions, above. In seventeenth-century New England, for example, the people who were considered the most pious were those who tried to maintain an awareness of God within themselves—as opposed to, say, focusing on the outer forms of religion or even the words of the Bible. Piety did not imply, in the pejorative way it does today, narrow-minded obedience or acceptance of the man-made rules and regulations of a society or church.

Piety, in the broader seventeenth-century and eighteenth-century usage (not confined to New England), carried the idea of humility in relation to a higher spiritual force—Providence, God—along with a non-egotistical adherence to principles. Thus someone who nobly fought a war against the accepted authorities and rules of his society for the liberty guaranteed by Nature and Nature's God—that is, someone who fought for the ideals of the American Revolution—might still be considered pious in this older sense of the word, and perhaps even exceptionally pious, despite fighting against conventionally held beliefs.

Think of George Washington fighting for the ideals of the Declaration of Independence—pledging his life, his fortune, and his sacred honor for a cause that he believed was favored by Providence. That's the kind of heroic piety he learned from the *Panegyrick* and the Duke of Schonberg: "It is an easie thing to talk Eloquently, and even Zealously of Religion. The World is full of Persons who can do it to admiration. But to lose for it Honors, Estates, Dignities; and readily to forsake all that can make our Life pleasing and happy, is given but to few.... that Heroick temper of Christianity, is almost worn out of the world."

Recently I spent an afternoon drinking vodka with a five-time Russian cosmonaut captain who tried to explain to me the qualities necessary to be a leader in such extraordinary circumstances as outer space. The qualities he said helped him to be a leader (and to be chosen a leader—not necessarily the same thing) reminded me of the attributes that helped George Washington succeed.

Beyond the obvious leadership qualities, this space captain was also pious—in a very similar way to George Washington. He started to explain this by telling me that he never really believed that the earth was round until he went to outer space.

I was, naturally, a bit surprised, until he explained himself.

Of course he always knew the earth was round. He'd seen pictures. He'd even been taught, and trained extensively, to recognize the pattern of stars in the sky seen from multiple angles (from all the angles you might see them as your space ship tumbled through the void encircling our globe).

But he never *really* knew the earth was round, he told me, until he saw it for himself, from outer space.

Also, for the first time, when out there, he told me he knew, he just knew, that there was an intelligence permeating the universe. In a burst of insight, he suddenly saw, understood, and deeply and life-changingly felt everything in an entirely different way.

As you might imagine, this was the last thing I'd expected to hear from a military man, and a scientist to boot. But then my images of military men or scientists are of quotidian ones, not the extraordinary ones who are chosen to captain space ships or chosen by popular acclaim to lead the nascent America.

The cosmonaut captain told me that, after his insight, all the petty problems of people on Earth (and even something like World War II,

I understood him to mean) seemed almost incomprehensibly small. After returning home, he viewed everything down here from—literally—a higher perspective.

He talked about all the ego-driven decisions people made, for their pride, vanity, and self-esteem, and how small these decisions and motivations now seemed. Like ants, he told me. It wasn't that he felt bigger than other people or their concerns—he felt that other people didn't understand how vast and magnificent *they* were or, at least, the thing that they were all a part of, in fact, was.

This same sort of awareness explains how it was possible for George Washington to eschew all the comforts and quotidian joys he could have had by staying home at Mount Vernon. He was able to feel how small those things were, compared with following the will of Providence.

When I asked the Russian cosmonaut to clarify one particular point, he told me he felt the intelligence that he perceived in the universe was "out there" somewhere. Not, necessarily, inside himself.

The cosmonaut's perception of a magnificent greater power evokes the piety that George Washington expressed. However, George Washington's Providence was more personal than the cosmonaut's all-pervading intelligence. George's Providence was not "out there" somewhere or, at least, not exclusively so. It was aware of the small distance between a bullet flying through George's hat and head. The Providence George believed in was concerned with the formation of the United States and the principles upon which the country was founded. It was not abstract and far away.

Like the cosmonaut's vision, though, Providence didn't speak to George through the Bible, or religion, or sermons. It spoke directly to something inside him, inspiring him to adhere, piously, to principles such as honor and chivalry and the ideals of liberty and freedom that were the basis of the struggle to create our country.

How broad and vast, and also how narrow and personal, was George Washington's piety towards that thing he called Providence?

When writing to his friend Landon Carter to thank him for his "kind and affectionate remembrance of me" during a difficult time in the Revolution, George exposed as much personal heartfelt emotion as he ever did in any surviving letter. He could not limit his thanks to Carter and his other friends. George felt that Providence had a "joint claim" on his gratitude. He had, he told his friend, no doubt that a Providential force had guided him, personally, and also his army through difficult and arduous tribulations: "My friends therefore may believe me sincere in my professions of attachment to them, whilst Providence has a joint claim to my humble and grateful thanks, for its protection and direction of me, through the many difficult and intricate scenes, which this contest hath produced; and for the constant interposition in our behalf, when the clouds were heaviest and seemed ready to burst upon us."

As many of us have spent our lives ensconced in the warm cocoon of post-modern Western so-called "civilization"—full of grocery stores, heated and air-conditioned houses, and lives in which advancement is to be had by filling out forms and obeying rules and regulations—it's worth considering what George had been through by this point.

Providence hadn't given him an extra tax deduction or a raise at his job.

Providence had made bullets aimed directly at his head pierce his hat but not ruffle a hair, had got his army through impossibly arduous times, and was, at the time of this letter, helping him beat the greatest and strongest military force on Earth, with little on his side but inalienable rights—which the British were doing their best to alienate—and his pious faith in Providence.

At a later point in his life, when talking to his close friend and confidant the Marquis de Lafayette, George portrayed Providence writing on an even larger canvas. Expressing his hopes and concerns about the ratification of the Constitution, he ascribed what he hoped would be a positive outcome not to the forces of history or mankind, nor to the extraordinary men who were involved, but to Providence:

> A few short weeks will determine the political fate of America for the present generation and probably produce no small influence on the happiness of society through a long succession of ages to come. Should every thing proceed with harmony and consent according to our actual wishes and expectations; I will confess to you sincerely, my dear Marquis; it will be so much beyond any thing we had a right to imagine or expect eighteen months ago, that it will demonstrate as visibly the finger of Providence, as any possible event in the course of human affairs can ever designate it.

Soon after this, George wrote to Benjamin Lincoln, also about the ratification process, revealing his belief that Providence, which he referred to as the "great Governor of the Universe," was a force of good, leading America to happiness: "No Country upon Earth ever had it more in its power to attain these blessings than United America. Wondrously strange then, and much to be regretted indeed would it be, were we to neglect the means, and to depart from the road which Providence has pointed us to, so plainly; I cannot believe it will ever come to pass. The great Governor of the Universe has led us too long and too far on the road to happiness and glory, to forsake us in the midst of it."

George and his compatriots were traveling to a place no one had ever been before—a land where, he hoped, the deepest hopes and aspirations of men and the inalienable rights granted to mankind by "Nature's God" would find full expression. He referred to the route they were taking as a "road" that seemed already to have been laid. For a road to exist, doesn't someone have to build it?

Long before this, when his father planted the cabbage seeds in the pattern of his name, George had learned that an unseen but intelligent guiding hand can shape the workings of the forces of nature. Throughout his life, George continued to see the fortuitous events of his life, and the life of his nascent nation, as resulting from divine paternal care.

We may speculate about the degree to which this belief might have been due to his own imagination or to his deification of a force or pattern science has yet to explain. Perhaps, though, it was a completely sober and accurate impression of the way the world actually works.

However, *that* he believed what he believed gave George the courage to do what he did. He was brave in battle, and he faced even harder psychological struggles, such as when, traveling to take up the presidency, he said he felt as if he were on his way to his own "execution." Without his belief that Providence was helping, George would not have had the faith to go forward in most of the great things he did in life.

Whether or not anyone can ever determine the degree to which George's belief in Providence was accurate, his piety was the cause of all he accomplished. He did not go into battle pumped up on amphetamines (a tactic used by many modern armed forces). On the other hand, neither did he face arduous circumstances with the spiritual weakness engendered by a religion that for centuries had been cast in the image of monarchy, with the supplicant begging for favors from an erratic, inscrutable, and mysterious deity.

The Revolution, of course, was overtly a war against a monarchical form of government. George's beliefs about Providence were a reflection of this same fight on the spiritual and religious plane.

George's piety recognized a relatively pragmatic, American-style Providence. The intelligence guiding the universe did some seemingly miraculous things but en route to a clear practical goal. That goal was the creation of a country in which the inalienable rights of man, and the laws of "Nature's God," would be paramount—a nation that would be the earthly manifestation of the fundamental ideal of liberty. George viewed Providence as a partner that guided him and his country—but that expected George Washington and his countrymen to pull their own weight, too.

How did George Washington pull such an enormous weight? Easy. He was a superhero.

More un-demythification coming up …

Chapter Three

George Washington's "Strength," "Vivacity," and "Soundness of Mind and Body"

"He had a Robust, and Strong Body, capable of the greatest Hardships. He was naturally Active, a great lover of Exercise...."
—H. de Luzancy, *A Panegyrick to the Memory of His Grace Frederick, Late Duke of Schonberg*

Here's the thing: some people really are better than you. At least at some things. More important than that, though, some people work harder, some people work smarter, and *some* people work smarter and harder at the *right* things.

Those are the ones to watch. Which is not to say you can't do it, too. Just do what George did.

When George Washington lived, where George Washington lived, he was the one to watch.

The way to succeed in colonial Virginia was relatively cut and dried. To be an amazing athlete, mentally vigorous in difficult circumstances—on a battlefield, on a horse, with cannons roaring—to be physically imposing (George was measured over six foot three at a time when the average height was much less than it is today), to be graceful and gracious—in essence, to be all the things George Washington was—was the ticket (and just about the only ticket) to the top of Virginia society.

At that same time in, say, London, things were different.

In London, you could be like one of George's favorite authors, Addison, and win success and prominence with your wit and wisdom.

Or you might become successful by sitting around a coffeehouse making insurance bets on cargo ships, as men who sat around Edward Lloyd's coffee shop did (that was how legendary Lloyd's of London insurance house got started).

Or you could be a great architect or a great painter back in England.

In George Washington's Virginia, though, there was virtually only one way to the top—and that was to be good at the things George Washington was good at. Who knows how many possible Shakespeares, potential Picassos, or almost Addisons there were in the colonies?

Think, for example, of someone with a literary bent in swampy Virginia. There wasn't a single printing press in Virginia until the 1730s; printing had actually been illegal in Virginia from 1682 until 1729. In those circumstances, what would a potential Addison have become? Or what would have become of the rotund, numerically inclined men who started making fortunes around Lloyd's coffeehouse about this time, had they been mired in the swamplands of Virginia? What buildings would a potential Christopher Wren have had to exercise his talents on in America? (Christopher Wren, of course, benefited not only from being born in England but from being alive and kicking just after the great fire that left half of London a blank slate on which he could create his magnificent structures.)

In a more sophisticated society, boasting a more complex economy with greater division of labor, George might have been only one of many great men in many diverse fields. In fact, in an extremely urban society, George might have been nothing more than a good-natured but annoying man who always got in the way, taking up too much room at the table—causing everyone to breathe a sigh of relief when he left, as they could finally stretch out their legs.

George, of course, believed that he was where he was because of an inscrutable intelligence beyond human reckoning—beyond even the clever calculations of the caffeinated odds-makers at Edward Lloyd's coffee shop. He viewed his birth in Virginia not as an accident but as an act of Providence.

However you want to look at it, George was built for the society in which he was born. He had the qualities necessary for success, and he exercised them to the fullest. He was either lucky or fortunate to be born where he was, as he was, when he was—at a time and a place where having "strength," "vivacity," and "soundness of mind and body" combined to create a ticket to the top.

Like the Duke, George had all those things in spades. Maybe that's one reason he was initially so struck by the *Panegyrick* that he had to own it for himself. The young George Washington saw that the Duke of Schonberg had possessed the very same natural advantages that he himself enjoyed. But the Duke had parlayed those qualities into achievements that, at the time George first saw the *Panegyrick*, he could only dream of.

George Washington Parke Custis was the unofficial adopted son of the father of our country. Although not related to my family by blood, he was raised by George and Martha as their child, along with his sister, Nelly. He was, in fact, Martha's grandson by her first husband, but the ubiquity of disease and death left him in a common circumstance in those days: raised from the age of eight by "cousins," that is, whatever relatives happened to still be alive, in his particular case George and Martha. George Washington Parke Custis thus spent his formative years perched, at times literally, on the shoulder of a giant.

You'd think his thoughts about his adopted father should be given more weight than the speculation of all the so-called experts who never even met my great-uncle. Yet, generally speaking, those few small histories whose surviving written origin is George Washington Parke Custis's *Recollections and Private Memoirs of Washington* aren't given much more credence by the people who are pushy enough to make their voices loudest than are those small histories whose surviving written origin is Parson Weems's *Life of Washington*.

It is always fashionable for historians—to the extent that any historian is ever fashionable (wait, I take that back—bow ties are cool!)—to dis non-professional historians, even the noted playwright and orator raised by George Washington, George Washington Parke Custis. I, on the other hand, tend to side with the amateurs—those who do things for love (amour, the "am" in amateur)—over the professionals—those who do things for money (or, perhaps, ego).

When I was fourteen, my friend had a father who was a psychologist, a professional in mental health. The man labelled his socks with the days of the week. From even that early age I, therefore, saw an inverse correlation, or at least no clear correlation, between professional certification and competence.

It tells even more in favor of George Washington Parke Custis's memories of his adopted father that, although he was an accomplished playwright and orator, his recollections about George were published only after his death. We, therefore, know he wrote them down for love of his adopted father, not money. He was not trying to write a bestseller nor to acquire more glory for himself.

As for any financial motive, he had inherited mountains of wealth. As for fame, he already had enough of that by virtue of his birth and the success of his plays and oratory. Even massive book sales wouldn't have made much difference to either his income or his public image had he published these memories when he was still alive, which, to repeat, he didn't.

Here is a story that comes to us through George Washington Parke Custis, in which the "strength" and "vivacity" of the young George Washington, along with his "soundness of mind and body" shine through. It is a little-known incident, almost never written about by those purchasers of bow ties who make the rules, perhaps because of their prejudice (and jealousy) against (and of) the man whose written account of it survives. However, this small history has the best provenance, besides George himself, of anything about George Washington's earliest years—coming directly from the boy who was raised by George Washington.

It is more than an interesting story. The tale reveals the mechanics—the smoke and mirrors, the hidden compartments where the rabbit waits to slip into the magician's top hat—that make an act of seemingly mythical heroism attainable through, yes, talent, but also training, experience, and a lifetime of hard work. (Sorry to spoil some of the fun, but you want to know how the trick works, right?)

The story involves George, a horse, and George's mother, along with George's "strength," "vivacity," and "soundness of mind and body." It also involves the horse's strength and vivacity, along with a noble equine will so strong that it would prove deadly.

George Washington's mother's character has been maligned by most biographers, although a few revisionists have attempted to resuscitate it. In the real world, of course, everyone is a mix of a good and bad. People seen as egotistical, for example, are merely, from another vantage point, overcompensating for insecurity. Bossy, selfish, and self-centered people—striking closer to home here, where George's mother Mary is concerned—are perhaps widows in a wild country, desperately trying to hang on to whatever scraps of property and dignity they may have.

It is, perhaps, easier to be graceful and gracious when you are, say, the Queen of England (although, come to think of it, most queens aren't either). It is, possibly, harder when you are scared, alone, and past the age of marrying, and you have nothing to give you support—financial or otherwise—except your children, even if one of them *is* George Washington.

In any event, surely we can forgive Mary Washington if her longing for her dead husband had a pragmatic element to it.

George's father, Gus Washington, had a favorite horse. Mary Washington, six or so years after her husband died, owned several of that horse's descendants. She loved the horses, in part, as mementos of her husband—but she also loved the horses because they were amazing horses. Wouldn't you love to have a driveway full of Porsches that sprang up of their own accord, descended from a vintage 1911 your husband had loved? If they flourished when you fed them bits of scrap metal and discarded motor oil, but only really showed their stuff when you took one out on the freeway at ninety miles an hour, you might be forgiven if, beyond being reminded of your dead husband as you raced down the highway with the wind whipping through your silvering hair, you also thought: "Wheeeeeeeeee!!!"

Anyway, this is something like the way Mary Washington was said to feel about these few horses descended from her deceased husband's favorite horse.

Beyond that, as these horses were to other horses, one of them was to the rest—that is, among them one outshone even its brothers, sisters, and cousins (sort of the way George did).

Horses, of course, need to be "broken." Predisposed as horses are to carry riders on their backs after countless aeons of breeding, each horse still has to be trained to accept a hundred-plus-pound hominid sitting astride him telling him what to do.

Genes are a funny thing, or perhaps it is spirit, but something occasionally shines through the ages of domestication and centuries of breeding, and a horse is too proud, too noble, too willful to be broken. Mary Washington's favorite horse was one of these.

George's step-grandson, in fact, believed that this particular animal was so spirited that he might be compared with that horse "which the brutal emperor raised to the dignity of consul."

It is arguable that—assuming the story is even true—Caligula wanted to make his horse, Incitatus, a consul not to demonstrate how much he thought of his horse but how little he thought of the Senate. (Some things never change.) In any event, this was the allusion George Washington Parke Custis used to indicate just how great this particular horse that belonged to Mary Washington was.

Caligula, incidentally, created a temporary bridge more than two miles long, across the Bay of Baiae, built on a row of pontoons. He then rode Incitatus across it. He did this to snub his nose at a soothsayer who had once said that Caligula had "no more chance of becoming emperor than of riding a horse across the Bay of Baiae." (Unlike the claim about Caligula wanting his horse to be consul, no one disputes that this really happened.)

George Washington, when barely a teenager, did something even greater. Caligula had an army to build his bridge, after all, which he then had merely to trot across. George Washington only had the neighborhood boys to help him when he decided to do something a lot more daring than the emperor had done.

George told his friends that he would break his mother's unbreakable horse. His friends argued that the horse was too proud, too noble, too willful to be broken—or at least that's what everyone believed, based on what had happened to a few people, with battered limbs and broken noses, who had tried to break him.

Yet George made a sort of dare to his friends.

Being a great leader never involves simply telling people what to do, after all, but instead, putting yourself in greater danger or peril than those you lead or, if this is not possible, at least being willing to share any burden with them.

Leadership also involves challenging those you lead.

George did both. He told his friends that if they could corral the horse in a space small enough that they could get a bridle in his mouth, he would ride and break his mother's unbreakable horse.

This, then, was George's Stephen King moment.

His mother's unbreakable horse was the monster in the haunted house, the giant in the forest, the dog that drooled acid from stainless steel teeth. His friends rose to the challenge.

Early the next morning after the challenge had been given, George's friends gathered 'round the monster, who made even gigantic George look less than the giant he normally seemed. With much struggle, through a combination of trickery and bribery, they finally got Mary's monstrous horse corralled in a small enclosure, expending a few apples and some sugar in the process, along with some of their own blood.

Once they had the horse in the enclosure, after several attempts, they managed to tie it up. Getting a bridle into its mouth then was not as difficult—the horse whinnied and neighed but could do little to resist.

Without waiting for fear to take over, George pushed his friends out of the way and leapt on the back of the horse. The horse exploded in a torrent of whinnying and writhing—though still tied up. George told his friends to untie the horse. The sounds of the animal mixed with the yells of the boys could be heard on adjoining farms as the horse now threatened to break George's legs against the sides of the enclosure.

George's friends somehow managed to open the gate, and the horse, with George on his back, shot across the field like a cannonball.

George Washington Parke Custis compares George's friends' evolving reaction over the next few minutes to the thoughts of the Indian marksman who, years later, had been ordered to shoot George in a battle. At first, the marksman was convinced that George had no chance. Yet as he fired shot after shot, he found his bullets mysteriously repelled from their target. After about seventeen shots, the Indian stopped shooting, concluding that it was a sin to shoot at George Washington. It was obvious to the Indian marksman that George Washington was "spirit protected." This is the way George seemed to his friends, staying atop the unmountable horse.

George first got the horse's attention by pulling the bridle sharply. Suddenly aware that George was stronger than any rider that had yet made the attempt, the horse exerted more of his own strength, writhing and bucking to get George off his back.

No matter how strong George was, strength would not be enough. However, coupled with his strength, his skill and balance, and his intuitive understanding of where the horse would move before the horse knew, made George begin to believe that he might actually stay atop the horse.

After a few more moments, George began to seem so attuned to the writhing animal that, to his watching friends, the two appeared as one, "centaur-like."

But no one could have predicted what happened next.

As George's friends looked on, "… the fears of the associates [George's friends] became more relieved as, with matchless skill the rider [George] preserved his seat, and with unyielding force controlled the courser's rage, when the gallant horse, summoning all his powers to one mighty effort reared, and plunged with tremendous violence, burst his noble heart, and died in an instant."

This was George's *Ferris Bueller* moment. The Ferrari had just crashed through the garage wall and plunged to the distant bottom of the canyon below.

His mother's favorite horse lay dead under him. As George Washington Parke Custis put it, "The rider, 'alive, unharmed, and without a wound,' was joined by the youthful groupe, and all gazed upon the generous steed, which now prostrate, 'trailed in dust the honors of his mane,' while from distended nostrils gushed in torrents the life-blood that a moment before had swollen in his veins."

At this point, George's "strength," "vivacity," and "soundness of mind and body" had led him to the brink.

Yet, for George, the soundness of his mind meant more than the quick reflexes and intuitive understanding of a horse that had allowed him to control the animal. His mind, after all, also contained one of his earliest memories: of the hatchet, the cherry tree, and his father. This part of George Washington's mind was about to come into play, too.

George and his friends all went to breakfast at George's house, during which Mary Washington asked the boys, "Pray, young gentlemen, have you seen my blooded colts in your rambles? I hope they are well taken care of; my favorite, I am told, is as large as his sire."

The modern mind immediately leaps to the obvious post-*Seinfeld* answer: "No, we've not seen your blooded colt, but we have seen your *bloody* colt."

But times were different then.

George considered the situation. He felt a compulsion to do the right thing towards his mother. Also, though George Washington surely would have done the right thing even if he and his mother had been alone, with his friends watching, the choice was made clearer.

"Your favorite, the sorrel, is dead, madam." George said.

"Dead?" his mother asked, incredulous. "Why, how has this happened?"

George continued with only a brief glance to see how his friends were reacting. Times may change, but boys will be boys. The utter unvarnished honesty George displayed amazed them more than George's superhuman performance on the horse. "That sorrel horse has long been considered ungovernable, and beyond the power of man to back or ride him. This morning, aided by my friends, we forced a bit into his mouth; I backed him, I rode him, and in a desperate struggle for the mastery, he fell under me and died upon the spot."

Mary's face flashed red, but she remained composed. "It is well. While I regret the loss of my favorite, I rejoice in my son, who always speaks the truth."

Neither of these two events—the ride nor the honesty about the ride—was a minor incident in the life of someone who was to inspire a nation, throughout his life and for hundreds of years after his death, by the exact combination of qualities he was now showing—courage, tempered with dispassionate honor; daring to do the brave thing, while feeling compelled to do the right thing and say the true thing, whatever the consequences.

Spoiler alert: Here's the trick. Here's how George managed to pull a superhero out of his hand-me-down tricorner hat.

It is claimed that courage is almost always a lack of knowledge—that is, if people really understood the danger involved in, say, jumping on the back of an "unbreakable" horse, they wouldn't do it. Is there really a difference between George's seemingly reckless leap onto the back of a horse that might kill him and a modern teenager's decision to drive a car ninety miles an hour down a highway?

There is.

George was still young when this incident occurred, but he had already been around horses for years—really, since the day he was born. He understood horses, understood this horse, and knew what he was doing. This horse clearly had more spirit and willfulness than the other horses, but the way any horse moves, the pattern of movements he would use to try to throw a rider, is imprinted in his genes. Horses, which must walk within seconds of being born, jump, buck, and try to throw riders in a specific pattern they are born with. They don't learn this. They *learn* to be ridden. Throwing someone off their back is instinctive.

George knew the pattern of this horse's movements, having seen him and his relatives his whole life. He had been riding on these horses since he was little more than a toddler.

George, therefore, knew exactly and precisely what he was doing and knew exactly and precisely what the risks were. It may have looked like idiotic daring to others, and of course there was some risk involved. George, though, knew what the risks were and how to master them. He knew this specific horse almost as well as he knew himself. His symbiosis with it, the fact that it looked to observers as if he and the horse had become one, "centaur-like," was not a fluke—it was the result of experience, exercise, practice, and training.

The lesson is not about taking ridiculous risks, but about a lifetime of refining your talents. It *is* about talent—but also about *developing* talent.

In other words, be cool, but know what you're doing. Shaun White has talent, but he also practices more than you.

⟡

Speaking of strength and vivacity…did George Washington really throw a silver dollar across the Potomac?

No. But he *did* throw a rock across the Rappahannock.

(For those non-Americans out there, along with the cherry tree story, this is the other "myth" about George Washington that every American learns as a child, and most Americans grow up to believe is a mere tale.)

While throwing a rock across the Rappahannock is less impressive in terms of strength and vivacity—it's a shorter distance than a dollar across the Potomac—it has the virtue of alliteration.

Also, it's true.

Although this will come as a surprise to reflexive doubters, the first story of George throwing things a long way is recorded, believe it or not, in George Washington's own words, in his own writing. This is obviously the best provenance of all.

George wrote the following in his notes to his friend and former aide-de-camp David Humphreys, who was living at Mount Vernon after the Revolution, before George became president. Humphreys was there beginning a biography of his friend and former commander. Because George and Humphreys were living in the same house, most of the interactions about the book between the two men were oral.

However, George did make some notes, seemingly oddly referring to himself in the third person. George said, about himself, that he had "never met a man who could throw a stone to so great a distance as himself; and, that when standing in the valley beneath the natural bridge in Virginia, he has thrown one up to that stupendous arch."

The "natural bridge" was thought, in George's day, to be one of the two great wonders of the Americas, along with Niagara Falls. In fact, it is higher than Niagara Falls, towering at 212 feet versus Niagara's 167 feet.

George's step-grandson, George Washington Parke Custis, said this about rock throwing: "The power of Washington's arm was displayed in several memorable instances—in this throwing a stone across the Rappahannock river, another from the bed of the stream to the top of the Natural Bridge, and yet another over the Palisades into the Hudson."

There should be no doubt that these incidents are true, because of the sources for them (George Washington and George Washington Parke Custis). Yet doubters will be doubters.

So, to debunk the debunkers, the rock-across-the-Rappahannock feat was demonstrated feasible, *MythBusters*-style, by retired Washington Senators' pitcher Walter Johnson, in 1936. On his second try, Walter Johnson threw a silver dollar across the 272-foot expanse of the Rappahannock River, landing it forty-two feet beyond the river's opposite edge.

As the tale has been retold and retold again since George first recounted it, it is not surprising that the river in the story has been changed from the one George knew in his youth to the one at his most famous home, Mount Vernon. But the essence of the story has always been true.

George was a phenomenal natural athlete.

More recently, the clever minds at the Aerobie company demonstrated that, in fact, a silver dollar *could* be thrown across the Potomac's mile-wide expanse at Mount Vernon. Although they could have thrown it any mile to prove the point, they chose, for publicity reasons, Mount Vernon, where one fine summer day an Aerobist threw a silver dollar, affixed to an Aerobie, across the Potomac from Mount Vernon.

George did not benefit from an Aerobie, but he *was* as great a pitcher as a legendary major leaguer. It is tempting to make an assumption and add the phrase "without any training," but this is probably not true. Who knows how much time George spent practicing rock-throwing? He doesn't record this. His ability to throw things a great distance was important enough to him, after all, that he mentioned it in his notes for a proposed biography.

Talent and practice, surely.

Remember, though, that today there are countless more things at which you can be talented, which will get you far. Someone had to invent the Aerobie, after all. Which means that even some engineers hover at the border of cool.

Before we get all dewy-eyed about George's greatness, it is worth pausing a moment to thank our lucky stars—or Providence, or the inexorable advance of Western civilization—for how much luckier we are than even Joseph Addison and Christopher Wren were. Or George Washington was.

Whether it is fate or luck, Providence or a roll of the dice, talent meeting opportunity is what makes men great. And it's so much easier for that to happen today.

Take tall Chinese guys playing basketball in New York. Only one or two decades ago, this would not have happened. To be an NBA star a few decades ago, you had to be tall, talented…and also born in the right place. Now, tall and talented is enough. The downside of this, of course, is that a tall, marginally less talented person born in what used to be the right place will, today, lose his spot to someone from Shanghai. The upside—which I'm convinced is bigger—is that, just as London offered many more opportunities than colonial Virginia did, the modern integrated world offers more opportunities than even a large metropolis in the eighteenth century could. Communications and transportation do give more opportunities, overall (the marginally less talented basketball player from what used to be the right place can now, at least, play for the Outer Shanghai Regional Basketball Association and Latex Sock Factory).

George Washington was great in the only way he could have been great in his society. We are fortunate to have a lot more ways and opportunities to be great.

Even so, being great is not for everybody.

Malcolm Gladwell has been ubiquitous in the media for several years, hawking his Horatio Alger–ish point, apparently based on his own informal meta-study, that the way—and he seems to claim the only way—to be great is to devote at least ten thousand hours to something you care enough about to devote ten thousand hours to. That much practice, along with whatever innate talents and abilities you may have, leads you to greatness, he says. He points to students at Julliard who entered at varying levels of ability, some of whom ended up successful concert pianists, some not. The difference is not their perceived abilities when they started Julliard but how many hours they practiced when they were there. No matter how talented they were, they didn't become great without a huge amount of hard work.

So work—exercise and training—seems to be a necessary component of greatness. But is it sufficient? Not for George. "Providence" was the vital core component, without which we never would have heard his name.

George Washington did work hard, he did strive, he did have alacrity and vigour. However, beyond this, he believed he was put here for a purpose. He was great in ways especially suited to his society. What he was able to achieve made him—beyond his own society, on the world stage, across all cultures, societies, and epochs—great, full stop.

A fundamental thing that made George Washington be the George Washington we know is that what drove George to true greatness was not a quest for personal glory, or self actualization, or whatever modern, egocentric labels we may choose to put on selfishness and small-mindedness. George became great by focussing all his abilities and opportunities in a quest to fulfil the destiny he had no doubt Providence had placed in his heart and also placed as potential in the world around him.

More than a century before Horatio Alger, George Washington was creating something great—himself—out of a uniquely American combination of talent, desire, and the liberty to do things his own way, alongside the perseverance and determination to get big things done, to get them right, and most important of all, to do them for the right reason.

Shouldn't people have hated him, though? Big, successful people, however pure their motives, are often the victims of jealousy. No. People loved and admired George Washington. Why? Well, we're about to find out what he did to make that happen.

Chapter Four

George Washington's "Affable, Candid, and Obliging Nature"

"He was of an easie Access, and incredible Patience. Never Angry, never Distasted, but always the same, willing to oblige, and averse from displeasing even the most ordinary People."
—H. de Luzancy, *A Panegyrick to the Memory of His Grace Frederick, Late Duke of Schonberg*

On the cold Monday morning of March 11, 1748, before the sun was even visible, George Washington and "George Fairfax, Esq." set out on the eighteenth-century version of a road trip, to help survey land owned by George Fairfax's cousin, Lord Fairfax, in the forests of the Ohio Valley. It was exactly the same as a road trip would be today, except, of course, there were no roads.

And, chances were, they'd run into Indians. And no, not the politically correct "Native Americans" you may have heard about in school. These were real Indians, drunk, with tomahawks, carrying scalps. (Spoiler alert: I said "chances were" they might run into these sorts of people, but do you really think I'd have said that if they weren't going to? Having the almost magical advantage of hindsight, I can assure you that, indeed, mere moments from now, these are precisely the people that the ill-prepared seventeen-year-old George is about to run into. Hold on to your hats. Better yet, hold on to your scalps.)

George Washington had impressed his neighbors, the Fairfaxes, that he was a rising star who could help "George Fairfax, Esq." return from a surveying trip into the wilderness with *his* scalp still attached to his head. George's slightly older contemporary, George William Fairfax, was richer in money but less heroic in every other way than George Washington. It was a plus that George Washington was studying surveying, but the real reason the Fairfaxes asked him to go on the trip was that in addition to having cultivated their friendship, he was clearly, already, a great teenager, if not yet a great man. He was better on his horse than his friends were on theirs, larger than almost anyone in Virginia, brave, and heroic. The Fairfaxes thought themselves fortunate to have big George help them with their business and perhaps to protect their own smaller George.

George's interest in surveying, though it wasn't the selling point for the Fairfaxes, was the primary reason George wanted to go on this trip. He wanted experience in applying the most important skill he was learning at his "country" school.

In a land-based economy, being a surveyor was as useful as being a stock analyst would be today (but slightly more exciting, as instead of water cooler breaks, George would be thrown into the water and almost drown. More on that later, too. Hold on to your boat—with the hand that's not busy holding on to your scalp.)

With no banks as we know them today, and money so rare that debts and bills were often paid with promissory notes passed around from man to man in lieu of cash (despite the very real risk that these could become worthless should the originator fall on hard times), the most stable wealth was land. You might grow crops with the help of your slaves, hire your land out to others, or sell it. But one way or another, land, not cash or stocks or bonds, was the way to acquire wealth in colonial Virginia. Potentially, by picking the right pieces of real estate at the right time, you might even get rich.

Not that being rich was the point. That's a modern corruption.

In George Washington's day, being rich was only a necessary stepping stone along the path to the real goal—being a great man, a gentleman. Having land, having wealth, having fine things—all those were the accouterments of being a great man, but the ultimate goal was to be someone like the Duke in the *Panegyrick*, not to have a number on a piece of paper with lots of zeros after it, or having even the trappings of wealth.

Still, George understood the inevitable importance of land in the equation of greatness in colonial Virginia and also understood that the way to get land and advance in life was to make the right friends. (Generally this meant people with land, who also tended to be the people with political, social, and business connections.) To make the right kind of friends, the right attitude for the up-and-coming young man was friendly but deferential—along the lines of the Duke's "affable, candid, and obliging nature" in the *Panegyrick*.

From our perspective, this may sound a bit smarmy. (Though just wait a minute, and you'll see how much smarmier people in the eighteenth century could be.) Today we think of "real friends" and people who "use other people" as polar opposites. This is an odd, and very modern, distinction.

Wouldn't we all be glad to be of use to our friends, to do anything good for them—especially if they're real friends? We have been brainwashed to think it is fair to get a job by our "merit" and unfair to get a job by our "connections"—when merit really just means answering questions on a test or getting a parchment which certifies that we have answered questions on even more tests. We complain about "favoritism." But who made the rule that being socially adroit is a lesser talent—or a worse measure of someone's overall worth—than ticking boxes on exam forms?

In colonial Virginia, your social skills were seen as part of your real merit, along with your intelligence and your physical strength. It was, if you consider the times, a new, different, and liberating state of affairs to be able to succeed in this way—on your real value as a man—rather than on inherited titles and family wealth.

Having said that, in George Washington's time, inherited advantage still was important. Compare the two Georges who were taking this eighteenth-century road trip together. George Fairfax, standing at his full height, stared straight into George Washington's chest. Yet he had many advantages George didn't have. The other George was the son of William Fairfax, who was a cousin of Lord Fairfax and administrator of Lord Fairfax's lands in America.

Lord Fairfax had inherited a truly astonishing amount of land in Virginia—over five million acres. Although many local colonists disputed the claim and resented Fairfax, most of the Fairfaxes were in England, close to the king, and, as the world was about to see, it took more than a few disgruntled colonists to affect the King of England. Nothing that happened in America—not local resentment, certainly, but beyond that no law, no court decision, nothing—mattered more than the king's opinion. And the king thought Lord Fairfax should have his five million acres.

Thus the short, portly, little Lord Fairfax retained his five million acres, such a vast quantity that he had actually decided to come to America to see it with his own eyes, surely at least in part to have something astonishing to talk about at dinner parties when he eventually returned home to England. In this way, George Washington was to meet the only titled Englishman to call America home (there were a few appointed officials with titles from time to time in the colonies, but they were only on temporary assignments).

The Fairfaxes were still mainly in England, and thus the Fairfax land in Virginia fell under the English system of primogeniture—the eldest son inherits everything, and the other members of the family get only crumbs from his table. Well, not exactly crumbs. Jobs suited to their station, like personal secretary or clergyman.

George Washington's father had been relatively wealthy, having about ten thousand acres. Lord Fairfax had *five hundred times* more land. He was more than loaded. He was outrageously, astronomically rich.

William Fairfax and his son George Fairfax, however, were caught in the middle between great wealth and a glass floor that cut off members of their class from what we might view as "work." Their only real choice in life was a kind of grovelling obsequiousness to their more highly placed relatives.

George Washington could have been sucked up into this world of flatterers, sycophants, and drones who buzzed around Lord Fairfax and his ilk, believing that the way to wealth and happiness was to court those who were more powerful than themselves. In fact, when George met Lord Fairfax, he was allegedly advised that it would be prudent to ride his horse less well than the rotund, unathletic nobleman.

George was impressed by the Fairfaxes' wealth and their Virginia house, which to him seemed a castle. (To George Fairfax, who had lived in England, it was merely a "tolerable cottage.") But he doesn't seem to have been impressed with Lord Fairfax himself, nor the system that insisted that in order for George Washington to advance in life he had to be or act, in some sense, inferior to Lord Fairfax.

Lord Fairfax was a textbook case of how enormous wealth—and the freedom it buys from ever having anyone question anything you do—can make people a little odd. (Think Michael Jackson, except that Lord Fairfax was known for his peculiarly long and hooked nose, not the complete lack thereof.)

Lord Fairfax, for example, had taken to arriving on the doorsteps of local ladies with a fox in a bag, to be released for their entertainment. When this happened, the poor women felt they had no choice but to stand on their porch smiling politely. As the show continued, they felt they had no choice but to express delight as the hounds tore the poor fox to bits.

In the normal course of events, Lord Fairfax could expect all his friends and neighbors to laugh at his unfunny jokes, to be impressed by cowardly shows of "heroism," and to compliment his faults. He was, after all, a fabulous font of wealth for many people, including George's own half-brother Lawrence. (Lord Fairfax once took a petition from Lawrence, shoved it into his pocket, and never mentioned it again. What could anyone say? It was never in anyone's interest to criticize Lord Fairfax.)

How different from the Duke of Schonberg, who—according to the *Panegyrick*—was immune to flattery: "truly Great...above the mean Insinuations of Flatterers. A famous wit in *France*, was commanded to Compliment him at his return from *Portugal*; and to make his Atchievements in that Country, the chief Theam of his Harangue. He did it to the Admiration of all who heard him, but the *duke*'s. His Modesty was more troubled at his Praises, than ever his Courage at the sight of the *Spanish* Battalions."

Lord Fairfax, lacking any natural luster, went instead for bumptious bluster. A lord or a duke, in fact, had to have quite a bit of genuine nobility of character to resist the temptations inherent in his station in life. The inner nobility that enabled the Duke to resist the flattery and the other temptations that came with his outward nobility was George Washington's ideal.

The unexpected path George took in pursuit of his ideal had begun in his school days, when his family could no longer afford to send him to Appleby, after George's father died. Yet George somehow had, one must logically conclude, the perfect education, the proof being that he ended up as near to perfect as most people could ever hope to be. Still, by English standards, George Washington had a terrible education.

At the end of an education at Appleby, George would have been able to translate passages of "Cicero into English, Demosthenes into Latin, the Latin Testament into Greek." He could have passed a "practical exercise on the Catechism" and composed verses in Greek. (Those were the requirements of an exam that some graduates of Appleby volunteered to take in order to receive a scholarship for Oxford.)

Had George's mind been molded by the rigid orthodoxy that was a legal requirement in England, it is very doubtful he would ever have become the George Washington we all know. Hidebound religious orthodoxy and brutal corporal punishment (including of boys by other boys) made English public school the perfect training ground for life in a rigid social hierarchy—the kind of system that Lord Fairfax sat at the very pinnacle of in colonial Virginia.

George couldn't speak ancient Greek as fluently as he could speak English (in fact, he didn't understand a word). He couldn't recite page after page of Latin off the top of his head as a "well-educated" boy in his day could have done. But more important, he was never beaten, bullied, and fagged by his schoolmates and schoolmasters.

He also, critically, was socialized in the American way by his schooling—not the English way.

Brutal corporal punishment was very much a part of a public school education in the England of George Washington's day. And while the "fagging" of boys was not something as widely discussed as caning, it was a tradition dating from at least the sixteenth century in English public schools and still considered good for one's character.

Overtly, fagging was the institutional subservience of younger boys to older boys—by virtue of nothing more than their respective years in school. It prepared students for life in a rigidly class-conscious society, in which certain people, regardless of their innate virtues (or lack thereof), but merely by their social position (primarily dictated by birth) had vast power over those lower down on the totem pole.

The "fagging" relationship in English schools included a wide range of duties, rights, and responsibilities. At its core, though, was the absolute power of the older boys over the younger ones. The sexual abuse that—not always, but not infrequently—tended to stem from this relationship was not admitted publicly. However, the modern term "fag" does come from "fagging."

There is a direct correlation between the bullying and abuse that was once an inherent part of the schools of the ruling class in Britain and the unquestioned autocratic instinct felt by those schools' graduates during Britain's heyday, as they and their country dominated a good portion of the earth's population. When we think about what George Washington did (and did not) get out of his education, then, it is clearly not just the intellectual aspect that is important.

There has always been a kind of viciousness between members of the upper class in Britain that was not a part of George Washington's colonial Virginia. On an island such as England, with a finite amount of land (land being the ultimate source of wealth), in which primogeniture was unquestioned (with the elder son getting everything, and the other sons getting nothing), competition for position amongst the landless portion of the upper class was intense. The further away you were from someone with some land, a title, or both, the more desperate was your struggle to maintain your position.

The legendary viciousness in English schools is clearly a reflection of the desperation to keep up with the Sir Joneses. The non–Lord Fairfaxes fawning attendance on the crude Lord Fairfax was the adult aspect of this same system.

Had George gone to Appleby, that obsequiousness—which he would later refer to as "the accursed state of attendance and dependence"—might have been so ingrained in his character that he would have groveled toward Lord Fairfax all his life—and never stood up to King George III. In fact, George Washington himself eventually came to believe that the typical English education was positively "unfriendly to republican government."

George, however, was living in a country in which land—the source of wealth and power in both England and Virginia—was seemingly infinite. For all practical purposes, and for the foreseeable future, there was more land than anyone could imagine ever using in America, even taking into account the five million acres locked up by Lord Fairfax.

The abundance of land in America made it possible to lay aside primogeniture and divide landed property between all the surviving sons. Eventually portions were even left to daughters. Rather than a constant vicious competition amongst younger sons for social position, there was a familial feeling of collaboration amongst all the members of George Washington's class in Virginia, as they tried to strengthen and keep intact the subtle fabric that enabled a society to exist where, within living memory, there had been nothing but wild animals and the Indians who were, in their view, savages.

Adding to this cohesive circumstance was the fact that there were only a very few—some historians cite seven extended families—that made up the Virginia gentry of which George was a member. Inevitably, the members of these families intermarried. Therefore, everyone that a person of George's class would meet as an equal in Virginia was a cousin, or at least related through marriage to one. (George's half-brother Lawrence was even married to a Fairfax.)

This American sense of collaboration, cooperation, and kinship, rather than vicious competition, was reflected in George's education. Although we might wish to know more about the details of George's schooling, we do know that the atmosphere in the type of school George Washington went to was collegial and nothing like a stereotypical English public school. (At a day school like George Washington's, you might even occasionally see a girl.)

Thus George's "affable" and "obliging" nature fell short of the truly smarmy toadying and flattery that was one of the worst characteristics of the British class system. He was affable enough to make friends with the Fairfaxes and obliging enough to take on this trip with George Fairfax. But George Washington was independent and American enough to relate to George Fairfax as his friend and equal—even, in some ways, as his superior—not as a flattering toady.

As we'll see, George Washington's quintessentially American social skills extended beyond his own class. George had a uniquely American aversion to "Displeasing" what the *Panegyrick* calls "even the most ordinary People."

As big and little George, George Washington and George Fairfax, set off, the thought of Indians was on both of their minds (ensconced as those minds were, they feared, for only for a short while longer beneath their scalps).

The idea of scalping does not have a visceral effect on most of us today. As a culture, we're generally desensitized to violence through exposure to mass media. In any event, in the mass media, Indians haven't been the bad guys for generations. Beyond this, political correctness has made it difficult to recall just how savage Indians could be. You will, though, in a moment, see American Indians the way they were seen by people who actually saw them. This might bring about at least a mild paradigm shift from what you've been taught in school.

Before the Indians, though, was the beauty.

George and George rode through brush and bramble, up and down the rolling hills. It was too early in the year for the mosquitoes and the other insects that tormented Virginians during the summer (and killed many settlers with the spread of disease). There were more buds than leaves on the trees, which enabled George to see through the forest in spite of the trees.

George Washington was normally diligent and punctilious, but on this first great adventure of his life, a sense of wonder opened his eyes, as he marvelled at the "most beautiful Groves of Sugar Trees" and wrote about spending "the best part of the Day in admiring the Trees & richness of the Land."

Although the hills and mountains over which they passed were uncultivated, in the valleys, for the first three days, the two Georges were in land that had been tamed by Europeans.

They saw, it might be said, the mirror image of what we would see.

We seek out forests for what we think of as a respite from the urban grind. We think we find nature in our national parks, but of course even these are highly cultivated. The wolves are gone from most of them, along with most of the bears. Saving the wolves and bears may seem a pure and noble thing from the comfort of your condominium's couch.

It was from quite a different vantage point that the two Georges saw nature—the perspective of potential wolf-meal or bear's dinner. They saw vast swaths of land, disordered and savage, with rare islands of cultivation and civility.

Even amongst the Englishmen, of course, it was still only a very few who were genuinely civilized. There were wild and relatively uncivilized Europeans out here, too. A well-ordered and prosperous farm with rows of tobacco was a wonder in the wilderness. A mere plate was a luxury and a meal at a table a small miracle.

For the first three days of George and George's journey, they stayed at the houses of planters of their own class. But the further west they went, the coarser the cloth of their hosts' clothes, the fewer and plainer the utensils—until, on the fourth night, they found themselves in a netherworld inhabited by Indians and those Englishmen disposed by class, background, or inclination to live amongst them.

George had not been taught the snobbery of the English. He naturally assumed, and rightly so, that some men were better than others, and he also saw that some men were in more fortunate positions in life than others. He did not see the two as necessarily going together, as a glance at the other George instantly told him. If the right people died, that other George would grow up to be a lord, but in any event he was born with more power and wealth than George Washington could reasonably imagine ever having for himself. For the Fairfaxes, George Washington was a mid-sized step down, even as George Fairfax, standing at full height, stared straight into George Washington's shirt.

George Washington had been born, bred, and educated in the partially tamed land that was to become the United States. He was now striving for success in this world. He had no compunction about finding friends and allies of the sort Lord Fairfax would disdain. George Washington was willing to be affable and obliging not just to those who could help him amongst the elite, but also to woodsmen and Indians. Snobbery would have got in his way. George had, indeed, if not the "common touch" of a modern politician, then a pragmatic ability to see beyond the superficial to someone's true worth, substance, and character.

His imperfect judgment, of himself and others, was still to get in his way, but he was already trying and often succeeding.

On the fourth night, George and George, along with a surveyor they had picked up along the way, stayed at "Penningtons." This was the sort of place "woodsmen" stayed. This was a class of men on the frontier, capable of living independently in the woods, surviving and perhaps even thriving by hunting, fur trading, and supplying hospitality and guidance to people such as the two Georges when they came through. The wars that were fought (and the Indians killed, subjugated, or at least cowed) that enabled these frontiersmen to stay in the woods with their scalps still firmly attached to their heads were largely invisible to them, although some understood the bigger picture enough to feel grateful, and to help those closer to the centers of power whose interests coincided with theirs, when they could.

Exhausted when he arrived at Penningtons, George Washington fell into a deep sleep, completely unaware that multitudes of "Vermin such as Lice and Fleas etc." swarmed over his body as he slumbered, leaving him itching and scratching in what ranged from mild discomfort to severe pain for weeks afterwards. He—affably and wisely—did not complain to Pennington about the pest-ridden hospitality. In this, George acted just like his hero the Duke, who was "averse from displeasing even the most ordinary People." Rather than complaining, George merely vowed privately to himself, in his journal, that he would sleep in the "open Air before a fire" in the future and leave Penningtons and places like that to real woodsmen.

Just a few days into his journey, my great-great uncle, at seventeen, was already becoming the sort of person who would be tough enough to wait the British out at Valley Forge. Had George spent those years ensconced by the fire in the library of an English school, as his father and he both had wanted, he would surely have been too soft to face the frost of Valley Forge. But more than that, he certainly would never have developed the ability to get along with people from backgrounds so vastly different from his own or to handle himself socially in the countless ways he was learning, even at the edge of the civilized world.

When old Westerns show Indians, they are almost always post–Andrew Jackson Indians, with the Indians on one side and us on the other. Nearly a century before the Trail of Tears, back in the 1740s, American Indians were not a unified group in anyone's mind, least of all their own. They were at war with each other—while Americans of European descent were seen by them as occasional allies, not yet the threat they were to become to all Indians.

Even bearing this in mind, it is perhaps still difficult to get your mind around George's first recorded reaction to American Indians. On March

23, 1748, twelve days after setting out on his first adventure, the seventeen-year-old George Washington was "agreeably surpris'd at the sight of thirty odd Indians coming from War with only one Scalp."

That he was agreeably surprised—rather than scared out of his mind—bears thought. Only one scalp? Did he stop to think the next one might be his?

The tone of his comment has the air of a Facebook photo caption of tourists in Mexico, who are agreeably surprised at thirty sombrero-wearing natives but somewhat disappointed that they only have one Mexican jumping bean among them. There is no expression of revulsion at the sight of a scalp, no word of disgust at the savage act of scalping one's victims, and, most tellingly, no fear.

The reason there was no fear is that in 1744, Virginia and Maryland had made a treaty with the Six Nations (also called the Iroquois), a confederacy of Indian tribes. The Indians who had met with the colonists possessed the power to make a treaty for all land near both the Potomac and Susquehanna Rivers, as well as certain areas beyond.

The reason a few Iroquois had the power to negotiate for so many Indians is that they had just won a bloody war of conquest and extermination against weaker, more vulnerable tribes. In what was to prove a fatal miscalculation, the Iroquois had also agreed, in those negotiations, to sell to the colonists whatever additional land they might want, whenever they might want it.

It must have seemed such a trivial thing to them at the time. There were, after all, so few British, and so much land.

Knowing of the Indian weakness for alcohol (though not yet knowing the cause—genetic markers D11S1984 and D4S3242, apparently, lead Indians to get drunk much more easily than most people and give them a higher propensity for alcoholism), George's party offered the scalp-carrying warriors enough alcohol to get drunk.

It is worth seeing it the way George did: "We had some Liquor with us of which we gave them Part it elevating there Spirits put them in the Humor of Dauncing of whom we had a War Daunce."

The reason the two Georges were carrying this much alcohol with them was not to fuel Bacchanalian parties for themselves in the wilderness. There was a strategic, diplomatic reason to be affable and obliging to the Indians. Keeping good relations with Indians meant not only that that British settlers could continue to live side by side with them, but also that the Indians, if and when they were needed, could be called upon to help fight Britain's enemies. Alcohol was a very cheap way for the English to get what they wanted. George himself said, a few years later, "The Indians are our Friends.… Nothing can more contribute to keeping them our Friends than contriving them the necessities of Life at the easiest rates.… The Indians…esteem those honestest who sell the cheapest."

Free is even better than cheap, and genetic markers D11S1984 and D4S3242 meant that alcohol, for the Indians, was something very close to a "necessit[y] of Life" for them.

Once the Indians had drunk their drink, a fire was built. Overtaken by the trance-like mood cast by the fire and fuelled by alcohol, an Indian speaker rose "telling [the other warriors] in what Manner they are to Daunce." Suddenly, "the best Dauncer," as if aroused from his sleep, leapt up and danced, according to George, "in a most comical Manner." Soon this "Dauncer" was followed by others, the dancing accompanied by a few Indian warriors who played a drum made with "a Pot half of Water with a Deerskin Stretched over it" and a few shakers, something like maracas.

We tend to imagine this sort of thing through the hazy prism of politically correct media images. So perhaps we have trouble seeing why, to George, Indians doing a war dance did not look proud and noble. Exotic, yes, but proud and noble, no. George seems to have had the same reaction that you or I might have encountering friendly homeless people dancing around a fire made in a trash bin. He felt no politically correct urge to see half-naked drunk people, carrying the scalp of their victim whilst dancing around a fire, through a soft-focus lens.

In the course of his career, George was to treat some Indians with respect, as partners and collaborators. He even prayed to their god with them at least once. But George did not imbue Indians with any imaginary "noble savage" status. In this first encounter, he candidly recorded his honest reaction, seeing them as exotic, interesting, and dubious.

George was "affable, candid, and obliging" to the Indians, but with balance and within reasonable limits—just as he was to the lords of his own world, just as he was to the woodsmen with their lice-infested blankets. George was polite and friendly to all sorts of people while making useful connections where he could. His attitude, though, didn't jibe with the prejudices of our day (in favor of the poor, the oppressed, and minorities), any more than he was blinded by the prejudices of his own time (in favor of the rich, the nobly born, and the powerful).

George took people as he found them and saw them clearly as they were.

Here, then, is something else we can learn from George (just as he, in his turn, was influenced by the Duke of Schonberg). An ability to judge people on their intrinsic merits is as valuable today as it was then. To intuitively relate to everyone in an "affable" and "obliging" way, without prejudice, is of great strategic advantage, in addition to, kind of, feeling good.

But let's be selfish. Think about it. Would you like to have more possible allies and friends? Or do you want to just stick to your frat brothers? Where would we be today if George had just stuck to people like the Fairfaxes?

George was to go on to effect a huge change in the world. It was necessary for him to start by seeing the world as it was. This began with his education—or, arguably, lack thereof. When George Washington had gone from his brother Austin's house to his school each morning—whether on foot or horseback, we can't be certain—he had *thought*.

George, on these journeys and in general, had had time to contemplate the world around him, to think things through. If George had been at Appleby School in England, as he and his parents had originally wanted, time by himself would have been more rare, and he wouldn't have been outdoors taking in the barely civilized new world of Virginia for himself. A rigorous school life would have inextricably shaped his character into a more standard English form. Instead, he was in Virginia, forming his own impressions of everything, learning in equal parts from life and books.

With our clock radios, morning DJs, Twitter apps, iPhones, and all the rest—the average person today rarely, if ever, reflects or thinks. This has real consequences. Where are the George Washingtons, Thomas Jeffersons, Benjamin Franklins of our day?

Would Einstein, sitting on the train in Zurich, have thought all the way through to relativity? Or would his phone have buzzed at the critical point in his train of thought with a reminder about his 2:15 Pilates class, which he misread, thinking it said something about pirates, which jarred him to google *Pirates of the Caribbean*, which led him to YouTube and eventually to an interview on E! with Keira Knightley, the movie's star? Rather than coming up with $E=mc^2$, he would have spent the rest of that bus trip fantasizing about getting Keira drunk and his relative chance of kissing her (E=0).

Goodbye, modern world.

George had a kind of education that is hopelessly old-fashioned today but was brand new then—the prototypical education that has created great Americans (however flawed some of them may be), from Benjamin Franklin to Steve Jobs.

This quintessentially American education has little to do with school.

Many bemoan and lament that there are no great men today while there seem to have been many, or at least more, in George Washington's day. There still exist today, though, those rare innovators who do things that could only happen in America. What is it that they have in common?

The first thing great Americans do is think for themselves.

That's exactly what George Washington, molded by his new kind of American education, was doing on his roadless eighteenth-century road trip. Whether he thought about the other George riding beside him, or George's illustrious noble cousin, or the woodsmen at Penningtons, or the Indians, he was forming his own impressions, something many people today avoid ever doing. He was affable and obliging to all, but not obsequious towards any. He judged everybody and everything on its merits. He would keep on doing that very American thing—thinking for himself—even as his experiences were about to turn, first his life and then the world, upside down.

Chapter Five

"His Duty Was His Greatest Passion"

"He would not presume to Command, before he knew perfectly how to Obey…. His Duty was his greatest Passion, and the Discharge of the Noble Trusts put into his hands, his only pleasure."
—H. de Luzancy, *A Panegyrick to the Memory of His Grace Frederick, Late Duke of Schonberg*

Most people died. They just died.

The bubonic plague wasn't the only plague, you know. People aren't really designed to live in cities, so throughout civilization there have been many kinds of plagues.

Of course even in those times between actual outbreaks of a plague, bubonic or not, people still died, left, right, and center. Children especially, but adults, too.

Despite all this, the average age adults reached before the twentieth century was not as low as is sometimes assumed. The average lifespan before the discovery of antibiotics is deceptively low. Before the era of modern medicine, a majority (literally) of children and infants, at least in some areas, died, lowering the overall average. (Cotton Mather, not entirely atypically, had fifteen children, two of whom survived to adulthood.) Therefore the average lifespan of those who reached adulthood was not nearly as low as we sometimes assume if we look at the average lifespan, while the maximum age that people lived was already on par with today's. Benjamin Franklin, after all, lived to be eighty-four, and Thomas Jefferson to eighty-three.

How could people bear so much mortality? Look at yourself. Many of us trundle along, blithely accepting that in the ten years after 9/11, more Americans died in traffic accidents than in all the wars we have ever fought with other countries (that is, excluding the Civil War)— more than died in the American Revolution, the War of 1812, all the way through World Wars I and II, the Vietnam War, the Gulf Wars, and Afghanistan. More Americans than all those who died in all of these wars, combined, died on the roads and highways in America in only the first ten years after 9/11. If you want to understand how people live in the presence of constant death, look at yourself.

Beyond the occasional devastating plague, other horrific and often deadly diseases such as scarlet fever and smallpox cut large swaths through the adult population of colonial America. These diseases have been so thoroughly eradicated that their names sound almost quaint to us. They were unavoidable, and therefore unremarkable, in all times before our own.

The most prevalent disease surely was tuberculosis, or "consumption," a constant threat, and one of the most common causes of death in George Washington's day. It had been ubiquitous since men started living in close proximity to other men and domesticated the cow. (Tuberculosis is thought to have originally been a bovine disease.)

George Washington's duty to his half-brother Lawrence, who was himself ill with tuberculosis, led to one of the greatest adventures of his life, which would, incidentally, involve a few other diseases and deaths and finally lead to Mount Vernon.

It started with a trip to Berkeley Springs that George took with Lawrence Washington, the elder of his two older half-brothers. The Berkeley Hills, in what is now West Virginia, were a popular health resort for colonial Virginians.

The assumption was that malaria, which was epidemic in Virginia, was caused by the "mal" (bad) air of the swampy lower elevations. It therefore seemed logical that the cleaner air in the mountains and the health-giving properties of spring water were preserving and enhancing the health of those who made the journey. This is the way even educated people thought before science. It was all guesswork.

In reality, of course, the malaria abated because the Virginians were escaping the mosquitoes that carried the disease, which were far more prevalent at lower elevations. It was not 'til much later that the association between mosquitoes and malaria was discovered. In any case it worked; going to the mountains actually kept people alive.

(To give the intuition of our forebears its fair due, the belief that spring water, such as was found in the Berkeley Hills, is especially health-giving has been scorned in recent times, thought of as being in the same category as bloodletting, no more than a pre-scientific superstition. However, people who drank spring water were surely healthier in at least one way, as spring water was the least likely to be infected with bacteria and, therefore, the least likely to cause disease. Spring water also tends to have more minerals than well water, and we now know that minerals enhance health. More interestingly, one of the minerals sometimes found in large quantities in spring water, lithium, gives someone who consumes it a feeling of well-being—in our times, of course, lithium is used in large quantities to treat manic depression. This feeling of euphoria may also have contributed to the impression that spring water was curative. Most interesting, as our understanding of things progresses even further, recent discoveries show that the amount of lithium found in some drinking water actually does seem to extend human life span.)

By 1750 Lawrence Washington's tuberculosis had become so severe that he felt forced to quit his job managing the Ohio Company, the organization he helped run, under whose aegis the Ohio Valley was, very slowly, being settled.

A year after quitting his job, nothing was helping. Not leeches, not bloodletting—nothing. His condition worsened despite the modern medicine of his day.

George and Lawrence knew that those who went to the Berkeley Hills did not get malaria. They also had no reason to dispute the common assumption that the spring water there was health-giving and might cure tuberculosis, too. In the fuzzy thinking that was common before the scientific age, the fact that people who went to the Berkeley Hills had less malaria led to the idea that the Berkeley Hills were good for one's health in general, even if the disease in question was an entirely different one, such as tuberculosis.

George and Lawrence reasoned that people who drank spring water got better. True, sometimes they didn't, but that was easily explained by the disease being so bad that even the water wasn't curative enough. Long before the age of antibiotics, it was, in any event, the best option and surely safer than the procedures that hurt and sometimes even killed patients, such as the bloodletting Lawrence was already undergoing.

So with the best of intentions, if with a pre-modern understanding, George Washington took Lawrence to Berkeley Springs, leaving Lawrence's wife, Anne, who was struggling to save the last of their five children, at their home.

George was indebted to his older half-brother Lawrence for much of what he had already accomplished. Lawrence's connections with the Fairfaxes (his wife Anne was the daughter of William Fairfax, Lord Fairfax's land agent) had already introduced George into the highest echelon of Virginia society, which had led to the trip west with the other George (Fairfax) and got him what might be called his first real job—as surveyor for Culpeper County. George was loyal by nature and nurture, but perhaps it was especially easy to give up his productive pursuits to help the brother without whom his own success would not exist.

But, no, that's not fair.

Duty, of course, has never meant doing something in a quid pro quo, you-scratch-my-back-and-I'll-scratch-yours way. "His Duty was his greatest Passion," says the *Panegyrick* about the Duke. But what did that mean?

George Washington got more inspiration and satisfaction out of doing what he knew to be right than most of us get out of getting what we want for ourselves. For him, "duty" had not been worn down to the threadbare, shopworn "duties" we talk about—not even duty to our family, to our employer, nor even to God and country. (After all, George Washington would spend more than six years trying to kill any armed representative of his country who came near him.)

No, for George, duty was above any of that. His duty was his passion, and his passion was the whole business of his life. It meant following in the path that he believed Providence had laid out before him, whether that meant neglecting all the other pressing calls on his time and attention to nurse his sick brother or giving up his loyalty to the British crown to lead a revolution.

George had a little more elbow room to pursue that passion than we seem to have, thanks to the place and time in which he lived. Virginia society was set up to allow at least certain people more scope to pursue greatness. As a member of the gentry, it was easier than it would be for a modern wage slave to decide to ride off into the wilderness on an adventure, or take the time to save your brother—or create a new country.

In our day, slaves as we are, most of us, to the corporations and taxman, we'd never have the time. Two weeks of paid vacation a year doesn't allow much scope for self-abnegating pursuit of duty as a passion.

But don't worry. If Lawrence Washington were living today, "the healthcare system" would take care of him, right? (Actually, I'm not so sure. Having lived overseas, and having had my life literally saved by coming back to America to see a real doctor in less than the eight-month wait I was subject to there, I'm not that impressed by government-managed healthcare "systems.") Plus today, why would we need a revolution, as George Washington felt was necessary, in order to be free? (We can save our country with a free choice between two cloned and clownish politicians, right? Problem solved. Now shut up, and get back to work.)

George had first seen the springs of the Berkeley Hills during his initial foray out west with George Fairfax. In just the few years since then, the springs had become a sort of colonial Lourdes. Tents of the sick and suffering surrounded a pine enclosure into which the waters had been directed. Bathing in it or drinking it were deemed equally medicinal.

Several times a day, a tin horn would blast three rough notes, indicating a switch of which sex would next be curing itself in the mud.

(Knowing what we now know about germs, large numbers of sick people bathing in and drinking the same water, however inherently curative that water may have been, was probably not the best idea.)

George, with no way of knowing anything about germs, still had a relatively pragmatic mind and was able to suss out something most of the sufferers did not seem to notice. He felt the whole setup was "… situated very badly on the east side of a steep mountain and enclosed by hills on all sides, so that the afternoon's sun is hid by four o'clock and the fogs hang over us till nine or ten, which occasion great damps in the mornings, and evenings to be cool."

Beyond this, neither George's passionate pursuit of his duty, nor all of his hopes, could change the laws of science. The water at Berkeley Springs did no good for his brother. George and Lawrence didn't blame the water, though.

The disease was, apparently, too bad at this point for the water to work.

It was gloomy, chilly, and generally miserable—enough to make any invalid, especially one who wasn't getting any better, long for a sunnier spot. As George and his brother mulled Lawrence's desperate circumstance, the idea of a trip to Barbados was eventually struck upon. George's sense of duty to his brother again trumped all his other plans. Work for the Fairfaxes was put on hold. Any aspirations he had to rise further in Virginia society were abandoned for the time being.

Duty first.

Sometimes, it had been observed, people who went to Barbados got better. Sometimes they didn't, but, again, that could easily be attributed to a disease being too far advanced. As some people got better by going to Barbados, going to Barbados might help.

Indeed, it is quite possible that there was a correlation between the more constant weather of Barbados and a respite from the symptoms of TB. Perhaps—even better than lithium in spring water—it was the plentiful rum in Barbados that made people feel better, if not get better. In any event, the cause of George Washington's only trip off the continent was to try to save his brother's life.

The way George's mind worked as a result of his relatively practical American education is clear from his journal of this journey. Had George been to Appleby and had a proper English education, his journal would more likely be filled with allusions to epics, and mythical sea voyages, and perhaps astronomical observations. (Or, perhaps comments on the quality of the fish he ate or the skill of the servants who cooked it, with comparisons between the ship's cooks and the cooks he would have become accustomed to at school.)

In fact, George recorded the ship's longitude and latitude every two hours, kept track of the wind and the weather, and before long was using nautical terms to record the positions of the sails at different times of day. A few more subjective phrases slipped in, but none burdened with the weight of classical allusions. The ocean, he said, was "merciless and fickle"—that was about as poetic as George got.

However Homeric this journey may seem to us, instead of allusions to Homer, George's journal was filled with nautical notations such as "RM: FS and DRFS," referring to the various combinations of sails that were up at any given time.

It was the season for hurricanes when their journey commenced, and George's ship had the bad luck to pass through one. It wasn't just any hurricane, either. It was to an average hurricane as George Washington was to an average man—bigger, stronger, and seemingly intent on getting what it wanted.

What it wanted, it seemed, was George Washington's ship.

Even the most seasoned sailors onboard were terrified, saying "they had never seen such weather." George somehow kept a page in his diary dry on which he wrote, "A Constant succession of hard Winds, Squals of Rain…." For several days the wind was so fierce that the crew was convinced the masts would crack, leaving the ship and everyone on it as good as dead.

That terrifying crack never occurred.

In the end, it seemed, not even a giant hurricane was bigger than George Washington. The seas finally calmed, the sun came out, and those with strong stomachs, including George, were finally in a condition to attempt to eat. When they looked, though, the cupboard was bare—the bread had been "almost Eaten up by Weavels & Maggots." However, casting their lines into the ocean, they were able to catch enough fish to survive the rest of the journey.

The ship with her haggard crew and passengers, including the two scraggly Washingtons, arrived in Bridgetown during the first week of November 1751.

Arriving in the rainy season, George Washington saw a landscape that looked like something from a dream. What he saw moved George to a state of near rapture. Out went his meticulous record-keeping. George, who had so scrupulously recorded the longitude and latitude of the ship every two hours, was now "perfectly ravished by the beautiful prospects which on every side presented to our View. The fields of Cain, Corn, Fruit Trees &c., in a delightful Green."

As you might expect if you were a Washington married to a Fairfax, a member of Barbados's governor's council—Major Gedney Clarke, who was related to the Washingtons through a Fairfax marriage—had come to meet George and Lawrence at the harbor. Wasting no time, he immediately recommended a local doctor for Lawrence.

The doctor, after a cursory examination, basing his diagnosis on the same science that had suggested first spring water and now an island as a cure for a bacteriological infection, gave Lawrence an ebullient and optimistic prognosis.

Continuing along a path marked by a surfeit of goodwill but an absence of scientific understanding, Major Clarke invited them to his house for breakfast and dinner, blithely ignoring the case of smallpox already in the household. However, the case of smallpox did not ignore George.

A few days later, George and Lawrence were sharing the house they had rented with the invisible hordes of microscopic guests carried along from Major Clarke's house in George's still apparently healthy body.

Although Lawrence was too fatigued to do anything at all in the heat of the day—nor for that matter was he strong enough to do much even in the early morning or evening— George, obliging and affable as always, made the most of his social opportunities. He had dinner with military officers, judges, and the surveyor general, and he went to the theater and church with his newfound friends.

At first glance it may seem odd that that the barely post-adolescent George Washington would so easily and naturally fall in with the most powerful men in a country the moment he stepped off the boat. The reason it seems odd to us, though, is that we have replaced the strict class structure of George Washington's day with a strict age structure of our day, which is arguably every bit as unfair.

In our own day, the most brilliant six-year-old is forced to stay in the same class in school as the stupidest of his contemporaries. The most promising nineteen-year-old, visiting a foreign country, might at best hope to be an "intern" at an embassy; he couldn't possibly expect to dine with the governor as an equal.

The fact is, the human instinct to form hierarchical societies seems to be universal. You can see it playing itself out in one way or another wherever you look. The Communist revolution in Russia, after all, merely supplanted one ultimate ruler (the czar) with another (the head of the Communist Party), and one small group of powerful people (the aristocrats) with another (Party members), who were also—well, at times far more so—at the complete mercy of their ruler. We modern people think we've shaken free from the class stratifications of George Washington's day. We've only replaced class discrimination with age discrimination.

In a society structured along class lines and not age lines, a sixteen-year-old could easily be a captain in the army, as in the case of Lafayette, and a nineteen-year-old George Washington would not instinctively feel inferior to older people of the same class with whom he would mix on a footing of equality, as a matter of course.

After some days of socializing, however, the dangerous effects of the hospitality the Washingtons had accepted the day they arrived in Barbados became clear.

On November 17, George was struck with "the small Pox."

He was in a sweating, suffering agony. Dr. Lanahan came by to do what he could, which of course was little but offer encouragement. Dr. Lanahan's "attendance was very constant till my recovery," wrote George. Of course, this sort of psychological encouragement does have a beneficial effect, as we now know—unlike the bloodletting the good doctor had also prescribed. Whether, on balance, the doctor's treatment helped or hurt, George survived.

Shortly afterwards George was out and about again, invited to dinner with a commodore, a general, and even the governor of Tortola. With an eye to a career in the army, he had a look at the island's fortifications and, knowing he would someday be in charge of at least some farmland, he carefully looked at the farms. He saw tropical fruit he had never dreamed of, noted the soil was richer and the farms more productive than those in Virginia, and yet remarked that many farmers were in debt.

George soon discovered the reason for this debt. He found that the debt of the farmers was at least partly caused by the rapacity of British officials—in combination with the commensurate docility of the local citizens.

George soon learned to see most of the British officials in Barbados with contempt. He found little of the *Panegyrick*'s nobility and honor among the government officials there. Their rapacity was, for the first time, planting a seed of doubt about British rule in his mind, a seed that would grow and finally bear fruit at the time of the Revolution.

Lawrence soon decided it was too hot in Barbados. He decided to set off for Bermuda. He told George that he would send for Anne, his wife, if he thought he would survive, but return to "my grave" in Virginia if not. George headed back for Virginia—encountering on his return trip even worse weather than he had seen on the trip down.

However, on Christmas Day George was surprised to find a sky "fine and clear and pleasant with a moderate Sea." It was so fine that everyone managed to eat a goose to celebrate. Other than that respite, though, the weather was so rough that at times the masts were left almost completely bare, leaving the ship to be tossed around like a nauseous roller coaster in an earthquake.

The first thing George did when he got back to Virginia was to deliver some letters from Lawrence to Governor Dinwiddie. This is probably when George first suggested himself as a replacement for Lawrence as adjutant general of the Virginia militia.

The adjutant's job was "instructing the officers and soldiers in the use and exercise of their arms … bringing the militia to a more regular discipline, besides improving the meaner people." George had already helped Lawrence out with the militia—putting in unremunerated hours to assist his ailing brother (yet another example of "His Duty was his greatest Passion"). He was not a complete neophyte. But he had never had any official position. Still, this did not seem an impediment to the appointment in his mind.

Nor in the governor's.

Shortly thereafter, although the post Lawrence had held was divided into four regional adjutants general, George was made a major of the militia and adjutant for the Southern District.

Lawrence chose to return to Virginia for the reasons he had said—to die and be buried at home. When Lawrence's daughter died, too, George became heir to Mount Vernon.

Whether it was a mere whim of fate or the will of Providence, there was another, hidden benefit of this trip, beyond putting George in a much better position to advance in his career. You may have noticed the passing incident of George catching smallpox in Barbados.

Did you notice, as he lay in bed those three weeks, how the entire future of the world changed?

Had George not had smallpox then and thus developed immunity, he very likely would have caught it when it swept through the army during the Revolution. In a harsher climate than Barbados, in the middle of a war, at an older age—it was much more likely it would have killed him. Had General George Washington died of smallpox, the

American Revolution was much, much more likely to have been lost. And had we won? Without him as president? We'd all be Canadians.

Stupid, bacon-loving Canadians.

It wasn't merely George's adherence to his duty during the Revolution that got us where we are today. In myriad ways we'll never be able to know or quantify—like the effects of a few million microbes—it was both the intended and unintended result of a lifetime of duty being George's "greatest Passion."

George, committed to the noble ideal that he found in the *Panegyrick*, spent his life making sacrifices for the sake of duty, beginning when he dropped all his own plans in order to help his brother recover from tuberculosis.

There is something special, deeper about doing your duty by following what you feel is the guidance of Providence, rather than following society's rules, that seems to make the effects greater and more mysterious.

When George was at Mount Vernon, doing his duty as a farmer, Mount Vernon prospered. (When even his well-meaning relatives took care of his farm while he was off at war, Mount Vernon did not do so well—in fact, it almost fell apart.) When George led the Continental Army, a ragtag group of ill-clothed, poorly trained, poorly armed soldiers handily crushed the world's greatest empire since Rome. When George agreed to join the Constitutional Convention in Philadelphia, voilà, the Constitution. When he agreed to be the first president of the United States, America got a president as close to perfect as possible.

When he did his duty, in line with what he called Providence, that is, with an inner feeling that he was in league with something greater and nobler than himself, he changed everything he touched.

He changed the world.

No wonder George found fulfilling his duty profoundly satisfying. In comparison with that deep and enduring satisfaction, mere pleasures are ephemeral, feather light.

Many people will never know that kind of satisfaction, but for those few who do, as George did, as the Duke of Schonberg did, as perhaps you will, duty cannot help but be your greatest passion.

Chapter Six

The Coolest American

"Temperance, which in most Men is an acquir'd Habit, and the reward of repeated Endeavours, was in him only the result of a happy Nature.... as for the evenness of his Temper, which in a hot and strong Constitution is the more to be admir'd, it can scarcely be exprest."

—H. de Luzancy, *A Panegyrick to the Memory of His Grace Frederick, Late Duke of Schonberg*

Some of these qualities sound so uncool. I mean, temperance? When I hear that word, the first thing I think of is the Temperance Movement—despite the fact that no one had yet dreamt of rallying against alcohol in the Duke's day. (I've always been astounded that a country whose Declaration of Independence was written by a wine connoisseur and whose first president grew hemp—albeit not for smoking—could think the government had the right to outlaw both hemp and wine, or indeed any personal liberty.)

In the Duke's time, and in George's, wine was still a sacrament, not a sin, and "temperance" had a more holistic meaning, having little to do with abstinence from wine, water, or anything. It basically meant having an even keel, taking things in moderation.

Being in control.

Today, if someone came up to me and said, "Yo, my bro, you be one temperate dude," I wouldn't exactly feel better about myself. Temperance sounds pretty tragically uncool to my ears. Still, since I've got bigger fish to fry than fighting against a cultural and linguistic tide just to make a point, how about if for the sake of this chapter, every time I say "temperate," you think "chillin' and willin' to be so cool that I rule"?

If I were Deepak Chopra, I bet I could sell a $1,495.00 course called "Balance Your Yin and Yang Energy" to make the point I'm about to make. If I offered my course in Los Angeles, everyone in Hollywood would come.

If, on the other hand, I came right out and said I was teaching temperance, I might just get just a little old lady from Tennessee to sign up. I understand that.

No little kid contemplating the Batman costume in the Halloween shop window thinks, *No, I'd rather go as Temperance Man.*

There's a very good reason for this, beyond the subtle changes in what "temperance" has meant over time. In George Washington's Virginia, people genuinely knew the real you. Therefore you had to be a genuinely great person to be considered a genuinely great person. Which seems a tautology, but it's not if you think about it.

Well into the 1800s, when most people still lived in farming communities or small towns, there were self-help books with titles like *The*

Elements of Character. The *Panegyrick* was a kind of precursor to these, advocating the qualities that people who actually knew you, and knew you well, would admire and appreciate, and find useful and valuable—such as temperance.

What happened in the twentieth century? Massive waves of immigration from abroad to America and from the countryside to the big cities turned American life upside down. I know an older woman with a very large house in Washington, in fact, right across the street from Senator (and Secretary of State under Obama) "Ketchup" Kerry's house. This woman's father, and his father before him, etc., had been businessmen in Philadelphia. She told me they regularly made monstrously large business deals, sealed with nothing but a handshake. This was at a time when Philadelphia was still relatively small (or at least a time when there was still a small coterie of people who remembered when it was literally small and continued to act as if it were small by associating only with each other). They conducted business just as George did in colonial Virginia.

It seemed to work out relatively well.

Today? Forget multimillion-dollar deals on a handshake. You can't even log in to a website without agreeing to give up your firstborn male child to Mark Zuckerberg.

What has this left us with? A society in which strangers with no "background" come to the big city and try to out-con each other to the top. The only thing keeping us from falling prey to each other's predatory instincts is our own wiliness, along with, arguably, the government's help. Government has stepped in and tried to tame the jungle with regulations and laws, but this only results in more expensive lawyers trying to outwit the laws, while outwitting each other.

Are we better off?

Did you know that the *New Yorker* was started by an uneducated cowboy who wished he was an urban sophisticate—and turned himself into, at least, a simulacrum of one? *Time* magazine, on the other hand, that great destroyer of the English language and lyric sheet to the tuneless song of the modern age, was created by what passes, in America, at least, for an upper-class toff. The modern city is a perfect petri dish of the modern American notion of self-invention, the idea that you can be anything you want to be. The cowboy wanted to be sophisticated, came to New York, and made himself the puppet master of Eustace Tilley and, if never quite his doppelganger, then at least his alter ego. The sophisticated Yale man who invented *Time* wanted to be richer than his ancestors had already made him, and, sussing out that there were more unsophisticated people (including, in fact, the creator of the *New Yorker*) in America than sophisticated ones, he created a monument of mediocrity to reinforce the masses' mediocre minds.

This sounds all well and good on the surface—or at least not too bad. One might ask, why not? Well, when sophisticated people are playing at being everymen, and cow rustlers are playing at being monocled gentlemen, what you are, underneath is irrelevant or even harmful—at least if anyone finds out about it. Of course character and background are different things, but when the way to advance is to pretend that you are something you are not ("fake it 'til you make it"), being genuinely anything ceases to be a prime concern of anyone.

Some people may still want to be genuinely good human beings. There's the Peace Corps for them. To really get ahead, a toff has to appear "regular" and a cow rustler has to buy a monocle.

Just a few generations after George Washington, ancestors of mine were drummed—well, nothing so noble as a drum was used; they were, in fact, violently expelled—from the house-moving business in Philadelphia in the decades after the Civil War. This was in a very different echelon of Philadelphia society than the one the Kerrys' neighbor's grandfather lived in. The Mafia, unfortunately for my ancestors, controlled house-moving in Benjamin Franklin's adopted city, the Quakers'

City of Brotherly Love. When people can be anything they want to be (and who you really are ceases to mean much of anything, and nobility has gone the way of the powdered wig), people often choose to be very bad things. This could never have happened in the Virginia of George Washington's day or even the Philadelphia of Benjamin Franklin's.

So we have Eustace Tilley and the Mafia. George Washington had—well, himself, and Benjamin Franklin, and Thomas Jefferson, and all the rest of them.

Are we moving forward on all fronts?

In modern America, flash and dazzle have replaced character and substance. "Name recognition" has replaced *actually knowing* the people you do business with. The books that advise the up-and-coming how to come up no longer advocate those qualities admired in George Washington's Virginia or the smoky rooms of gentlemen's clubs in antebellum Philadelphia. We no longer read *Poor Richard's Almanack* and *The Elements of Character*. Instead we resort to the shallow exhortations to "believe in yourself" and "go for it" that have followed in the wake of twentieth-century books like Dale Carnegie's *How to Win Friends and Influence People* and Og Mandino's *The Greatest Salesman in the World*.

Did you know that "Dale Carnegie" was originally "Dale Carnagey" but, in a shrewd career move, changed the spelling of his name to give people the impression that he was related to steel magnate Andrew Carnegie? What kind of success do we want for ourselves? The kind achieved by used-car salesmen? A quick transaction, wham, bam, thank you for your money, I'll be seeing you around, maybe?

Instant success, over timeless substance, is "The Secret" aspiration that has permeated our whole culture. There are books, there are seminars, there are legions of greedy sheep herded by soulless shepherds towards the almighty dollar sign on the hill. De Tocqueville warned that we would eventually measure everything in dollars. "How is that movie?" "It earned 32 million last weekend." Does it occur to you how fundamentally wrong it is that the media doesn't measure a movie by telling us how uplifting it may be for our souls but by how much money it made?

This soulless, transactional, anonymous materialism has even infected our love lives: there's a whole subculture of guys who teach other guys how to "pick up" women by tricking them into believing they are cooler than they really are. In the best kind of society, a girl would know what a guy was really like by his reputation, by his character, by his *honor*. To get the girl, you'd have to be great, really, not just "fake it 'til you make it."

In Philadelphia in John Kerry's neighbor's ancestors' days, or in George Washington's Virginia, you would entrust your fortune (and possibly your life and your sacred honor, too) to other men whose families had known each other for generations, men whom you yourself had known since you were a child. Those connections weren't valued just out of habit; they meant actually knowing the people you were dealing with.

In the egalitarian pandemonium which has replaced that way of life—that is, in today's society, where everyone is supposedly "given a fair shot"—none of us has much of a fair shot at honest dealings with trustworthy people.

Take the Madoff scandal.

People were captivated by Bernie Madoff's salesman's charm and the too-good-to-be-true "returns on investment" that his company paid out—of course, really, just money stolen from other "investors." If a client, or potential client, ever doubted his personal integrity, they reassured themselves that government regulations and lawyers (those modern substitutes for character and honor) would keep their money safe. After all, Bernie Madoff himself used to be the chairman of NASDAQ, one of those large government-regulated institutions that provides safety and security in the modern world, in lieu of such outmoded things as personal honesty and actually knowing the people you do business with. Bernie Madoff's customers knew *of* Bernie Madoff. They had heard of his "charm," even if they didn't experience it firsthand. Some of them felt lucky to have met him personally.

But they, demonstrably, didn't really know him.

They surely never even asked themselves the first question anyone in George Washington's society would have asked: Is Bernie Madoff temperate enough to be content to provide investors with a reasonable and moderate return on investment? Does he have the self-restraint to keep his hands off his clients' money? But of course the clients were greedy and intemperate, too. Many of them, apparently, were convinced that Madoff was doing something unethical, taking advantage of his elevated position and connections in order to bring them regular out-sized returns. These clients were happy to have Madoff act unethically on their behalf. (They were too lacking in fundamental principles to reject any dealings with someone lacking honor.) Had they instead been like a Virginian of George Washington's day, and refused to engage in business with someone lacking honor, they still would have at least *some* money.

And their honor.

In George Washington's day, before you handed somebody your cash…or a job or government post…or even your personal trust and friendship, you had a lot of evidence about his character. You could see whether or not he was temperate enough to be trusted and relied upon.

After all, a man without self-control can't trust *himself*. Why would you rely on him? He's not his own master. An intemperate person will be tossed to and fro by greed or bad temper. He'll be reliable until he's not. Temperance, on the other hand, means being master of your emotions. One way to do this is to harness your emotions to a more elevated passion, such as doing your duty.

Temperance may *sound* uncool, but it's really all about keeping your cool. What could be cooler than that? Mr. T plays it cool (no, not *that* Mr. T—Mr. Temperance).

George Washington was that kind of cool.

Perhaps somewhat surprisingly, this coolness was the furthest thing from George Washington's innate temperament. Remember the horse that George tried to break but ended up killing?

George's natural temperament was something like that horse's.

Coolness didn't come easily to George, as it did to the Duke. George's self-control was "an acquir'd Habit, and the reward of repeated Endeavours"—endeavours, surely, to imitate the hero of the *Panegyrick*. It can be truly said of George, as the *Panegyrick* says of the Duke, that "the evenness of his Temper" is "the more to be admir'd" because of his naturally "hot and strong Constitution."

Naturally, George had a notoriously bad temper.

Reports of his bad temper stretch back to the beginning of his military career, in his not infrequent harsh treatment of soldiers. On the other hand, you don't win wars, nor lead men into a hail of deadly lead, by being Mr. Nice Guy. Some of George's temper, especially at this early stage of his life—some of it—must be attributed to the difficulty of trying to maintain order and discipline beyond the bounds of any external framework that might support him, alone in the woods, an almost untrained officer, far from civilization, far from a commanding officer, far from anything else that might help him maintain control over a small army of scraggly "soldiers."

Some of his temper, however, especially when it was expressed towards servants or social "inferiors," was clearly of the same order as the temper tantrums of children. George was not perfect. George's temper, in fact, was one of the hardest things he ever had to work on. He never fully succeeded in taming it.

Even years later, after George had become president, Lady Liston, the wife of a British diplomat, called him "Naturally hot-tempered." She confided that he had "acquired a uniform command over his passions on publick occasions, but in private & particularly with his Servants, its violence sometimes broke out."

Thus, even after he was president, George was more hot-blooded than he seemed in portraits and statues. That stolid expression was an achievement of self-control, not evidence that George was wooden. (Not even his teeth were really made of wood—as we'll see below.)

That he was *working* on his temperate exterior was made clear by something George said to Lady Liston when she once told him "that his countenance indicated the pleasure to which he looked forward. You are wrong replied he, my countenance never yet betrayed my feelings."

George was not meek. In fact, he had something of a volcano inside of him. It is therefore all the more impressive that he could keep his temper under control when he needed to.

When did he need to?

In the woods, surrounded by duplicitous enemies with guns and tomahawks, as one example.

Just after George had returned from Barbados, Virginia's Governor Dinwiddie made him a major in the Virginia militia, appointing him the adjutant for the colony's Southern District.

Shortly after George got his appointment, France asserted its claim to the same land that Britain had recently granted to the Ohio Company. In essence, the British and the French kings were both claiming to own the same land. As both George Washington's family and Virginia's governor were large shareholders in the Ohio Company, their interests in the area may not have been entirely dispassionate. Still, no one wanted the French taking English land. (Except the French, that is.)

Although the French had considered the territory their land for decades, they had never done anything with it. When the French caught wind that the Ohio Company planned to do the eighteenth-century version of developing the area—getting people to move there, although instead of building roads and sewers, they planned to build forts—the French made a move in a few months that they'd been delaying for sixty years. Before the Ohio Company had laid the first log of their first fort, the French had built several forts, solidifying their claim to the Ohio Valley. The King of England, hearing the news, ordered Virginia's governor to demand that the French leave.

No one really expected that they could convince the French to leave by knocking politely on the front gate of a fort and asking, "S'il vous plaît." But this was the necessary first step. When the French said "Non," as the English knew they would, the English would then have to make them leave.

Knowing all this, the king had authorized force before the diplomacy even started.

Learning of the crisis, George appeared in Williamsburg, went to see the governor, and volunteered to serve the French their eviction notice. It might be argued that he was volunteering for nothing more than political theater, an empty gesture. Then again, in the eighteenth century, you didn't go around shooting people without being polite about it. It was, therefore, important—in the way it is important that boxers tap gloves before a match.

Why did George think himself capable of what was, given the bigger picture, a serious task? Well, perhaps he thought his paucity of military experience had not prevented him from training military officers, so there could be no reason that he should not represent the King of England in a diplomatic mission. His lack of experience in diplomacy and complete ignorance of the French language bothered neither him nor the governor. The King of England had also requested that his emissary gather as much intelligence as possible. George knew nothing of espionage, either.

George got the assignment. After all, what the governor wanted was good character, especially a reputation for handling things with aplomb. Cool.

On his way through the forest to the French fort, George did think to pick up someone who spoke at least some French. This was a Dutchman, Jacob van Braam, who spoke French the way a diligent tourist today might. George also took along Christopher Gist, who had acted on behalf of the Ohio Company before. Rounding out the party were four Indians and some servants. (The servants are almost entirely ignored in everyone's written record, as today we wouldn't mention the tires on our cars. They were just sort of there—vital, but not thought of.)

The first important encounter on George's first diplomatic mission was with an Indian leader called Half King. His name came from the fact that he had given away some of his power to the Iroquois. The Half King could live with this mild indignity but not with the gross lack of respect the French had recently shown him.

Both the French and the English knew that it was crucial to get the Indians on their side in the conflict they were all anticipating over the

Ohio Valley. They therefore knew they needed to court Indian leaders to secure Indian backing for their side. When it came to the Half King, the French had gone about it in entirely the wrong way. The French had made the Half King hate them.

How? A French commander had lost his temper. Or acted like it, perhaps. Maybe he was just being offensive on purpose—haughty contempt being something of a French specialty. The particular Frenchman in this case had profoundly offended the Half King by, essentially, throwing a temper tantrum. The French commander had been intemperate enough to throw the Half King's belt of wampum in his face after screaming that the French could and would destroy every Englishman in the Ohio Valley, along with any Indian foolish enough to support them. He had called the Half King a "child" and said that he and his Indians must live under the rule of the French or not at all.

Kings, even Half Kings, don't like being spoken to that way. Come to think of it, nor do *actual* children. Temperance is not an unimportant thing. This one intemperate act by this intemperate Frenchman may have tipped the balance of an entire war.

Perhaps the French commander was just having a bad day. If so, you might call it "the temper tantrum heard 'round the world."

As the assassination of one man led to World War I, this insult with the wampum had huge repercussions. Had the Frenchman instead subtly implied, or shown through action, that the French would outgun the English and respect at least some of the Indians' rights, the Half King, naturally more concerned for his own people than for either the English or the French, might have joined the French side. Had these Indian allies chosen the other side, the Seven Years'—"French and Indian"—War would almost surely have turned out differently.

But this is not what happened. The Half King had been insulted by the French. By the time George came along, the Indian chief was ready to be charmed by the English.

But ready in a kind of Half Kingly way.

This is where the relatively temperate George first became valuable. George was "affable" and "obliging" to the Half King, maintaining an unruffled demeanor, finally flattering the Half King into submission. This wasn't as easy as it might sound.

George had understood that the Indians, formally allied with the English, accepted the Ohio Company's plans to "settle" the Ohio Valley. But that wasn't the Indians' take on the situation at all. The Half King told George that the Ohio Valley belonged to no one, and "the Great Being above allowed it to be a place of residence to us." "Us" the Indians, that is, and not the French—but not the Indians' English allies, either.

The way the Half King saw it, the French had stepped out of line by coming not only to trade, "like our brothers the English," but to "BUILD HOUSES UPON OUR LAND." Apparently the Half King was unaware that the French had built those forts only because the English were threatening to build their own. Despite a treaty that seemed to ally these Indians with the English, the Half King was now saying that the Indians would "stand by" whichever side "will have the greatest regard" for the Indians' rights.

George remained unflappable. He kept his cool. Some might judge George for being too cool a customer, as he got the Half King on board the English side without disabusing the Half King of his illusions about English intentions for the Ohio Valley. George, unlike his French counterpart, did not throw a temper tantrum, throw wampum in the Half King's face, and thus throw away all chances of Indian support for England.

Temperance brings rewards.

The Half King and some of his warriors agreed to accompany George and his party on their mission to the French. On December 4, the expanded party arrived at the house of a certain John Frazier. Troublingly, the house was there, sure enough, but without John Frazier. The house, instead, contained French officers—eating Frazier's food underneath the French flag they were flying on top of Frazier's roof.

They had thought, though, to bring their own wine.

⁂

This provided another opportunity for George to exercise his temperance in the aid of his mission. This time "temperance" both in the eighteenth-century sense and also in the more modern sense.

In what may seem to us the quaint style of eighteenth-century diplomacy, the French officers invited George and his men to "sup with them, and treated us with the greatest Complaisance." Everyone was polite to each other, knowing they would most likely soon be trying to kill each other in the fight for the Ohio Valley.

This is a particularly astonishing idea for us, perhaps, as our wars are always sold to us as wars for a higher purpose—never, for example, for oil. It's all about "democracy and freedom," we're told (though somehow it always seems we care most about spreading democracy and freedom in close proximity to large amounts of oil).

In George's day, no one denied that wars were for money and power. George and his hosts might soon be killing each other, not for an idea or ideal, but because two kings (and certain of their powerful subjects, such as the owners of the Ohio Company) wanted the same piece of land. Imagine if the makers of Ford and Toyota met for a beer, preparatory to lobbing missiles and hand grenades at each other's factories in order to dominate the minivan market.

Lubricated with *beaucoup de vin*, the French seemed to be turning their arrogance up to eleven—which proved inadvertently beneficial to George in his nascent outing as a spy. George had already been advised that a general, a few miles away, was the man to whom he should take his petition, so the conversation at John Frazier's erstwhile house had no official purpose. *Naturellement*, over the course of a few hours, the French began to talk more and more about themselves.

They were French, after all.

While they drank and bragged, George stayed sober and listened.

The Frenchmen at Frazier's, George noted, claimed "an undoubted Right to the River, from a Discovery made by one LaSalle sixty years ago; and the Rise of this Expedition is to prevent our [the British] settling on the River or Waters of it, as they had heard of some Families moving-out in Order thereto."

In other words, after waiting six decades, during which they had done nothing to settle the area, the moment the English wanted to do something productive with the land, the French had suddenly decided to enforce their sixty-year-old claim. The French officers spoke of "their absolute Design to take Possession of the Ohio, and by God they would do it; For that altho' they were sensible the English could raise two Men for their one; yet they knew their motions were too slow and dilatory to prevent any Undertaking of theirs."

By staying sober, George had gained intelligence he would never have gained had he kept up with the French in their intemperate drinking. George learned that the French expected the English to outnumber them two to one in any conflict. They were pinning their hopes of victory on the English being "slow and dilatory." Beyond that, they had a really, really high opinion of themselves—their arrogance was at a level that might lead them to act foolishly. Indeed, George had evidence that it was already having that effect—obviously, the French thought so little of the George and the English they had did not mind revealing their weakness in numbers to him.

Rain and snow delayed their journey, but George's party finally arrived, a week later, at the fort where the French general was. After receiving George's message, conveyed in a letter from the governor, the French officers retired for a council of war, which gave the neophyte spy the opportunity to do a bit more espionage. He decided to measure the "Dimensions of the Fort, and mak[e] what Observations I could." He reported that there were about a hundred men in the fort. His Indians counted two hundred twenty canoes.

Although the French had the manners of gentlemen, they did not have the characters to match.

While some French officers were courteously handing George a letter with their response, others were trying to bribe George's Indians to desert him. This wasn't as small a thing as it may sound. Leaving George and his party to make their way back *sans* Indians through the howling winter wilderness of the Ohio Valley would have left the group far more vulnerable to Indian attacks and, more than likely, dead. In fact, George later said, "I can't say that ever in my life I suffer'd so much Anxiety as I did in this Affair."

But he kept his cool.

The French finally failed in this treacherous scheme—which is the only reason we know of it, or have ever heard of George Washington.

On the way home, George and his party, with their Indians and canoes, would be traveling upstream, up the Monongahela River. Fighting their way against the flow of the water was arduous enough, but things got horribly worse as they began to find the river frozen in places. They had no choice but to carry everything—canoes and supplies—around sections of the river that were frozen solid.

After a few days of excruciatingly slow progress, George recalled what he had learned from the French at John Frazier's house. The French thought they could beat the English, even outnumbered two to one, as the English were "slow and dilatory." Maybe that was true of the English, George reasoned, but not of the Americans and certainly not of George Washington. The English were "slow and dilatory"? George would show the French what Americans were made of.

This thought in mind, he then made a quick calculation that the message for the governor was too urgent to wait. After consulting with Christopher Gist, the more experienced woodsman, he told the rest of his party that he and Gist would break away from the group and travel back to Williamsburg on foot.

The next day, when George and Gist were alone in the middle of the forest, a group of "French Indians" fired directly at them, missing them both. George and Gist were able to escape in the woods and somehow managed to make their way to the Allegheny River, not knowing whether the Indians were close behind them or had thought the chase not worth their time.

When the two Americans finally got to Allegheny River, out of breath, hungry, and fearing they were still being followed, their hearts sank. They now had the opposite problem they had just had with the Monongahela. Expecting to find the Allegheny solid with ice, and thus to cross it on foot, they saw a freely flowing river, impossible to cross.

Or almost impossible.

George doesn't tell us what his emotions were, but two people, alone in a vast forest, a few hours after Indians had shot at them, might well have been frightened to death.

Yet George, who would be calm even when bullets were whistling about him in battle—he was shortly to declare that he found the sound "charming"—remained temperate. He coolly assessed the situation, rather than letting his emotions get the better of him. A lesser man might have panicked, might have scrambled back to try to rejoin his party. George's presence of mind—his ability to retain a cool head in a heated circumstance, to restrain his emotions—continued to stand him in good stead.

George saw they had to cross the river if they could. It didn't seem possible, but George reasoned their situation out. He realized that finding their party would take days, and anyway the Indians who had shot at them were still out there, somewhere. Finally, of course, the only reason George had left the main party was he thought it was urgent to get the French message to the governor as soon as possible. He wouldn't let a little thing like an impassable river—and no boat—stop him.

The only tool he and Gist had between them was "one poor Hatchet." (George doesn't mention if it was the same one his father had given him when he was a child, but in a society with no corner hardware stores, it just may have been.) And, of course, they had a forest full of trees.

This was enough.

George quickly decided to make a raft and make it as quickly as possible. Driven by at least some fear that the Indians were still on their trail, and hurried by the urgency of their mission, they quickly put together a crude raft. Stars were already emerging when they finished building it, but it never crossed their mind to wait for morning. If they slept where they were, they both saw, they might wake up scalped.

Just after "Sun-setting, after a whole Day's Work, we got it launched, and on board of it, and set off; but before we were Half Way over, jammed in the Ice, in such a Manner that we expected every Moment our Raft to sink, and ourselves to perish."

This is a moment to recall that swimming was not considered a normal thing in the eighteenth century. The polymath Benjamin Franklin famously learned to do it, but he was the exception. The general assumption was that if you fell into water deeper than your nose, you died. This was worse than that, though. If you have ever fallen into water in winter, fully clothed, you'll know that winter clothes when soaked with water add fifty or sixty pounds of unexpected weight. You sink. I've done it myself. Not a pleasant feeling at all. (I struggled out of my coat and made it out okay. But one, I can swim, and two, I was in a pond, not a rushing river.)

With this in mind…"I put out my setting pole to try to stop the Raft, that the Ice might pass by, when the Rapidity of the stream threw it with so much Violence against the Pole, that it jerked me out into ten Feet Water."

Even George Washington was not ten feet tall.

He sank.

He doesn't say so, but he must have fallen in upstream of the raft. At this point, even in still water, George was dead. In a raging river, he was doubly dead. Or he would have been if he weren't George Washington.

Somehow, he caught hold of one of the logs they'd lashed together to make the raft, perhaps smashing against it with the current. However, he had lost the pole.

Now with no pole to guide the raft, drenched in literally icy water as the darkness blackened everything out in the middle of the roaring river, George and Gist had no way of getting to either shore.

They found themselves near an island, miraculously, and were able to get the raft close enough that they could wade to its shore, where they gratefully spent the night, safe from both Indians and the river.

Perhaps they were able to start a fire using flint, although this is not mentioned in George's account. It is hard to imagine they could have survived without fire, drenched as they were in freezing water. Their clothes would have become suits of ice. Gist did suffer the excruciating pain of frostbite on all his fingers and some of his toes. (George, in a further testament to his virtually supernatural physical abilities, made it through this ordeal with no injuries whatsoever.)

The biggest redeeming result of that frozen night was that the next morning the river was frozen solid as the New Jersey Turnpike. They walked the rest of the way.

When George finally made it to Williamsburg, just before Christmas, the House of Burgesses had already adjourned and its members gone home. They would be back for another session on February 14. Without the Burgesses, no money could be allocated for defense of the Ohio Valley.

George's journey had not been in vain, though. After reading the letter that George had risked his life to bring back, the governor had an idea. What if George wrote a report to rally the government to action even if the legislators were away from the capital?

The starting point for all of this was the letter the English had expected from the French commander. It was written with the unflinching politeness of the time, which did nothing to mitigate its unflinching resolve:

> As for your summons to me to retire, I do not feel any obligation to do so, whatever may be your instructions. I am here by orders of my general and I beg you, Sir, not to doubt for an instant that I have the fixed resolution to conform to them with the exactness and firmness expected of the best officer.
>
> I made it my particular duty to receive Monsieur Washington with a distinction, equal to your position and to his own quality and great merit.

The governor asked George to make his pitch as quickly as possible. In fact, he gave George just twenty-four hours. The sooner the burgesses—and everyone else in Virginia—knew that the French would not cede the Ohio without a fight, the sooner they would rally to its defense, and thus the more likely that French would not benefit from English dilatoriousness.

George stayed up late enough to burn through three candles. He had his report ready in the morning. It was then printed and given to members of the Governor's Council (a twelve-person appointed committee who had to approve the laws passed by the House of Burgesses). The governor also had it sent to the burgesses in their homes.

Hoping he was not alone in seeing the French incursion as a major issue, affecting more than just the interests of Virginia or the Ohio Company, the governor also sent George's report to the governors of the other colonies and finally to London, where it was reprinted and passed on yet again. This made George Washington known for the first time to his future rivals and allies throughout the Western world as a tough and resourceful young officer.

The modern view of history is that grand historical forces sweep the world this way and that, determining the outcome of events.

But I beg to differ.

The drunken comment by the French officer that the English were slow and dilatory may well have been the deciding factor in George's decision to break away from his party and head back to the capital with only Gist. This timing brought the English to prepare for war earlier than they otherwise would have done. Thus the English were engaged before the French had the opportunity to bring more soldiers and forts in the area. In a "butterfly effect" kind of way (a butterfly flaps its wings on one side of the world, setting off a chain of events that ends in a hurricane on the other), George's temperance at his adversaries' dinner table arguably saved English lives and ultimately brought English victory more easily than otherwise would have been the case.

George learned to moderate his temper, and appear temperate, in a wide variety of important moments throughout his life. He had kept his cool with the Half King and didn't lose his cool when he stood between gun-wielding Indians and an impassable river. Even in the heat of battle, George's levelheadedness would be said to be his "usual" state of mind. Much later, at the Constitutional Convention, and when George became the first president of the United States, what others saw as his statue-like demeanor was the outer evidence of an inner temperance, a determination to remain unflustered even when taking a leading role in the most momentous events of our epoch.

The caricature of George Washington is that he is stiff, upright, uptight, and almost inhuman. To some extent, we can blame his portraits for his austere image. Eighteenth-century dentistry accounts for his expressions in those paintings—including the real grimace and strangely shaped mouth that are most in evidence in the iconic Gilbert Stuart portrait. (Although George Washington never, in fact, had wooden teeth, he did have several sets of rather cumbersome artificial teeth made from such things as elephant ivory held together by iron fittings. If modern braces are uncomfortable, it is a safe bet that eighteenth-century spring-loaded dental contraptions were something like mild dental torture by comparison.)

Disregarding his dentistry, George had a tremendous amount of self-control that would have made him seem austere, anyway. Knowing this self-control was a constant, life-long struggle for him perhaps makes it easier to see the man shining through the mask.

His was "a tremendous temper," said one artist who painted him, but "under wonderful control." According to Thomas Jefferson, George

Washington's "temper was naturally irritable and high-toned, but reflection and resolution had obtained a firm and habitual ascendency over it."

The thing that set George on the path to master what he thought of as a "defect" in his constitution had been the *Panegyrick* and its call for "reflection and resolution."

This is something we can all do. If "temperance" still sounds uncool, you can still always think, instead, "chillin' and willin' to be so cool that I rule."

Chapter Seven

"The Most Surprising Dangers, Never Betray'd in Him Any Fear"

"He neither Courted, nor Fear'd Danger;
ever Himself, ever Fortunate, ever preventing the worst,
and surmounting the greatest Difficulties."
—H. de Luzancy, *A Panegyrick to the Memory of*
His Grace Frederick, Late Duke of Schonberg

The space around George Washington seemed to bend by infinitesimal degrees, as bullets aimed at him missed, again and again. His hats, his cloaks, his horses were not so fortunate. They were all ripped to shreds by the bullets aimed at George. Is it possible this was because George held strongly to the image of the of the Duke's "Invincible Courage" in the *Panegyrick*?

Or was he just lucky?

All we can say with certainty is that George Washington held certain beliefs, and he got certain results. *Post hoc, ergo propter hoc* is a logical fallacy, but it's not a counter-proof. Quentin Tarantino has said that when he was young, he didn't care about wearing a seatbelt, didn't care for his safety one bit. He knew—he just knew—that God wouldn't let him die until he made his first film. It is unknowable to us (it can't be tested in a double-blind study with multiple Tanatinos) whether such beliefs are self-fulfilling prophecies, the illusion of hindsight, hormonally based post-adolescent overconfidence, or actually what George Washington and Quentin Tarantino thought they were, which was something like this: if you are striving to live your life for the purpose Providence has for you, then Providence is more than willing to flick a few pesky bullets out of your way.

People in the future will laugh at the people of our day—or highly evolved cockroaches, or whatever follows us, will laugh (or quizzle, or whatever highly evolved cockroaches will do when amused)—for our naive, simplistic, mechanistic view of the world. At the level of quantum mechanics, after all, even something as seemingly obvious as cause and effect is not always what it appears to be. Effect sometimes precedes cause. We don't yet understand our universe well enough to know how these things work, if we ever will. Perhaps the thing that George called Providence will someday be explained in ways scientists can document. Perhaps George's effort to align himself with Providence had some kind of outward effect.

In George's view, at least, the thing he called Providence was guiding him, while he was, in turn, trying to follow Providence's lead. One result of this was that "The most surprising dangers never betrayed in him any fear." It is at least possible that George's fearlessness was justified.

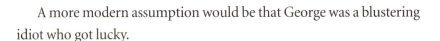

A more modern assumption would be that George was a blustering idiot who got lucky.

From our armchairs, this seems the obvious call. But you go, without real military training, and fight a war in the middle of the forest with and against Indians, and against professional French soldiers, and see how you feel about the world.

There are no atheists in foxholes, it is said. George Washington, Providence or not, was still too green even to know how to build the eighteenth-century version of effective foxholes—that is, he had no clue how or where to build forts, or how to avoid stumbling into the open to be shot at, as we're about to see—yet he retained, as the Duke had done, a sublime confidence.

In fact, George was about to report that he found the sound of bullets whistling overhead "charming." Was this hubris, the sort of stupidity we recognize in Darwin Awards winners, or in the life (and gruesome death) of someone like Timothy Treadwell, the man who loved grizzly bears, lived with them, and was eventually eaten by them—on camera?

Did George just have better luck?

Maybe.

But hubris and and the kind of confidence George Washington had are different things, even if they seem the same on the outside. One comes from ego. The other comes from knowing in your gut that you are in line with, in league with, something bigger, greater, stronger, and more miraculous than you could ever understand, or explain, even to yourself.

George, in what might to us seem an astonishing act of boldness for someone with his almost total lack of experience, asked to be second in command of the army that was now being raised to confront the French. (The army had finally been authorized in the late winter of 1754, several months after the report George had written about his initial encounter with the French.)

He was twenty-one years old with no military experience. In fact, he lacked any real military training beyond observing and then helping train local militias. These militias were comprised of soldiers and officers who had, for the most part, never seen combat, either. Despite this, George became second in command, and then de facto commander, of an army representing one of the world's superpowers in a confrontation with another superpower.

How did George pull this off?

It is sometimes easier to use a little imagination to recast the past in a modern context. If you want to understand how it seemed to the people involved, it is not so useful to imagine yourself a governor of a British colony several centuries ago, bewigged and berobed. To really understand how it seemed to the players, imagine yourself sitting in a dorm room, the overworked president of the Inter-University Tiddly-winks Society (IUTS) stressing about who you're going to send to a rival university next weekend to captain your team at a big match. Just as your brow is furrowed with worry, some guy you know, like, and trust walks in and offers to do it. I don't mean to diminish the events, or to equate a Tiddlywinks match with a world war, just to make a small point about subjective impressions.

"Subjective impressions" is, in fact, the point. People in the eighteenth century tended to go by their impressions, more the way things still happen in high school and college, less like our modern "professional" worlds. The governor and his council, when deciding who to put in charge of the army, had no bureaucratic criteria to fulfil, no exams the candidate must have passed, no certificates of equine competence, no military schools.

In this context (back to the dorm room), imagine the guy walks in and offers to be the captain of your team. You don't just know, like, and trust him. He's also the same guy who has already arranged the match, at great peril. He traveled through dangerous neighborhoods, perhaps.

He visited a rival fraternity. You feel loyalty, and obligation. Beyond this, he dresses well, and you are friends with his relatives (Lawrence and Austin). Beyond even this, he's a member of the best frat at your school (which is to say, George was an, albeit obscure, member of a prominent Virginia family). Of course you say yes. This is what, in essence, the Governor's Council did in offering George the job of a leading officer in the army.

It didn't happen simply because George wished for it, or simply because he was George Washington. Even for George, a little hustle was in order. George had written to Governor's Council member Richard Corbin (whose family was to intermarry with mine over the following generations).

> In a conversation with you at Green Spring, you gave me some room to hope for a commission above that of major, and to be ranked among the chief officers of this expedition. The command of the whole forces is what I neither look for, expect, nor desire; for I must be impartial enough to confess, it is a charge too great for my youth and inexperience to be entrusted with. Knowing this, I have too sincere a love for my country, to undertake that which may tend to the prejudice of it. But if I could entertain hopes, that you thought me worthy of the post of lieutenant-colonel, and would favor me so far as to mention it at the appointment of officers, I could not but entertain a true sense of the kindness.
>
> I flatter myself, that, under a skilful commander, or man of sense, (whom I most sincerely wish to serve under,) with my own application and diligent study of my duty, I shall be able to conduct my steps without censure, and, in time, render myself worthy of the promotion, that I shall be favored with now.

As it happened, the "skillful commander" George Washington aspired to learn from was nowhere to be found in a colony that had thus far been free from any major conflict. In lieu of anyone with actual skill and experience, the frat brothers back in Williamsburg—well, the bewigged and berobed gentlemen of the Virginia colony's government—hit upon a mathematics instructor at William and Mary College.

Not exactly General Patton, but, then, George Washington wasn't exactly George Washington yet, either.

This choice was to mean that George's career as an autodidact would continue—he would have to learn the art of war by figuring it out for himself. Not that the William and Mary math teacher necessarily lacked innate military talent, or was completely untrained, it was just that Joshua Fry's allegedly corpulent body and demonstrably dilatorious pace meant that he was on a course to arrive at the action long after the action was over. Even following that dilatory course, in the end, he never made it at all, for a reason even George could not have guessed.

There already was a small group of Virginians occupying a British outpost on the edge of the disputed territory. Word had been coming back to Williamsburg, through them, that Indian scouts were tracking a huge French war party coming down the river. "You are to act on the defensive," said the governor to George, ordering him out immediately to aid the outpost with a small group of soldiers, with the hope that Fry and additional troops would soon follow.

To prevent any misunderstanding, "defensive" was defined further on in that same order: "Defense" meant, according to the governor, to "kill and destroy" or "make prisoners of" anyone who might "interrupt our settlements." This was a slightly different message from the one that had come to the governor from the king, who had stressed that in no circumstance should the English be the first to use force. Closer to the action, the governor put a more aggressive spin on the king's message— some would argue this Ohio Company partner outright changed the order.

It all sounds relatively straightforward to us, perhaps. We are likely to assume, for example, that George simply had to lead his armed soldiers to the English garrison, and then protect it.

But it wasn't that simple. First George had to acquire the soldiers the governor was expecting him to lead.

Well, no, even that would have been too simple.

George actually had to create the soldiers from whatever recruits he might be able to round up. Then he needed to get them guns and ammunition, and finally he had to work out a way to get all his men and guns through the woods to the garrison.

Did you assume George had money to do this?

George soon wrote to the governor, begging for money. An initial grant finally allowed him to convince a few men to join him.

Did you assume that the soldiers had clothes?

George immediately had to ask the governor for more funds, reporting, "There are many of them without shoes; others want stockings, some are without shirts." (George's soldiers were evidently not recruited from the seven leading families of Virginia.)

Now, George needed to find guns and gunpowder, and wagons to carry it all.

As you might imagine, the local farmers' wagons all disappeared the moment word got out that George was impressing them. (He had no legal authority to impress anything, but such formalities did not yet disturb the mind of the man who would fight a war, a few decades later, inspired by similar incursions on the rights of Americans by the British.)

Having collected 159 soldiers and at least some munitions and supplies, George set off for the "Forks" garrison near present-day Pittsburgh, where the Allegheny and Monongahela Rivers meet. As his men chopped through the woods to make way for the few dilapidated carts they had been able to impress, filled with the few munitions they had been able to obtain, George rode ahead, scouting the best possible path. Word continued to come back from the garrison, ever more desperate, urging them to hurry. Indian scouts were reporting that the French were closing fast.

Suddenly, through the woods, George heard movement.

It did not seem threatening. It sounded too boisterous to be Indians, and as no state of war yet existed, George and his men should—if everyone played by the rules—not be in immediate danger even if it were the French.

George stayed atop his horse.

As the sound grew nearer, he heard a few English words. Suddenly, through the trees, thirty-three Englishmen stumbled upon the still figure of George Washington, sitting like a statue on his horse. Next to the thirty-three Englishmen, two silent Indian warriors emerged from the trees. The Englishmen were carrying a few belongings, including their guns.

These were the soldiers George had been coming to aid. All of them accounted for, unwounded, uninjured, with all their ammunition unspent.

Earlier that day, they told George, as they had looked over the still-unfinished walls of their garrison, these thirty-three soldiers and their several Indian allies had seen sixty boats, three hundred canoes, and "more than a thousand French" pour into the river below.

As soon as it was offered, English soldiers had wisely accepted the French commander's offer to hightail it, hoofing it towards undisputed land as fast as they could.

George considered the bigger picture.

Losing a battle—or being kindly offered, and accepting, the opportunity to be checkmated before a battle began—did not necessarily mean
losing the war.

The Half King had also been at the garrison, and, in the manner of
Indian kings, if not European ones, he had screamed contempt at the
French as the French commander granted the Englishmen both their
lives and freedom. The two silent Indians were two of the Half King's
men that he had sent along with the English to suss out whether the
English were going to live up to their promises.

The English had promised "big guns." The Half King wanted to see
them.

The two Indian warriors carried strings of wampum from the Half
King. These strings of colored beads, made from shells, had many purposes. They marked marriages, they served as memory aids for the
illiterate Indians, they were even used for money. In fact, by virtue of a
bit of magical thinking, long strings of beads were the most valuable
because, as the Indians saw it, they contained so many memories. In this
case, the purpose of the wampum was to signify that the visit to the
English was official and that agreements arrived at would be binding,
even without the Half King's physical presence.

The Half King's message, conveyed by his warriors (who finally
spoke), was clear:

> We are now ready to fall upon them, waiting only for your suc-
> cor. Have good courage, and come as soon as possible; you will
> find us as ready to encounter with them as you are yourselves.
>
> We have sent those two young men to see if you are ready
> to come, and if so they are to return to us to let us know where
> you are, that we may come and join you. We should be glad if
> the troops belonging to the two Provinces could meet together
> at the Fort which is in the way. If you do not come to our

assistance now, we are entirely undone, and imagine we shall never meet together again. I speak with a heart full of grief.

George had, indeed, run into a "surprising danger." It might not sound like that to us. Had he gone over a hill, looked out, and suddenly seen a thousand Frenchmen with guns pointed at him, that might seem a more surprising danger. He was, in fact, about to encounter that kind of nasty surprise.

But facing these two Indians, he was in a more precarious position than we might initially perceive. The isolation of those times—no radios, no phones, no GPS—put anyone in the middle of the woods, many days journey from help, in a precarious position. (Not that there was, really, any help to send. George's army was, at this point, virtually the entire Virginia army.)

This also put George in a position of greater responsibility than anyone in a similar position would be in today. In our time, people sail across the ocean, or even row across the ocean, "alone"—all the while being guided by billions of dollars' worth of GPS satellites, accessing weather reports from satellite phones, updating their blogs, and always a short time, often mere hours, from rescue via SOS signals sent to nearby ships, perhaps even the Coast Guard. People fly down the highway at ninety miles an hour knowing that, if they smash themselves to bits, they will, at least, be helicoptered to a hospital.

George had no one to rely on but himself, and his few fellow officers. So he called a meeting.

It was clear from the Half King's message that a bold display of force was needed to keep the Indians engaged on the English side. Yet even a man of George's virtually nonexistent military experience could see that his 159 barely trained soldiers, pitted against a thousand experienced French soldiers, would have been crushed like a plate of escargots in a no-holds-barred match with a half dozen of Hannibal's elephants.

George and his officers decided on a compromise.

They wouldn't withdraw, but they wouldn't advance, at least not directly towards the French. They decided to sidestep the thousand French soldiers (later deduced to be closer to six hundred) and head to a different strategic point, about thirty-seven miles from the Forks.

Their destination was an Ohio Company storehouse where the Monongahela River met Redstone Creek. This, George reasoned, could be the basis for some kind of temporary fort. Of course, thirty-seven miles in a land where trees had to be chopped down to create a path large enough for the wagons that carried your supplies was a lot farther than thirty-seven miles on the Hollywood freeway (except at rush hour, when it's about the same distance).

Keeping a cool head at unexpectedly hot moments is a virtue. Pitting fewer than two hundred barely trained soldiers against a thousand veterans would have been reckless folly.

George's lack of experience, though, seems to have left him blind to what he was still getting his soldiers, and himself, into. Calm, rational, and fearless decisions, with no experience to guide you, will not necessarily get you where you want to go. As George saw it, the task was simply to clear a "road broad enough to pass with all our artillery and our baggage, and there to wait for fresh Orders."

What could go wrong?

As their journey progressed, George and his men encountered more and more desperate traders fleeing from the French. These men clearly thought that George was crazy to bring a few score of soldiers to engage the thousands of French they believed were filling the Ohio Valley.

If George was afraid of this unexpected danger, he didn't show it. Whatever he actually thought of the news, he dismissed it as exaggeration, and convinced his compatriots that he was right.

Onward they went.

Despite his own skills as a surveyor and the excruciatingly careful maps he had drawn, George, lacking satellite phones and weather maps, cut his road directly into a flooding river.

As he and his soldiers waited for the flood to subside, word came that, at the recently lost Forks, the French were now building a massive fort with eight hundred men already there. Meanwhile, the thirty-three Virginians who had abandoned that key point had also abandoned George, or, more accurately, had been sent home by him, as they didn't accept his authority over them. George had decided it was better to have 159 disciplined soldiers than 192 soldiers among whom dissension might spread.

As the small army waited for the river to become passable, the officers George had brought with him had time to develop doubt. They had heard news from Williamsburg confirming that mere soldiers in other companies, more closely linked with England, were getting more money than Virginia's officers. Long before any of his soldiers had got to the point of dissension, George's officers began to threaten resignation.

Their indignation had less to do with the amount of money they were receiving than the offense they felt to their honor, as a result of the disparity between their pay and that of the English soldiers. Were they not Englishmen too? Asked to fight for their king, why would they be treated with less respect merely because they were born in America?

The procedure for making a complaint in an army is up the chain of command, which in this case meant through George, who was asked to send his officers' letters of protest on to the governor.

The problem was becoming serious. Idle troops and idle officers, while not quite at the point of mutiny, were engaging in the closest legal alternative. If the soldiers saw an exodus of their officers, what could stop the soldiers from leaving, too—whether legally or illegally?

As far as George knew, at this point, he was outnumbered by the French at least six to one, while promises of reinforcements had yet to materialize. He could not let this go any further.

But how could he stop it?

George did face this unexpected danger…but not exactly head on. Rather than getting angry, or directly confronting his officers, he performed a kind of judo move, allying himself with those who complained the loudest. He would show his solidarity with them by complaining louder still.

George did not show fear in the face of the potential disintegration of his entire army. He, instead, agreed with his officers' complaints, going on to say to them, and the governor, that he was more offended than they were. How dare the governor, sitting in comfort in his mansion, dishonor these brave men, who were fighting for "the heroic spirit of every freeborn Englishman…and privileges of our king.…"

George's letter to the governor regarding pay was not merely a strategic or pragmatic move on his part. He himself had objected to this sort of pay disparity before. Here, though, was a chance to use his personal grudge for a greater goal.

He agreed to send his officers' letters to the governor, while insisting on sending his own, foremost among them. He did not make the content of his letter a secret to his fellow officers. His letter said, in part,

> Giving up my commission is quite contrary to my intention. Nay, I ask it as a greater favor, than any amongst the many I have received from your Honor, to confirm it to me. But let me serve voluntarily; then I will, with the greatest pleasure in

life, devote my services to the expedition without any other reward, than the satisfaction of serving my country; but to be slaving dangerously for the shadow of pay, through woods, rocks, mountains, I would rather prefer the great toil of a daily laborer, and dig for a maintenance, provided I were reduced to the necessity, than serve upon such ignoble terms; for I really do not see why the lives of his Majesty's subjects in Virginia should be of less value, than of those in other parts of his American dominions; especially when it is well known, that we must undergo double their hardship.

To give up his pay was a truly brilliant move, and a long-sighted one, especially for someone who actually needed the money. George was, at one level, taking the longer and higher view—honor before anything else.

It was also cagey and expedient.

By giving up his pay and continuing to serve as a volunteer, George made it clear that it wasn't the money, but the principle, that he stood for. Why should he, as an American officer, be paid less than a mere regular soldier who happened to be English?

There were, of course, arguments on the other side. It might have occurred to George that inducement, or at least fair compensation, for a soldier from further afield, in a strange land, might account for at least some of the disparity in pay. He might also have thought, as indeed many burgesses did, that someone as connected with the major shareholders of the Ohio Company as he was should perhaps, along with his friends and relatives, pay for the whole enterprise themselves, and not whine about the salary.

The disparity went further than pay, though, and to any objective observer it would have been troubling. For example, English officers would often send local soldiers on the most dangerous maneuvers. The invidious distinction between English and Americans was, at its core, an important issue that eventually would contribute to the full-scale rebellion of the Revolution.

For the present, though, George, by allying himself with the men serving under him, now had all his officers, and himself, on the same side. This was as pivotal a moment as any battle for George, as he wanted more out of this expedition than mere money, or even the success of the Ohio Company. He wanted to be a man like the Duke of the *Panegyrick*—a hero, a great leader. If he were to achieve this most fundamental goal, he could not afford to let his first military mission fall apart.

When the heat had died down, and no one was paying much attention any more, George reversed himself and asked for, and received, all the back pay he had refused at the time.

In the meantime, though, the officers, hearing his words of sacrifice for a greater good, could not—their honor would not let them—abandon George Washington. They would have been ashamed to do so.

George still had a lot to learn about military strategy and tactics. He was already, though, clearly, a consummate leader of men.

Perhaps that's one reason that the Duke, whose "Genius" had also led him to "Martial affairs," was such an attractive role model for George. With time, the *Panegyrick*'s praise for the Duke's military achievements would be applicable to George, too: "Nature had had fitted him, for what Europe [and America too, in George Washington's case] admir'd him afterwards; that is, for an Excellent Commander. And really, this is the scene of that Great Man's Life. It is the Theater, where his actions have replenish'd the world with astonishment; and made him, if not Superior, at least Equal, to the…CAESARS of our age."

George, at this point, clearly had a long way to go before he'd be thought of in those hagiographic terms. But he was on his way—although not without accidentally causing a world war, and a few other mishaps along the way.

⚬

About the time the river became passable, word was en route from Williamsburg that the math professor/newly minted military commander, Joshua Fry, was on his way with reinforcements. He was coming to take command. Ignorant of this, George and his 159 soldiers were already on their way when word from the Half King of yet another "surprising danger" did, in fact, reach him.

According to the Half King, the French had sent an army—although no one seemed to know of how many soldiers that meant—to "strike" and presumably kill George Washington and his soldiers. Besides passing along this news, the Half King also said that he and other Indian chiefs were on their way to hold council with George.

Rather than frightening George, this unexpected news about French activity emboldened him. In fact, he lamented that he could not find the French more quickly, to "annihilate" them.

George eventually made it to a place called Great Meadow, which he picked out as "a charming field for an encounter" with the French. An important battle would take place there, though not yet—and when it did, the experience would fall somewhat short of "charming," at least from George's point of view.

Some would think it *charmant*, however.

Meanwhile, as he waited for the French, George naively cleared branches and undergrowth away from two shallow indentations in the ground, mistakenly believing that they were deep enough to serve as trenches, and also mistakenly believing that clearing the brush away would give his soldiers a clearer line of fire. In fact, it would make them exposed targets.

As George's officers and men were as green as he was, none of them objected to his plans.

The French nearby did not seem inclined to attack yet, although a few dozen seemed to be close. Piecing together different reports, George reasoned that about fifty Frenchmen, led by a wily officer known as La Force, were searching for him. He believed they had come by canoe but had now left their canoes behind them. George split his troops, sending out various scouts, bareback, on the horses that were meant to pull the carts, to look for the French—to no avail.

Finally word came that Half King was nearby. George immediately rode out to meet him, finding him late that day. The Half King's scouts were now sent out. Perhaps unsurprisingly, they were able to see what had been invisible to the Americans. They quickly found the French, tipped off by two footprints on a trail.

A French contingent of thirty-two soldiers were sleeping near those footsteps, hidden in a hollow. Being hidden did not mean, however, protected. The French were, in fact, utterly exposed.

George rode back to his camp that night, almost immediately leaving with about seventy-five of his troops, along with the dozen or so Indians that had accompanied the Half King. The plan was to surround the sleeping French.

As rain was pouring down, the Americans were fairly sure that no scout would spot them. Any sound was muffled by the downpour, their footprints disappeared as soon as they took the next step, and the light of the night sky was blotted out by the clouds, the rain, and the forest.

George led what would be the necessarily exposed right flank in the attack, while a captain led the left flank. The plan was to surround the French, sneak up on them, and kill them.

Actually, it was a little more complicated than that, because of the way fighting worked at that time. Specifically, what, in fact, you did in George's day, or at least in classic, European battles, was march, in a specific formation, three soldiers deep, towards your enemy. You didn't flinch, you didn't blink—you marched. You didn't fire your gun, you didn't aim your gun in more than a general direction—you just marched. Because the guns were wildly inaccurate, a shot at farther than fifty yards was almost not worth taking. After the other side shot, there was a pause before their soldiers' next round could be fired, as it took time to reload.

During this pause, you got a bit closer, waited for the order to fire, and fired—ideally before the other side could fire their second round. You then went to the back of the three-person deep formation that comprised your unit, and began reloading your gun, as the row now in front fired. That row of soldiers, after firing their guns, then moved to the back, putting you in the middle row. The row that was now in the front fired, then went to the back to begin reloading their guns, which brought you to the front with your newly loaded gun again. And so on.

This battle wasn't, of course, a classic battle on an open field, and no one actually remembers who shot first. What is clear is that George Washington stood, exposed, as the man next to him fell, shot by the French. He didn't flinch.

In the end, ten Frenchmen were killed—some of them by George's hatchet-wielding Indian allies—while twenty-one were wounded. Unknown to George at the time, one French soldier had escaped. The whole thing was over in fifteen minutes.

But it started a world war that would last seven years.

Why? Before the smoke had cleared, a few of the French prisoners began yelling at George, while one ripped papers from the pocket of a dead (and scalped) compatriot and waved them in George's face. At least three interpreters started to make sense of what was being said.

The French claim, backed by the bloody documents, was that their party was an ambassadorial expedition to deliver a message to the English. The message was from the French king, telling the English to remove themselves from his territory.

Their mission had been, it appeared, a perfect obverse of what George had done a few months earlier when he took the message warning the French to get out of the Ohio Valley. All the documents they had with them seemed to argue a perfect parity with George's mission of the prior December.

Along with the message they were to give the English, and orders to deliver this message, they even carried orders to make a report on the size and strength of the English fort they presumably would be allowed to enter in order to deliver their message—exactly as George had done when in the French fort.

George remained convinced, or at least continued to claim, that more than thirty soldiers was too many for a mere embassy—and besides, he was swayed by the concurrent reports he had received, telling him about a French expedition sent specifically to attack him.

Beyond this, he believed that the French had tried to murder him and Gist as they had returned from their own embassy, although he couldn't prove it. Whether George realized that these were not mutually exclusive contingencies—the French could have tried to murder him in the woods and still, now, be sending out an embassy—is not clear. He always maintained that the papers the French had carried were only a ruse, meant as a justification for their presence in case they found themselves outnumbered. He claimed that no embassy would be hiding in a hollow—diplomats would be traveling openly.

Then again, traveling openly in an area where Indians felt justified in relieving you of your scalp might not be the wisest plan.

Although the evidence is ambiguous, it was always clear in George's mind that all of the diplomacy had been, basically, a charade. Both sides wanted the same land, and both sides intended, sooner or later, to use force to claim it.

Joseph Coulon de Villiers de Jumonville, the commander of the French soldiers in the hollow (thus the name of this encounter, "the Battle of Jumonville Glen"), was not as lucky as George had been on his diplomatic mission. He ended up dead, and possibly—at least, that is how one account has it—scalped, with the Half King washing his hands in his, Jumonville's, brains.

George's fortune was about to take a further downward spike. At least that's how it would look to everyone else. George wasn't going to see it that way, though.

Maybe the vision George had of being, one day, like the Duke—rather than trundling through life with no clear vision or goal—helped give him his almost supernatural ability to snatch emotional victory from the clenched jaws of literal defeat. This defeat was to leave him standing in a pool of his dead soldiers' blood, mixed with the rainwater on which he blamed—rather than blaming himself—his first inglorious defeat.

Perhaps the experience of psychologically transcending this first major defeat was necessary to build in him the kind of almost super-human perseverance—the true American grit—that it would take to wear down the British in the war of attrition that would be the American Revolution.

By a strange twist of fate, George's most inglorious defeat would come on...the fourth of July. This "coincidence" would seem to reinforce

George's own perception that beyond his personal ambition there was a kind of Providence, as he called it, guiding his life.

George didn't have enough experience to prepare for battle well, but he did do his best. He had his men stick logs upright in the ground in the Great Meadow that he, with his naive eyes, saw as a "charming" battlefield. This created what looked like a high log fence. George saw it as a fort.

He called it Fort Necessity.

The Half King, assuming George knew what he was doing, at first kept his thoughts to himself. However, it soon became clear to the Half King, who had seen countless French forts throughout North America, that George needed help. A wooden fence, he tried to explain to George, would be a "trifling" thing in the face of a competent enemy. Also, the Half King said, the whole thing—call it a "fort" or not—was too near the woods and thus in dangerously close range of soldiers who could fire from a hidden position, as he knew they had adapted to the new type of warfare that the American landscape engendered (pragmatism over honor being, in many ways, the new American ideal).

George remained unflustered by this criticism, writing the governor, "even with my small numbers, I shall not fear the attack of 500 men."

Although not precisely hubris, this was a point when George's confidence and fearlessness, untempered by wisdom, would not be enough. To believe in yourself is useful. To want to do what no one has done before is noble. But to do something without reference to the past, without the context provided by experience or the advice of those with experience, is rarely the best plan.

George, in this case, seems to have acted his age. He didn't need the Half King's help, he thought. He could do it all by himself.

He was wrong.

The scene around the fort was suddenly becoming, if not festive as in Christmas, then festive as in Woodstock. Queen Aliquippa, another Indian ally of the English, had appeared with about twenty-five Indian families in tow, fleeing in terror from French anger and reprisals in response to the recent Battle of Jumonville Glen, which the French were now interpreting as the murder of their ambassador by none other than George Washington. All the members of the families who followed their queen appeared, with the notable exception of the grown men. These men, who would have been useful warriors, seem to have had other plans that week.

Squalling babies required food, as did their plaintive mothers, the squabbling toddlers, and the coy teenaged girls who ran playing through the "fort" that the soldiers were still constructing. George's men, who had chopped a road through the forest to get their supplies in, saw much of their hard-won food disappear into the mouths of this gaggle of Indians.

The Half King meanwhile promised reinforcements. George could not fight with mere promises, though, and everyone knew that an attack was imminent.

About this time the news finally reached George that Colonel Fry had died and that he, George Washington, was now the commander of all the Virginia forces. George still wanted an experienced commander above him, something he wrote to Governor Dinwiddie at the time, although he was too busy with the preparations to give this much thought.

Unfortunately, he was also too blind to see that he already had an experienced commander with him in the person of the Half King, whose advice he continued to dismiss. In George's defense, it is perhaps understandable that, as he may have learned of, or even seen, the Half King washing his hands in Jumonville's brains, George was not inclined to take orders from him, nor even advice. But whatever the facts, ignoring the Half King would turn out to be a mistake.

Finally, reinforcements did arrive. About three hundred new soldiers appeared in Great Meadow. Two-thirds were reinforcements for George's own regiment. The other third, about a hundred soldiers, seemed to come from another planet.

Dressed differently, in regular British uniforms, they also walked differently, talked differently, and even stood still differently. They were in all all ways stiffer, more formal, and less American than George's regiment. These one hundred soldiers were technically British, although many had been born in America. But the technical distinction made all the difference. They were under the command of Captain James Mackay, a Scotsman from a family rich enough to have purchased him a commission granted directly by the king. (In Britain, younger sons of landholders sometimes found their way in the world with the purchase of an officership in the army). To be fair, after his parents had purchased his position for him, Captain Mackay had already, at this point, been in the army eighteen years. It is therefore possible that his prideful arrogance had some justification—he did, after all, have more experience than George. But this was not the distinction he chose to press. The distinction he chose to make an issue of was the last one George wanted to hear, although the first one George expected to hear.

Here was George Washington, a recently made colonel and also, albeit by default, the commander of all of Virginia's forces. He was serving his country as a volunteer because his pride would not allow him to accept less pay than a regular British officer. As he stood there, towering over the pipsqueak "old country" officer, a mere captain, the pipsqueak had the effrontery to tell George that any officer from Britain—a mere captain, for example—outranked any officer from the colonies—for example, a colonel and the commander of Virginia's army.

This interaction between George and Captain Mackay was not forgotten by George when, two decades later, he made the decision to expel from American shores anyone who reminded him of Captain Mackay, or who reflected the same attitudes this arrogant "old countryman" embodied. These small indignities—Gandhi's experience on a train in South Africa, George Washington's experience with Captain Mackay in the Ohio Valley—can have far-reaching consequences. If you want to hang onto a large empire, you have to be very careful whom you insult.

Unfortunately for both of them, Governor Dinwiddie hadn't made it clear whether George Washington or Captain Mackay was supposed to be in command. So Captain Mackay insisted—astonishingly, at a fort that everyone believed was under imminent threat of attack—on staying in a separate camp. "Fine, whatever," is a modern translation of what George thought. Or, as he put it when writing to the governor, "I have not offered to control Captain Mackay in any thing, nor showed that I claimed a superior command, except in giving the parole and countersign, which must be the same in an army consisting of different nations, to distinguish friends from foes. He knows the necessity of this, yet does not think he is to receive it from me.... its absurdity is obvious."

Did you catch that? Mackay wouldn't even allow his company to accept the Virginians' passwords—the "Who goes there?" kind of thing. (Maybe the sign and countersign George's men were using weren't aristocratic enough for him? After all, during the Revolution, Americans would pair the password "Industry" with the countersign "Wealth," and "Neatness" with "Gentility." Perhaps Captain Mackay would have preferred "British" paired with "Insufferable Twat.")

To put it another way, Captain Mackay behaved like an arrogant jackass. And, as George saw it, acted like a moron, willing to get his head blown off, and his soldiers', too, because of his ego.

Early in the morning of July, 3, 1754, George learned that the French were within four miles. Four miles in the forest is not four miles on the highway, but it was still close.

George scrambled everyone, dashing about making last-minute preparations.

About nine in the morning, word came that the French were nearby. George lined his men up, awaiting the arrival of the French. Within minutes, the French appeared on the edge of the forest, directly across from George's "fort."

Exactly as George had imagined.

George immediately ordered his men to leap behind the fortifications he had so carefully built. The soldiers couldn't actually fit in the fort itself, as the fort he'd build, to the extent it was a fort at all, was too small for much beyond supplies and gunpowder. Instead, George had had his soldiers build earth and log entrenchments—a kind of hill of dirt and logs. During the final days of preparation, George had the idea to extend this wall of dirt and logs down beyond a creek, to give George's soldier's water, in case the French attempted a siege, which is what George expected, perhaps from reading about battles for castles.

Fort Necessity may have been many things, but it was not a castle.

Not that George's men had, after feeding the Indians most of their supplies, enough food left to endure a siege, but it was too late to do anything about that now.

They'd make the best of what they had.

George felt ready for the battle. As he had written to the governor during his preparations, "I have a constitution hardy enough to encounter and undergo the most severe trials, and, I flatter myself, resolution to face what any man durst."

So far, George was proved right, the Half King wrong—or so it seemed. The French seemed to be ready to advance in a straight line, directly into George's line of fire.

They say a common error in preparing for wars is preparing to fight the last one, not the next one. George seems to have prepared to fight a battle he read about in a book, in a war from a different era, certainly not one taking place in the woods, behind a balustrade of wood and mud. Whatever may have possessed George to believe the French would continue to walk straight into a line of fire, beyond what he'd read in dusty books about classic European strategy, is unknown.

In fact the French had merely stumbled into the clearing by accident, before realizing where they were. After jumping behind the entrenchments, George's soldiers had time to get off one volley before the French disappeared back into the woods, never to be seen again.

But they would continue to be felt. And heard.

A constant bombardment ensued, from hiding places in the woods. So much for classic European warfare. The Half King had been right, as it turned out. The Fort was situated too low, as the Half King had realized, while George's keen surveyor's mind had somehow failed to see the angles and lines of sight that made his defenses defenseless.

Every time one of George's soldiers would let his position be known by standing up enough to fire a single shot, usually blindly into the woods, out of the morass of trees would come dozens of carefully aimed shots, falling as close to that spot as guns of that era allowed. The only reason George's soldiers were not mown down in a single round is that guns, at that time, were so inaccurate.

The Half King had thought the battle already lost before the French had arrived in the Great Meadow. By midday of July 3, 1754, it surely seemed lost to many of George's soldiers. Yet as late as that afternoon, as George slipped on the blood of his many fallen and injured soldiers, he still did not consider surrender or defeat.

Then the rain came.

It did not come in drops or drizzles, but in torrents. This was the rain on which George would blame his defeat—along with blaming the powers above and beyond his control that had left his soldiers without bayonets, which prevented them from going out of their fort (or at least in front of the mounds of dirt and logs) and driving the French from their position in hand-to-hand combat.

The rain, in addition to forming rivulets of bloody water, soaked and destroyed much of George's gunpowder, which would have been no surprise to the Half King, taking into account the fort's low position on the meadow (the same one George had initially called a "charming field for an Encounter"). I say this *would have been* no surprise to the Half King because the Half King had not stuck around for the battle and was therefore not there to witness George's inglorious defeat.

For a while George's soldiers fought on, fueled in the end by the rum that still performed its function despite the rainwater that had mixed in with it, stored next to the gunpowder that did not function at all. Although rum might provide a temporary fire in the belly, with no fire in their flintlocks, and vastly less food than they had hoped to have, finally, by that evening, George's soldiers had nothing left to fight with.

Still, even after all this, when the shots from the woods momentarily died down, and a lone voice called from the forest, "Voulez-vous parlez?" George rejected it. He did not want a representative from the French coming into his "fort" and reporting back to the French commanders any lines or angles of attack that had thus far eluded the French.

Pas de problème, came the French response, you can send your representative to us. When George's representative returned with the terms of surrender, George had a few changes to make.

Again, pas de problème. George's suggestions were accepted with no hesitation. The French did not even want prisoners, except two hostages, to be kept only until the ten "prisoners of war" George had detained after his first "battle" were returned.

Finally, in a *petit bonbon* designed to delight the eyes of a boy brought up with dreams of glory, the French would even allow George and his surviving men to march out of their "fort" with the "honors of war." This meant a drummer could beat a drum, and a flag—although not the heaviest, as that would prove too heavy for George's exhausted soldiers— could fly above their battered and heads, empty stomachs, and bloody bodies.

So, on the morning of July 4, 1754, George Washington marched out with "the full honors of war." Wounded soldiers were carried by famished soldiers, a small flag limply hung overhead, while the one symbolic cannon they had been allowed to keep trailed behind. (They were to abandon it three miles away, as it was too heavy to carry.) All this while a lone drummer beat a martial beat. When George's troops were halfway across the field to where the French stood at attention, the whoops and hollers of Indians suddenly screamed from the woods. Had George been tricked? Yes, but in a far more clever way than appeared. It would not do to have the British forces scalped, so the French stopped their Indians. An act of nobility?

No. They had a slimier snail to sautée.

Although the French stopped their Indians from scalping George and his soldiers, they did allow them to loot their belongings. With no energy to complain, glad to be left with their lives, the defeated soldiers stood mutely for this last indignity.

George, who had been brought up in the American way of direct dealing, did not see that the new lines of French attack had nothing so petty for their goal as scalping by Indians, but instead extended around the world, to the courts of Europe. The story as usually told is that George, who did not know French, was tricked into signing a document, in French, in which he admitted to assassinating the French ambassador Jumonville.

What George failed to fathom was that—admission or no admission, assassination or no assassination—the easy yet wily terms of the French surrender were predicated on the notion that there was no state of war, so that of course George and his troops should be allowed to leave. Therefore, call it an assassination, call it what you will, if you are not at war with a country, and you kill a citizen of that country—what else can it be but murder?

By offering such easy terms of surrender, the French were angling for the moral high ground in Europe, in what they hoped might be nothing more than a diplomatic struggle—not, as it turned out, a war that would engulf the world and cost a million lives.

As word of his initial skirmish in the woods spread around the world, George Washington would be known, in Horace Walpole's words, as the man who "set the world on fire." Or as Voltaire put it, a "cannon shot" in America had "set Europe ablaze." (In fact, there had been no cannon at Jumonville Glen.)

George Washington, it would eventually be claimed, started a war that spread around the world, lasted seven years, and killed, some estimate, over a million soldiers and civilians. (Allowing for population growth, if the same proportion of the world's population were killed today, that would be something like ten million people.) That's an awfully big responsibility to put on one twenty-two-year-old, bumbling about in the wet woods of the Ohio Valley.

In his first military command, George Washington never flinched. Yet he was defeated—on the battlefield, and even more ignominiously in the court of public opinion.

There would be nothing for us to learn, of course, from my great-uncle if he had started out perfect.

George's stumbles should encourage to us.

Consider—whatever mistakes you've made, you probably haven't been accused of committing a murder and starting a world war.

Yet that's how George Washington started his career. Still…still…he went on to glory. He really did become the kind of hero he was aiming to be, the Duke (2.0).

In fact, despite the gargantuan setbacks in the Ohio Valley, George was already on his way to his goal. Imperfect as George was at this point in his career, why did the Half King—while simultaneously believing that George and the English had acted "as fools"—admire him? And why, in the first place, was George the commander of an entire army, at only twenty-two?

He was doing something right, already.

Perhaps it was talent. George saw it, as we shall soon see, as having more to do with Providence, along with the inspiration of the Duke never flinching, even at the "most surprising danger."

All the rest—George's inexperience, his foolish decisions his overlooking the Half King's potential help—is understandable in someone beginning his progress through life. No one is born perfect, filled with all wisdom and knowledge.

George Washington worked, grew, and struggled, always with great courage. As the *Panegyrick* says of the Duke: "surmounting the greatest Difficulties."

Chapter Eight

"Exact to the Rules of Civility, Breeding, and All the Accomplishments of Men of Quality"

"As fit for the Cabinet, as he prov'd after for the Camp.... He is as admirable in his Private, as in his Public Capacities; and there is as ample a Catalogue of his Vertues, as of his Exploits."
—H. de Luzancy, *A Panegyrick to the Memory of His Grace Frederick, Late Duke of Schonberg*

What could be more frightening than being shot at?

Well, different people are scared of different things. "The most surprising dangers" on the battlefield didn't seem to phase George Washington. But he *could be* intimidated in social circumstances. He was, after all, terrified when he traveled to take the office of president—he said that made him feel as if he were on the way to his own execution.

Yet, despite how he may have felt, George, like the Duke, was as successful socially as he was martially.

How did George become cool, socially?

⟨※⟩

George's ambitions weren't only military.

Would you find it shocking if I told you that George was thought of as a kind of "Dr. Love"? What if I told you that, later in his life, teenaged girls came asking him for advice about love?

When we think of love, the first person that pops into our head probably is not George Washington. In fact, George may be, for many of us, the very last person we'd think of.

Still, one assumes that if teenaged girls were bugging him for love advice, they must have seen him as especially wise about love.

All the things you didn't know about George …

⟨※⟩

Beyond girls, George also needed to make his way in society. He also needed money. He had to succeed in private life as well as achieving public acclaim. But how?

The *Panegyrick* told him how to get started. To be "Exact to the Rules of Civility, Breeding, and all the Accomplishments of Men of Quality."

But what exactly were the "Rules of Civility"?

In a society in which only a very few men had hereditary titles, a man's behavior mattered. With no title to keep you afloat, your surname might have meant *something*. It surely helped, in Virginia, if you were a Lee or a Carter or a Washington. In many ways, your family's connections were necessary.

But they were not sufficient.

To count as a gentleman, you had to *be* a gentleman.

People then, as now, judged other people on the subtlest of clues. A king of England once remarked that he could tell who was a gentleman and who was not by what he did with the tails of his jacket as he sat down.

A gentleman would simply sit.

Someone who was not a gentleman would flip the tails of his jacket back to avoid sitting on them. This was because a gentleman would have many jackets, and many servants to ensure that his jackets were always in top shape and always wrinkle-free. Someone who was not a gentleman would have fewer jackets and fewer, if any, servants to take care of them.

This might seem silly to us, but this sort of subtle thing was of profound importance in a class-based society.

So George *was* careful to do the right things and behave in the right way.

These behaviors were not confined, at least for someone like George, to things as superficial as coattails. After all, quite early in his life, he had met some of the "best" people in America. Many hadn't impressed him at all. Men such as Lord Fairfax or the corrupt officials, well-mannered but morally bankrupt, that George and Lawrence had met in Barbados.

George, at the same time, also met many men who were *not* the "best" people in America, according to the sit-on-your-coattails standard—yet whose real merit strongly impressed him. Men such as Christopher Gist, the experienced woodsman who had shared George's first mission in the Ohio Valley.

George knew that following the outward "Rules of Civility and Breeding" was not enough to make him a hero in the same league as the

Duke of Schonberg. George did, as he had to, enough of the sit-on-your-coattails-or-you're-not-a-real-gentleman thing to fit into the highest stratum of Virginia society—in fact, to achieve an impressive position in that society.

The more important and fundamental rules that George followed, however, the ones that set him apart from men with wrinkled coats and soiled souls, were rules that encouraged expressions of innate morality, of the duty toward other people that George felt as a "Christian gentleman." This type of civility is something that cannot easily, if at all, be put into lists of maxims. It seems it must be intuitively felt—even if it could be rationally thought through.

To understand this, let's start by thinking about sex. (I think about it all the time, anyway. Why not put these thoughts to good use?) We are (well, we soon will be) talking about marriage (George's marriage, that is), so the subject of sex seems as good a place as any to start.

Why do all societies have rules about sex?

Most people don't think this through.

Sometime around the dawn of civilization, it was noticed that people who had promiscuous sex got horrible diseases. Therefore, spontaneously, organically, rules developed to discourage promiscuity. As people at this time—thousands of years ago—didn't have any ideas about germs, they ascribed divine or supernatural causes to the diseases, and tended to think of them as divine retribution.

There came an idea that it was on pain of divine punishment that one must obey the rules, which, inevitably, got more complicated than they needed to be, and sillier than they ought to be—because that's what people who don't truly understand things tend to do. Complification, whether it's a word or not, is what it is.

This has given rules, *per se*, a bad name, at least among people who consider themselves worldly and sophisticated. It's obvious to "cool" people that the *complificated* rules are daft. Yet, unfortunately, they often fail to see there is at least a vital grain of truth hidden in many of them.

So these cool, rule-ignoring people got venereal diseases and, before antibiotics, often went insane and sometimes died.

George, though, was a different kind of cool. We already know that he had extraordinary self-control—the kind of cool that made it possible for him to imbibe sparingly and never lose his temper while the French got Bacchused and bragged about how easy it would be to beat the "slow and dilatory" English.

George wasn't only able to make himself obey rules—such as moderating his appetite and keeping his temper—rules that many people find it very hard to follow. He also had the discernment to know which rules were worth following and which could be safely ignored. The trick to being cool like George Washington (although it was described as honorable back then, we can view it as "cool"), is to get the essence of the rules, the deeper morality behind them, while rejecting superficial nonsense. Which is to say, there is an element of balance in George's understanding of what the rules of civility truly are.

As George was later to explain, "the composition of the human frame" contains "a good deal of inflammable matter," but love "ought to be under the guidance of reason." In other words, passion and reason must be in balance. Inflammable human nature makes rules necessary—still, the rules should be reasonable, not arbitrary.

For George, this kind of balance seemed to work. His balanced, reasonable "Civility" made him a social success in the highest circles of colonial Virginia. It paved the way for his spectacularly successful marriage. Indeed it served him well in places he never could have imagined he would be.

Contrast.

Perhaps the easiest way to see how George was "Exact to the rules of Civility and Breeding" is to see how others were not. Martha Washington's first husband, in fact, was a character in a multigenerational soap opera more sordid than a Frenchman's imagination.

There once was a woman called Martha who was as short as George was tall. She had already been married. However, in colonial Virginia, early death from the myriad diseases overwhelming that swampy, pre-antibiotic world ended more marriages early than divorce does today.

She was twenty-six, single, and perhaps the richest woman in America (many, at least, say she was).

Martha was, as she said of herself, "a fine, healthy girl" who was "cheerful as a cricket and busy as a bee." Others saw her as a soul overflowing with kindness. Throughout her life, she loved nothing more than nursing the sick—from soldiers to servants to George himself—back to health.

She also had other loveable qualities, but perhaps, as George allegedly did, you stopped paying attention at the sentence about her money. That's an allegation often levelled against George Washington—that he married Martha Dandridge Custis for her fortune.

Where is his defense? George insisted that his letters to his wife be destroyed at his death, but even without them we still can establish that George's marriage wasn't as mercenary as some have claimed.

Did George have any pragmatic motives for marrying Martha? Even one such motive mixed in with purer ones may sound scandalous to us. However, prudent reasons for marrying were acceptable, and even encouraged, in colonial Virginia. Whatever the ratio of pragmatism to passion, George and Martha's marriage was clearly filled with a vastly higher and more noble kind of love than you have ever seen in a Hollywood film. And a more lasting kind than perhaps the purest love of all—Romeo and Juliet's.

But we don't have to dig into literature, nor dive into Hollywood trash, to put George and Martha's love in context. As we'll see, reasonable and prudent look pretty good when compared with the riot of passions that had roiled the family of Martha's *first* husband.

Daniel Parke Custis had been the descendant of a very rich man whose family emphatically was not "Exact to the Rules of Civility and Breeding" in any sense. That is, the Parkes and Custises did not tend to follow the outer rules of their society, while they still seemed like bastards on those rare occasions when they did.

Actually, technically, a lot of them *were* bastards.

More on that in a moment.

Daniel Parke Custis's grandfather, Daniel Parke, had the self-control of Byron, the taste of Donald Trump, and the political wisdom of Groucho Marx. He did what he wanted, seemingly without regard for anyone else. His penultimate act in public life was being appointed governor of the Leeward Islands by Queen Anne. His ultimate act was inspiring the people of the Leeward Islands to rise up and kill him.

But he wasn't through yet. His legacy of lasciviousness would outlive him.

Before his death, Daniel Parke had done something that was clearly not "Exact to the Rules of Civility and Breeding," something that would have posthumous effects so far-reaching that George would feel them on the day of his marriage, half a century later. Daniel Parke left a will so vile that even today it would be splashed across the front page of the *National Enquirer* as one more bit of evidence for the imminent doom of civilization. (No, wait, the *National Enquirer's* mere existence is that. Anyway ...)

He wasn't all bad, though. He started out in life as a member of the King's Council of Virginia. (Always start at the top, I say.) This gave him access to the governor, whom he, notoriously, struck with a horsewhip. I've never heard of a governor who couldn't do with a sound beating, so, in my eyes, at least, Daniel Parke was off to a stupendous start. Not, of course, in keeping society's overt rules, but as for the innate morality of it, I, personally, give him a pass. Still, that was only one commendable act in a life otherwise seemingly devoid of such things.

He left his wife and two daughters in Virginia and sailed back to England. This was not necessarily done in opposition to his society's rules—it was the sort of thing that had to be done from time to time. After all, George would spend a lot of time away from his wife during the Revolution. Yet, pretty clearly, Daniel Parke did what he did in opposition to the innate rules that most people's consciences would scream at them to follow. He didn't just abandon his family, he left them in something close to penury as he spent great gobs of money on himself.

Then again, who could really blame him (other than his conscience)? Virginia was drab and England grand. Daniel Parke took most of the profits from his Virginia estate, leaving his family poor. He became colonel and aide-de-camp to Marlborough—and, in those pre-telegraph days, he carried the news of the miraculous victory at Blenheim back to Queen Anne, who gave him a diamond-encrusted memento and £1000, which was serious money at a time when you could buy a house for £15. In addition, he was given the governorship of the Leeward Islands.

Did I mention a governorship in those days did not involve work? It was, pretty much, a license to effortless profit. (Often the *actual* governor would appoint someone else to *actually* govern, taking the profits for himself, never bothering even to show up at the place of which he was governor. However, Daniel Parke had the—misguided, as it turned out—idea that he could simultaneously actually govern and fleece the Leeward Islanders. In their presence.)

The Queen rewarding the man who delivered the message of the victory at Blenheim with the governorship of the Leeward Islands would be something like rewarding the mailman with a new car for bringing you good news—well, it's exactly like that, really. Unless…unless the mailman has done you a few other favors, too?

Only Queen Anne knows for certain.

The reason Daniel Parke was killed by an angry mob—assuming angry mobs have anything so rational as a reason—was that he failed in epic proportions to be exacting to the innate morality of the islanders. Specifically they were protesting policies he enforced as governor that enriched himself at their expense.

To some degree Daniel Parke's enrichment of himself was to be expected—financial opportunity was a main point of his being made governor, after all. However, he went much further than he should have gone.

"How much you can get away with" is not something that would have been, or could have been, written down. This episode, then, illustrates that the "Rules of Civility and Breeding," ultimately, have to be intuited. Daniel Parke was too blinded by his passions—particularly, by his greed—to be able to *feel* the unwritten rules.

But he wasn't done yet, even though, now, he was dead.

It turned out Daniel Parke had another—a second—family in the Leeward Islands, with several offspring.

Again, this was straying pretty far from the "Rules of Civility and Breeding"—and it still would be, even in our own day, even if society's overt rules about such things as marriage do change over time.

However, Daniel Parke's actions seem, beyond this, to have run against what he should intuitively have felt was wrong, rules or no. His passions caused him to hurt others—his original wife and children, of course, but also people generations away from himself, people he would never meet.

Daniel Parke's will—the one that caused a great scandal—stipulated that while his Virginia family got to keep his vast landholdings in Virginia, his Leeward Islands family got to keep everything there. So far, not so terribly bad (though not terribly civil or well bred either, according to the mores of his day, or ours).

But then came the zinger. All of Daniel Parke's debts in the Leeward Islands—and those debts turned out to be as big as the ocean that separated Virginia from the Islands—were to be paid from the Virginia estate. Surprise! You've got bastard sisters and brothers—oh, and please pay all their bills. Remember, this was a time before Mary had two mommies and bastards were "special siblings."

Beyond what society expected—and it didn't expect him to create bastards—Daniel Parke was also *being* a bastard.

Meanwhile John Custis, yet another man who was noticeably *not* "Exact to the Rules of Civility and Breeding" in any sense, had married one of Daniel Parke's semi-abandoned daughters in Virginia.

But not for love.

This claim is not made as the result of scrupulous academic research, comparing and contrasting verb and adverb frequency in letters written at the time (people—not me, though—really *do* things like that).

No, nothing quite as subtle as that. John Custis had it written on his tombstone.

Yes, his tombstone.

Bastard.

Walking through an ancient graveyard in the Virginia countryside, one can still find these words on a moss-covered tombstone, just across from another one that has almost completely collapsed. Perhaps someone felt this particular tombstone was worth preserving. Even people who work in graveyards have a sense of humor, after all. Or, perhaps, they have a better idea of what it means to be "Exact to the Rules of Civility and Breeding" than John Custis did, and want this counter-example preserved.

Who knows?

> Beneath this marble tomb lies ye body of the Honorable John Custis, Esquire of the city of Williamsburg and Parish of Burton.... *Aged 71 years and yet lived but seven years, which was the space of time he kept bachalor's house at Arlington on the Eastern Shore of Virginia.* This information put on this tomb was by his positive order. William Colley, mason in Fenchurch Street, London, England. [Emphasis added]

The seven years are the period of time he lived *after* his wife died.

It's one thing to feel that way. But to put it on your tombstone?

Not, really, in keeping with "the Rules of Civility and Breeding," in any sense. John Custis married Nancy Parke for her money, was absolutely unhappy because of her allegedly unpleasant personality (damaged by her father's abandonment?), then went through his entire married life afraid to spend any of her money because of the lawsuit from the bastards hanging over the family (they *were* bastards, after all, whether or not they were "bastards"). In his own words, he refused to pay "to enrich a kennel of whores and bastards," yet he couldn't risk spending the money, lest he lose the lawsuit.

This pressure seemed to make him nasty. Or perhaps he was born that way. Maybe, who knows, his wife and he were a perfect match (she didn't choose to leave her opinion of him on her tombstone).

One other thing John Custis did that seems astonishing, both by the mores of his times and by our values, was to free one of his slaves (good), and threaten to leave his estate to the freed slave if his son—Daniel Parke Custis, who was to be Martha Washington's first husband—didn't behave (not quite as good, thereby leaving the motivation for the first act in question).

(But hey, still good for the now ex-slave.)

The degree to which Daniel Parke Custis's father had any genuine justification for his, in any event, astonishing behavior is not clear from the record.

One of the things a Virginia gentleman was supposed to do, after all, was get married, but his father refused to give him the property that was expected when a son got married. Although Daniel Parke Custis tried a few times, no one would marry him without the estate he ought to bring with him. Finally, when he was thirty-seven—grandfather age, almost, in that society—he married the eighteen-year-old Martha Dandridge. The Dandridges were respectable but poor, so the marriage, for her family, was a large societal step up, if a personal step down.

For some reason, John Custis relented and gave his son the property he would need to support his bride. Oddly enough, one thing that preceded the marriage, and the change of heart of her father-in-law-to-be (or change of mind, more possibly, in this man with the miniature heart) was that Martha had given a couple of presents (a pony and a saddle) to the freed slave who was being used as a pawn in John Custis's game of power with his son. Though this seems to have tipped the scale in her favor, we don't know the details.

In any event, John Custis, beyond providing the property necessary for his son to marry, also made Daniel Parke Custis his heir, cutting out the freed slave from the bulk of the estate. Perhaps John Custis had never really been interested in the ex-slave but was using the threat to leave him his estate as leverage in his quarrel with his son.

There is not enough evidence to know the details of this conflict, and perhaps the fault was more evenly spread than it seems, but still, somehow, you can't imagine George, nor anyone in his family, being involved in anything remotely resembling this colonial melodrama

Anyway, then John Custis died. Power game over. His son Daniel Parke Custis got the estate, lawsuit and all.

Although the lawsuit was still hanging over their heads, Daniel Parke Custis and Martha raked in barrels of cash—well, barrels of tobacco, which were what passed for cash in colonial Virginia—lived in a splendid house, and managed to have four children before Daniel Parke Custis died.

Now let's see how George Washington did things.

It is arguable, and almost surely true, that George had more passion, more fire in his belly, and more get-up-and-go than Daniel Parke, John Custis, and Daniel Parke Custis combined. The "composition" of George's "frame" was not lacking in what he called "inflammable matter," either. Yet he did not allow his passions to make his social or private life an ugly mess. He did not start up second families or get into tabloid-worthy disputes with his relatives, as the Parkes and the Custises did.

George is rather well known, inarguably, for violating some very basic tenets of his society—for fighting against "king and country." Yet no one argues that he violated the "Rules of Civility and Breeding." How can this be? Simple.

He conformed to his conscience, not just outward forms of politeness. George acted as a "Christian gentleman" as did the Duke, regulating his passions by reasonable "Rules of Civility and Breeding."

There were legions of Virginia gentlemen, in fact, who were not gentlemen, at least not the way George was. Remember Lord Fairfax?

There is, to spread the net a bit wider, a notorious diary, written in code only recently decoded, by William Byrd. Byrd was one of George's fellow Virginia gentlemen, about a generation before George. He lived his life seemingly for little but his large appeties—or at least this is what he felt was worth recording. Something like Hugh Hefner, which isn't exactly evil or even so very ugly. Just not terribly noble, nor good.

What George did, on the other hand, was take his own large dose of passion and decide to direct it. He did this for something he perceived as a higher goal, a grander vision, a more noble ideal.

He didn't snuff his passion out. He focused it.

George's focus did not just manifest itself in how he appeared to others, but in what he did and how he did it. He wasn't wild and crazy, on the outside or even the inside, as many men of power in that day were. He was focused, like a laser beam. And it worked.

Perhaps this is a ridiculous example, but think of Jim Carrey versus James Dean. They arguably have the same amount of inherent energy. Yet James Dean somehow commands our respect, generations later, because he focused his abundant energy, directed it. Rather than just letting it all out. Every hyperactive child has energy. A rare genius focuses it with great clarity.

Here is how it actually looked: a friend of George's, about this time, describes what Martha would have seen as George sat in Martha's parlour, gaining her trust, and finally her hand in marriage. "His features are regular and placid with all the muscles of his face under perfect control, though flexible and expressive of deep feeling when moved by emotions. In conversation he looks you full in the face, is deliberate, deferential, and engaging. His demeanor at all times composed and dignified. His movements and gesture are graceful."

When he got up to leave her parlour, she would have seen that "his walk [was] majestic," and as he rode away, that "he is a splendid horseman."

What girl could say no?

George had shown up shortly after Martha became a widow—not so short a time after her husband's death as to be disrespectful, but not so long a time as to be imprudent. He was hero in a non-cynical age, so no one looked askance at what may have been his obvious motive. Marriage was both a business and personal transaction.

Society generally accepted that there was a very strong pragmatic element to marriage. It was, after all, a time and place in which land, not a job, meant wealth, and the primary way you got land was by marrying (or pleasing your father, as with Daniel Parke Custis, and then marrying). Besides, a twenty-six-year-old woman at that time needed a man, and a military hero was about the best catch a woman could land—especially a woman who didn't need any more money.

As Daniel Parke Custis hadn't been expecting to die quite so soon, he hadn't even left a will. This meant that Martha automatically, by law, got one third of the estate, and each of her two surviving children got one third.

George ended up managing each of these estates, doubling their value over the next fifteen years, while never taking a farthing in payment (don't look for that kind of service from the trust department at your local bank). The lawsuit from the Leeward Islands never ended in a judgment against the estate, but at the time of George's marriage to Martha, it was quite possible that much of her wealth might be wiped out.

If you want to look for a cynical motive for George's marriage, consider his selfless stewardship of his stepchildren's estates. It's as absent there as anywhere else.

Imaginative cynics, with no historical understanding of Virginia society at that time, sometimes accuse George of mercenary motives for his marriage, on the theory that he didn't care passionately for Martha, and that in fact he cared for someone else instead.

This would be a great drama, and I would love to write about it if there were any facts to reasonably support it—hey, I love a good love story as much as anyone and would, furthermore, love to humanize George even more. He has always been seen as too much like a statue.

Sadly, I have to go where the facts take us.

George once said, the proponents of this non-affair point out, that "there is no truth more certain, than that all our enjoyments fall short of our expectations and to none does it apply with more force than to the gratification of the passions."

Might the reason George felt that "enjoyments fall short of our expectations" be that he compromised too much in marriage? Did George choose, by marrying Martha, pragmatism over the joy he might have had—maybe even over the joy he once did have, and lost as a result of following society's rules, rather than his own heart? Perhaps whoever ignited the "inflammable matter" in George Washington's "human frame" was not, for whatever reason, acceptable marriage material.

Some have claimed that, right around the time George married Martha, George also had a romantic passion for Sally Fairfax, the wife of his old friend, the other George, George Fairfax, of the non-road road-trip fame.

However, these conclusions are due to an ignorance of context, which is to say, assuming other people are exactly like us. George wrote his grassy knoll letter to Sally Fairfax late in life, after the War of Independence and his presidency.

By the time of the letter, Sally Fairfax was a widow and had been living in England for decades (her husband had been a Tory who could not return to America after the War). Here is what George wrote: "So many important events have occurred, and such changes in men and things have taken place, as the compass of a letter would give you but an inadequate idea of. None of which events however, nor all of them together, have been able to eradicate from my mind the recollections of those happy moments, the happiest of my life, which I have enjoyed in your company."

George also wrote the same sort of thing to Lafayette. It doesn't mean he was gay.

In a world with no Twitter or Facebook, no airplanes or steamships, half a world away meant more than two movies and a three hour nap interrupted by chicken kiev, a packet of peanuts, and a bit of turbulence. To miss someone was to really, really miss someone.

To long for a past that existed before the entire world changed, as a result of the Revolution—to long for a youth when your greatest cares, however great, were less than being the leader of the newest and most momentous nation since Rome—these feelings would have been accompanied by a kind of nostalgia no one, without these experiences, can fully appreciate.

To imbue this nostalgia with something low or dishonorable seems small-minded, soulless, ignorant, and ultimately unimaginative.

Years later, after George and Martha had had many years of a mutually supportive life together, filled with love, George wrote Martha's granddaughters (his step-granddaughters) letters of advice on their own love lives. In one letter to Nelly Custis, George argued against the

Romeo-and-Juliet kind of love, painting "[a]n involuntary passion" as undesirable.

It may be hard to imagine a voluntary passion—passion by its very nature would seem to be involuntary—but he went on to explain what he meant. A latent or "dormant" passion should be kept away from a spark that would inflame it. This is where he wrote about human nature as "inflammable" and yet argued that "all our enjoyments fall short of our expectations": "In the composition of the human frame there is a great deal of inflammable matter, however dormant it may lie for a time, and…when the torch is put to it, that which is within you must burst into a blaze."

He advised, in other words, keeping the torch at a safe distance. Because if you don't, as George may have particularly considered when writing to Nelly Custis—you might just end up like your Parke and Custis ancestors, a complete mess. Whereas if you let reason govern your passions—you might end up happy, and not just in the short term.

George went on to summarize his balanced view of happy marriage in a letter to another step-granddaughter. He started by letting Betsey Custis know that he understood how she felt about love, referring to "emotions of a softer kind, to wch the heart of a girl turned of eighteen, is susceptible." But he also warned her, "Do not then in your contemplation of the marriage state, look for perfect felicity"—by which he meant rapturous, Romeo-and-Juliet–level emotion—"before you consent to wed. Nor conceive, from the fine tales the Poets & lovers of old have told us, of the transports of mutual love, that heaven has taken its abode on earth: Nor do not deceive yourself in supposing, that the only mean by which these are to be obtained, is to drink deep of the cup, & revel in an ocean of love. Love is a mighty pretty thing; but like all other delicious things, it is cloying."

By "cloying" he meant sickeningly sweet, or at least sickeningly sweet in excess. I personally don't find love sickeningly sweet, but, then, I don't find the sound of bullets whistling overhead "charming," either. I guess I'm not as wise yet, or experienced, as uncle George.

George went on, "and when the first transports of the passion begins to subside, which it assuredly will do, and yield—oftentimes too late—to more sober reflections, it serves to evince, that love is too dainty a food to live upon *alone*, and ought not to be considered farther than as a necessary ingredient for that matrimonial happiness which results from a combination of causes...."

George seems to say that love is necessary, but not sufficient. I suppose, as George implies, you can find love about twice a week—as a teenager, at least (or do I speak only for myself?).

What else did uncle George think was required for "matrimonial happiness"?

"A combination of causes; none of which are of greater importance, than that the object on whom it is placed, should possess good sense—good dispositions—and the means of supporting you in the way you have been brought up." So cash does come into it. But the "sense" and "dispositions" of your potential partner in life are also crucial. Everything in balance. "Such qualifications cannot fail to attract (after marriage) your esteem & regard, into wch or into disgust, sooner or later, love naturally resolves itself."

Love resolving itself into disgust. That would be a very bad—and lengthy—punishment for your mistake in an age before divorce was commonplace.

Of course George was talking about marriage, not teenaged girlfriends and boyfriends, which didn't exist at the time. Did you realize that a monogamous boyfriend and girlfriend would have been unacceptable in George Washington's day? A girl in colonial Virginia could show no more than a hint of favor to any particular boy, at least in public. This, of course, is the antithesis of the "Rules of Civility and Breeding" in implied force today, under which a girl showing equal favor to all boys would be seen as something quite awful.

If the modern regime of girlfriends and boyfriends—serial monogamy, punctuated by inevitable break-ups—had been specifically designed to prepare boys and girls for divorce, it could not have been better designed. Amazingly, there was no such thing as a breakup in George Washington's day.

Then, you only chose once.

Possibly that style of "Civility and Breeding" led to better outcomes. Then again, besides the happy lives of George and Martha, we have the unhappy lives of John and Nancy Custis to look to.

George did, by all accounts, have a happy life with Martha at Mount Vernon. His marriage was satisfying to him in a more lasting way than a mere "gratification of the passions," which, as he warned Betsey Custis, will inevitably "fall short of our expectations."

Speaking of expectations, we live in an age overwhelmed by corporate media. No one believes that the standardized plot of the corporate romantic comedy (the rom com) is meant to reflect real life. Yet, seeing this so often—and hearing the words of so many songs reinforcing these ideas—we can't help but be influenced in our expectations.

George seemed, on this subject, to take the world as it really is, or at least to take a balanced view of things. He didn't deny passions existed, but, in his mind at least, the solution was to keep them under control— to live by the rules. He found the best life was one of balance, an even keel, a steady course.

It certainly seems obvious that people who indulge their passions without restraint end badly. Born just three years before George, Catherine the Great, whose rise to power was as ignoble as George's rise was noble, was virtually uninhibited in the indulgence of her passions. She ended up a toothless, fat laughingstock. (Don't believe her portraits; painters painting portraits of people with absolute power will go so far as to replace their subject's entire head with a more beautiful head, rather than risking their own.)

The "Rules of Civility and Breeding" would have kept the extreme passions of people like Catherine the Great in check. They're rules meant to raise civilized life above a nasty and brutish free-for-all. The rules don't always succeed. Sometimes, as in the lives of Daniel Parke and John Custis, the rules are disregarded. Sometimes they're silly and irrelevant, like that whole thing with coattails.

But sometimes a great man sees through the superficial requirements of society to the fundamental standards of true civility toward other people, and he allows those fundamental standards to shape his behavior and life. The Duke of Schonberg seems to have done this.

So did George.

Even if George had had any passion for his friend's wife, which an informed look at the evidence does not show, whatever passion he might have felt in those circumstances would have been checked. What he in fact did was marry Martha, whom he called his "agreeable partner for life." He was an honorable husband, a kind stepfather, and a responsible, and in fact rather brilliant, custodian of her and her children's estates, managing them as well as he managed his own, with no thought of personal profit.

Around the time of his marriage, something brought about a great change in George Washington's outlook on life. Maybe it was marriage itself, or Martha, or domestic happiness, or possibly a close brush with death. (George, despite his normally bountiful health, went through a dangerous bout of tuberculosis around this time that nearly carried him off.)

For whatever reason, his personal ambitions changed. He no longer yearned for advancement in society. Instead, his desire was focused on happiness at Mount Vernon, with Martha. He left public life, writing that he was now "fixed at this seat…and I hope to find more happiness in retirement, than I ever experienced amidst the wide and bustling world."

Unfortunately for him, but fortunately for all of us, his earlier personal ambition had left him with the skills of a leader and the reputation of a hero. All the things that made him famous still lay in his future (with the small exception of having, it was said, started a wee world war).

But for the rest of his life, all the things that were to make him truly famous would be done from a sense of duty, and Providence. He truly would have preferred, personally, to be with Martha at Mount Vernon.

Still, George was to discover secrets that helped him change the world.

How do you change the world, or even just your small (or midsized) slice of it?

Don't you think that the best person to ask would be the person who changed more than any man in modern history? I do. That's why I wrote this book.

Read on to ride along as George changes the world.

Chapter Nine

Commander in Chief

"The Name of SCHONBERG [and, it can also be said, the name of Washington] alone was an Army."
—H. de Luzancy, *A Panegyrick to the Memory of His Grace Frederick, Late Duke of Schonberg*

In a way that is hard to understand but clearly true, the person at the top of an organization—a company, a country, a football team—really does change the nature and character of the entire thing.

The Chinese once felt that their emperor simply had to be great. He only had to exist, as a good and great person. Somehow, through a kind of ethereal, empire-wide glow, his goodness and greatness would radiate throughout the land.

At first blush, this seems superstitious to the point of insanity, but the Chinese weren't fools, China has endured a long time, so maybe they were on to something.

Closer to home, an obvious example of this phenomenon in the news the last few years is Steve Jobs (who no doubt would have found it completely natural to be compared to emperors). Steve Jobs, by his own account (in the biography he asked to have written about himself), was a sociopath in all ways but one.

A sociopath cares about nothing but himself.

Steve Jobs cared about little but the beauty and perfection of his products.

When John Sculley, who had been the head of Pepsi, took over Apple, he almost destroyed the company. Sculley thought about making money. He thought about fooling the consumers with slick advertising, appealing to their emotions rather than focusing on the reality of something truly and fundamentally great.

Steve Jobs was brought back, and Apple became the biggest company on Earth, at least by some measures.

Steve Jobs, for all his eccentricities, personality problems, and seeming cruelty towards and utter disregard for the feelings of others, was able to change the world.

People now think, communicate, and create in an entirely different way because of one man. The world, and all of our lives, would be very different without him. The name of Steve Jobs *was* Apple. That kind of career gives a tiny contemporary clue about what it means to say that "the Name of Schonberg"—or, in our case, Washington—"alone was an Army."

In 1774, the British had what seemed an invincible army. It was big. It was strong. However, it was different in a fundamental way from George Washington, and the American army.

There surely *were* a lot of British soldiers.

And those soldiers surely had a lot of stuff. Gunpowder and guns, cannons and cannonballs.

But stuff doesn't *make* an army. People do.

How was a British soldier, and thus the British Army, different?

Their army was a career. The British Army at this time fought not for any grand principle, but to feed their wives and mothers, while giving themselves the sort of social position and dignity that the army, at that time, gave. Joining the army in Britain was something like a career in banking is today. Prestigious and well paid, yet not filled with passion.

It was different for the Americans. Joining the army of a country that did not yet exist was not the psychological equivalent of joining a bank. The Americans were not fighting to put bread on the table. They were fighting for a feeling located somewhere in their souls.

By the time the American Revolution actually happened, the British had already caved in on every issue the Americans were angry about, except for one purely symbolic tax. Britain had, in the end, insisted on keeping in place a nominal three-penny-a-pound tax on tea. This last vestige of British authority was meant to show that the British could— they *wouldn't*, but they could—lord it over the Americans. The Americans, who could, and often did, just as easily drink coffee, could afford the three pennies if they really wanted tea.

Yet the Americans—our forebears—went to war over the uncomfortable feeling in their souls that a merely symbolic reminder of British dominance was worth dying to abolish.

If you went to a football game, and you knew that one side was fighting for their honor and lives and the other for a slightly better cut of beef for their mothers-in-law, who would you put your money on?

The British fought with the brains of bankers, the Americans fought with the hearts of heroes.

Still, it wasn't going to be easy.

We know the end. I can't keep you in suspense over that. But what you don't know, is...well, this:

In the period leading up to the First Continental Congress, George Washington did not seem to be in a position to lead much of anything. He wasn't, really, a political leader, and it had been a long time since he had worn a military uniform.

Although he had been elected to Virginia's House of Burgesses—serving in the legislature was the sort of thing that someone of his class did, something like jury duty—he had confined himself almost exclusively to regional issues of local concern.

George was happily married to Martha and happily living on his farm. Not only had he never considered volunteering to lead the armed resistance to British oppression, he wasn't even sure there should *be* an armed resistance.

When large issues affecting all the colonies came up in the Burgesses—mainly the pre-Revolutionary issues regarding the colonies' relationship with England—George did not take the lead, instead weighing these issues carefully in his mind, often turning for greater understanding to his neighbor, George Mason.

Mason gently prodded George in a revolutionary direction.

It was slow going, though. George Washington had spent his life being British and had, of course, fought in the British Army. He was nowhere near the forefront of revolutionary thought.

The only idea that George Washington *was* beginning to accept (at the same slow pace at which America was coming to believe it, too) was this: the corrupt people in England were straying—through the same sort of decadence and degeneration that had destroyed Rome—from the principles and ideals that make men and nations great. The Americans, not degraded by the corruption inherent in large cities such as London, but instead breathing the (literally and metaphorically) pure air of America, were more truly English than the nouveau Romans that the Americans' distant and largely invisible overlords across the ocean seemed to them to be turning into.

According to this view, Americans were the true defenders of the rights of Englishmen and therefore had a right and a duty to resist any kind of descent into tyranny.

To have these thoughts in the abstract was one thing. To actually do something about them was an entirely different thing. It was something like the difference between having a dream about flying and actually flying.

No one gives up his entire world without grave, deep doubt.

We tend to assume that all this was somehow easier back then, because…well, just because. But why would that be true? All of these people had at least as much to lose as you would today. At the same time, today, if we look around ourselves, we see we are facing vastly worse oppression than a three-penny-a-pound tax on tea. Would you be willing to fight for your rights, at the risk of your life? Those few people who do so today are largely considered crazy.

But they're not crazy. They're just more like George Washington.

George's progress toward taking up arms against Britain, helped along to a large extent by George Mason, was slow and plodding. George Washington thought the Boston Tea Party was a mistake; he believed it would give the British an excuse to treat the colonists with even less justice. However, the British reaction to the Tea Party—in the form of the Intolerable Acts—was, to George Washington, intolerable.

The official name of one of these acts, in a startling presentiment of Orwell, was "The Administration of Justice Act." It allowed British soldiers accused of murdering Americans to be whisked away to Britain "where," as George said, "it is impossible from the nature of the thing that justice can be obtained."

All of these things that nudged George in a revolutionary direction were pushing any American with a sense of dignity and honor, too. George was slower than some, going through a deliberate process of decision-making that he was later to describe as "balancing in my mind and giving the subject the fairest consideration."

Thomas Jefferson, who said he "knew General Washington intimately and thoroughly" and who helped ensure that he became the Commander of the Continental Army, would say later that George's mind was "slow in operation, being little aided by invention or imagination, but sure in conclusion," and that, therefore, "as far as he [Jefferson, that is] saw, no judgment was ever sounder."

Once George made a decision, he was confident in it, as it was the result of such thorough contemplation of all sides of an issue.

In order to lead an army, of course, one must be able to make decisions in difficult circumstances, almost always with incomplete knowledge. No one, therefore, would want to entrust an army to someone who could not be relied upon to come to the best conclusions in the harsh uncertainty of war.

When Thomas Jefferson called George's mind "slow in operation," it almost sounded perjorative. Slow can't be good, can it? Jefferson would also say that George's mind was "great and powerful, without being of the very first order." This, too, at least out of context, almost sounds like an insult—until you realize to whom he was comparing George. Jefferson went on to say that George's mind was "strong, though not so acute as that of a Newton, Bacon, or Locke." In other words, George was in the same league as a mathematical or intellectual genius, just not the flashiest player at the table. An elephant is slow and powerful. A mouse is quick and weak. George Washington's thought process, Jefferson was saying, was more like an elephant—slow and powerful.

Of course, this wasn't being scored solely on brains. If brains were all that mattered, Nerdy McNerd should be King of the World.

We know, in our guts, that this would be a very bad idea.

Brains without wisdom have a history of being more dangerous than stupidity. Fortunately, George's intelligence, coupled with his careful reasoning, made him a natural real-world leader. This was an especially valuable type of character in a Revolution otherwise led by men who wrote words that were more beautiful than pragmatic or even flew kites in thunderstorms.

In a leader, steadfastness is vital.

Beyond this, the inexperience responsible for George's unforced errors at the beginning of the French and Indian War was now twenty years behind him. He had now had twenty years to develop patience and long-term thinking as a farmer. He out-farmed many neighbors by rotating crops or even leaving some fields fallow, making long-term gains through deliberate short-term losses, something many farmers were too impatient to do. He had learned pragmatism, careful thinking, and wisdom, yet still had the reputation of a war hero.

What else did George have that the Continental Army—once it came into existence—would need from its commander in chief?

Let's look once more through Thomas Jefferson's eyes and see what he saw when he looked at George.

Jefferson followed up his assessment of George's intellect with a contrast of two seemingly opposing ideas. Jefferson said that George "was incapable of fear, meeting personal dangers with the calmest unconcern," yet he follows that *immediately* with, "Perhaps the strongest feature in his character was prudence."

Unless Jefferson was an extremely poor judge of character, or capable of forgetting the last sentence he wrote—he was neither—one has to find a reason for this seemingly incompatible contrast. How could George, whose "strongest feature," according to Jefferson, was "prudence," face "personal dangers with the calmest unconcern"? One answer was George's belief in the thing he called "Providence," which is to say his lack of fear was not due to impetuousness or foolishness, but to a kind of conscious collaboration with something larger and more powerful than the thing that, to others, may have seemed fearful. A belief, as we recall, that George shared with the Duke of Schonberg. (Kids, don't try this at home without parental supervision!)

Jefferson went on to talk about other qualities. According to the sage of Monticello, George Washington's "integrity was most pure, his justice the most inflexible I have ever known, no motives of interest or consanguinity, of friendship or hatred, being able to bias his decision."

This is a perfect echo of the Duke of Schonberg's "Character of Honor, Truth, and Justice, which was Natural to him." Young George's "I cannot tell a lie" seems to have blossomed, under the guidance of the *Panegyrick*, into a character of absolute integrity and perfect justice in his dealings with other people.

Jefferson summed up his assessment of George's character this way: "He was, indeed, in every sense of the words, a wise, a good, and a great man." Once again, shades of the Duke of Schonberg—in whom, as the *Panegyrick* tells us, "*That Greatness and Goodness, so seldom united in others*" were "inseparably linkt." Good, great, and wise. George Washington had actually succeeded in becoming the kind of person he had wanted to be—somebody like the Duke he read about in the *Panegyrick*.

These ideals, embodied in George Washington, appealed to Americans across the colonies. The Puritans in New England had no use for the dashing ideals that made a Virginia gentleman shine but still appreciated integrity. Pennsylvania's Quakers didn't like war but still admired a good character.

George Washington seemed to have turned himself into George Washington. But was that all it took?

No. The most surprising episodes and useful lessons are still to come.

George and his fellow burgesses reacted to the Intolerable Acts as one might expect Virginia gentlemen to react, which is to say, markedly differently from the rowdy working-class Bostonians. Their words were strong—very strong—calling the British actions "the hostile Invasion of the City of Boston, in our Sister Colony of Massachusetts bay." The burgesses went on to complain that the Bostonians' "commerce and harbor are, on the first Day of June next, to be stopped by an Armed force."

However, the only action the burgesses proposed was a Martin Luther King–style protest. There was, though, a subtle threat of a Malcolm X–style reaction—or, more accurately, of a George Washington–style reaction, thrown in for good measure, in case the MLK tactics didn't work. George and his fellow burgesses declared that the "first day of June be set apart, by the members of this House as a day of Fasting, Humiliation, and Prayer, devoutly to implore the divine interposition, for averting the heavy Calamity which threatens destruction to our Civil Rights, and the Evils of civil War...."

A war takes two sides, so the mention of "civil war"—even if the burgesses chose to call it an "Evil"—made the statement less benign than it might seem at first glance.

After all, there would be no war without the colonists' participation.

The burgesses' next statement was deliberately ambiguous. It could be seen as backtracking from their implied threat.

Or not.

The Virginians said they hoped for "one heart and one Mind firmly to oppose, by all just and proper means, every injury to American Rights." Notice that "just and proper means" were not defined. After all, the burgesses were still hoping—or so they *said*—that the "Minds of his Majesty and his Parliament, may be inspired from above with Wisdom, Moderation, and Justice."

However, in fact, more and more minds, including George's, were coming to the conclusion—as event followed event—that wisdom, moderation, and justice were the last things they could expect from the British government.

George's first act of political insurrection would take quite a mild form. He and his fellow burgesses would walk out of their chamber at the beginning of the last day of the term, and instead go to church to hear a sermon "suitable to the Occasion."

"Suitable to the Occasion"? It is worth remembering that sermons, in those days, were the intellectual lifeblood of communities, people's main connection with the outside world. In a time before regular newspapers (much less the internet), sermons conveyed not just religious messages but news, political ideas, and indeed almost all the thoughts that were shaping and shifting society. Sermons in some cases stretched to many hours. (In some colonies, church attendance was mandatory—

imagine being required, by law, to sit through a four-hour sermon every Sunday.)

The point being, much of American's revolutionary fervor was spread through sermons. Therefore, the idea of going to a church to hear a sermon was, again, perhaps less benign than at first glace it might seem to us.

Still, it's not throwing tea into a harbor. It was a relatively cautious first step.

But it was a first step.

The governor responded by immediately disbanding the Burgesses. This was unwise.

Denying men their dignity was not the sort of thing you did to men for whom "honor" was the primary virtue, nor to those whose sense of justice was piqued to a high degree when something they perceived as unjust was done to them.

The House of Burgesses met anyway. The governor had no power to stop them. They might obey him out of habit and custom (or choose not to), but not in response to threats of force. At least not yet. At this point the governor's only direct power, after all, was to write and speak. Any enforcements of his edicts would be up to the colonists themselves. The memory of this kind of balance of power surely has something to do with why the Constitution was to deny the federal government power to use force against its own citizens, by denying it the power to create any kind of police force, or even criminal laws (other than those dealing with piracy, treason defined very narrowly, and counterfeiting).

George and his fellow burgesses ignored the governor's order and met, instead of in the House of Burgesses, in the Raleigh Tavern. These Virginia gentleman, who included but were not yet led by George, made a one-for-all-and-all-for-one kind of declaration to join with the other colonies to boycott British imports, which they duly sent to their compatriots in the other colonies. They also called for a congress to be made up of representatives from all the colonies, to coordinate American opposition to British encroachment on their collective rights—what would be the First Continental Congress.

Beyond reacting against the slap in the face to the Americans' collective honor, George was impelled by a sense of justice. He made this clear when he took his first leadership role in the realm of politics:

> Fairfax County Resolves
> July 18, 1774
>
> At a general Meeting of the Freeholders and Inhabitants of the County of Fairfax on Monday the 18th day of July 1774, at the Court House, George Washington Esquire Chairman, and Robert Harrison Gent. Clerk of the said Meeting....

George had now risen to be the chairman of an unofficial county commission.

Hey, you've got to start somewhere, right?

The local landowners had come together to ratify a document that George Washington's neighbor, George Mason, had drafted. Going beyond both vague, ambiguous threats—of the *we don't want a war, but if you keep doing what you're doing, what choice do we have?* variety—and practical and pragmatic resolutions—to severely limit trade with Britain until matters were resolved in the colonists' favor—the Fairfax Resolves invoked ideals that were, more and more, being seen as universal benchmarks of natural justice. The members of the commission were willing to proclaim those ideals even though, on one important point, they went completely against their own interests.

The seventeenth resolution (of twenty-four) seems at first to be just another instance of the general boycott of British commerce: "Resolved…during our present Difficulties and Distress, no Slaves ought to be imported into any of the British Colonies on this Continent." But then it goes on in quite a different vein, sounding a note that was ahead of its time—and especially surprising coming from slave owners in the slave economy of Virginia: "we take this Opportunity of declaring our most earnest Wishes to see an entire Stop for ever put to such a wicked cruel and unnatural Trade." George Washington was committing himself to liberty— even at a significant cost to his way of life. That was a commitment he would ultimately make good on, freeing his slaves in his will at enormous cost to his estate, which, by law, and practicality, had to provide a good deal of money to support freed slaves. (Unlike Thomas Jefferson; Mr. *All Men Are Created Equal* talked a good game, but he left his slaves to his heirs.)

Late in that same summer of 1774, while arguing for American rights, George chose to describe the colonists' situation by saying that if they didn't do something sharp, strong, and hard to stop the British encroachment on their rights, over time they themselves would become "as tame, & abject Slaves, as the Blacks we Rule over with such arbitrary Sway." The next year, writing to his old friend George Fairfax, George Washington compared the American people as a whole to the slaves: "the once happy and peaceful plains of America are either to be drenched with Blood, or Inhabited by Slaves. Sad alternative! But can a virtuous Man hesitate in his choice?" He meant the choice to fight.

George, as the months rolled on, understood more and more clearly what liberty would require of Americans—including himself. He did not blink at what he was beginning to see, although it would turn his world upside down and consume most of the rest of this life. What was right for George was what was right, not what was expedient. (Surely the best we can expect of a man is that he be at the forefront of any change for good, relative to where his society is at the time.)

George's commitment to liberty—and his acceptance of its price—
was vital, if Washington's "Name alone" was to be "an Army." What other
force, what other power did George Washington have to lead an army?
For that matter, what army would there be for him to command? It was,
ultimately, the ideal of liberty that he believed in, that he shared with his
fellow Americans, that brought that army into being and made him its
commander in chief.

Up 'til this time the world had been, with a few fleeting exceptions,
ruled by strong men of one sort or another. Renouncing their loyalty to
the crown and taking on the British Army would require that ordinary
American soldiers be committed to the ideal of liberty. However, it
would also require something more. The soldiers would also have to
trust that the officers who commanded them—and most especially their
commander in chief—would not become the very thing they were fighting against. What guarantee was there that the man who led them would
not, if they won the war, turn into a tyrant as bad as George III?

George Washington's character. That was the guarantee.

George had now arrived at the precise point in history where the
"Greatness and Goodness" he had learned from the Duke was exactly
what was required.

Nothing else would have fit the bill.

George didn't say much at the Continental Congress.

He seemed to be doing his best imitation of a Chinese emperor
whose virtue alone guaranteed the safety and prosperity of his empire—
sitting still, being quiet, and letting other people do the talking.

However, George's demeanor and his reputation did, in fact, speak
for him. George may have been largely silent, but he gave other people
plenty to talk about. Despite the flaws and failures of his earlier military

career, he was remembered as a great military hero of the French and Indian War.

It helped that he still looked the part.

George alone showed up to the Continental Congress wearing a military uniform—ready for the war that he knew now was the only way to preserve American liberty.

But George wasn't the only candidate for commander in chief of the American forces. There was also, most notably, Charles Lee, a professional soldier from England (not one of the Lees of Virginia). John Adams wrote at the start of the Continental Congress that the delegates, almost to a man, "shudder at the prospect of blood." The notable exception was Charles Lee—plotting, planning, and even seeming to hope for war. Even before it was seriously considered that America needed an army, Charles Lee looked like the clear choice to become commander in chief of any force that might be needed.

War was both Lee's profession and his avocation. Having retired from the British force on half-pay, he had still continued to ply his trade, serving as aide-de-camp to the king of Poland, among other European adventures. While the other delegates avoided the thought of war, Charles "Boiling Water" Lee agitated for it, even devising war plans. (During the French and Indian War, he had married an Indian princess, fathered twins, and been given the name "Boiling Water" by the Indians—apparently not without some cause.)

Later, during the Revolutionary War, Charles Lee would be captured by the British. Before being traded back to the American side, he would concoct and write down plans useful to the British. To be fair, perhaps he was acting under threat of death (for desertion of the British Army). Still, Charles Lee did have the air—and the career—of a gun for hire.

Unlike George Washington.

In the Continental Congress, George continued to take the emperor-of-China approach, letting his reputation speak for itself.

Besides the character that he had earned for military prowess in the French and Indian War, rumors were circulating about George Washington's wealth. It was being said that George planned to raise a thousand troops, to be paid at his own expense, to go to the aid of the oppressed Bostonians.

The rumor was not accurate, but it contained an important kernel of truth about George's character. Charles Lee expected pay for commanding the American forces—which he justified, at least in part, as compensation for the land in England he would lose by throwing his lot in with the Americans. George Washington, on the other hand, refused to profit one penny from the Revolution. He wouldn't take pay, nor any other benefit, for his military service; he would accept only reimbursement for his expenses.

In fact, George was willing to serve at great risk and accept heavy (and unreimbursed) expenses, over and above his official expense account. Not only did he risk dying by a British bullet in the War. Not only did he risk being hanged as a traitor if the Americans lost the war— as any objective observer in 1774 or 1775 would have said the Americans inevitably would do, if a war actually happened. His farm—which was his wealth and his family's livelihood—even if it wasn't destroyed or confiscated in the course of the war, would certainly degenerate horribly in his absence. The very best case scenario for George, should the Americans have the freakish luck to succeed, was that he would end up exactly where he had been before the war started—except older, poorer, and in worse health, having gained but one solitary thing: liberty, for himself and his countrymen.

And for you and me, if we are still willing to fight for liberty even a little bit.

Can you imagine marching against the might of the world's best army—something roughly comparable, in eighteenth-century terms, to the U.S. military today—with hunting rifles, to take your freedom back?

That's what the American Revolution felt like at the time to the soldiers who actually fought in it.

Today, the people in charge (the Machiavellian sociopaths we call politicians, our media and advertising industry, etc.) have convinced most of us to believe that cynicism is the only thing that is real, that Madison Avenue–style prepackaged emotional manipulation is as close as anyone is likely to get to goodness and greatness.

Yet lest we get all misty-eyed for the good old days, we have to remember that the courage to defend liberty was rare back then, too. It has been said that not even a majority of Americans at the time were in favor of the Revolution. Clearly an even smaller percentage of the population were actively involved in the struggle. As Samuel Adams said, however, "It does not require majority to prevail, but rather an irate, tireless minority…." History shows him to have been right, though he forgot to add—*led, and inspired, by a good, great, and wise man.*

Charles Lee was the contender for commander in chief who had the most military experience and skill. But George Washington was the personification of the ideals of the American Revolution. If America had been able to field a well-paid professional army, and to keep it well trained, fed, and supplied, Charles Lee might have been the right choice. But the job was, it would turn out, to lead a ragtag half-frozen force through the nightmare of Valley Forge; to negotiate successfully with the French, the Hessians, and toughest of all—then as now—the American Congress; to transform a bunch of mismatched militias into a national army and a baker's dozen of colonies into a nation, against all odds, in the face of Everest-sized obstacles. In these circumstances, a mere professional with a surfeit of European arrogance, who was in it at least partly for the money, would never be able to pull it off.

It was a job for a very different kind of man: A man of military experience, but also a man with an unequalled reputation for integrity. Someone whose established character proved him to be completely trustworthy, so that soldiers would never fear that they were risking everything for nothing more than an exchange of one tyrant for another. The commander in chief would need to inspire men to join an army that did not yet exist to die for a country that had not yet been invented. He would have to be completely identified with the cause of American liberty.

There was only man in America who fit that description.

George was finally (and unanimously) elected commander in chief on June 15, 1775.

Commander in chief of what?

The military George was about to take over was nothing but "a mere chaos"—at least that's what he called it. On the upside, a multi-year war fought against the greatest empire on earth was not truly imaginable at that point. So, while George Washington was officially made commander in chief of the Continental Army, what this actually meant, at the time, was simply that he was "pressed to take the supreme command of the American troops encamped at Roxbury," as one delegate put it, in somewhat less earth-shattering tones. This put things—completely incorrectly, as it was to turn out—in a slightly less intimidating light.

We are so accustomed to the wooden image of George Washington on the dollar bill, or to all the iconic statues and paintings, and even to the fact of George's success as "The Commander in Chief of the American Armies" (and all the rest—there was his brief stint as president, too) that we may find it hard to believe what it looked like at the moment everything changed—in his life, and the world's history.

Patrick Henry said that tears rolled from George's eyes as he said, after the vote that made him commander in chief, "Remember Mr. Henry, what I now tell you. From the day I enter upon the command of the American armies, I date my fall and the ruin of my reputation."

Tears.

George Washington, the giant who would command the Continental Army, the man who could throw rocks farther than any man in America, who was propelled into a raging icy river on the darkest night in the middle of winter and survived, who dodged bullets like a character from *The Matrix*, and who found it amusing, rather than frightening, to encounter twenty Indians emerging from the woods carrying a scalp, was now crying in front of Patrick Henry.

George had an inherent sense of dignity, and therefore probably remained ramrod straight as the tears welled in his eyes. It is true that, at this time, tears in men—even in generals (or commanders in chief)—did not carry the taboo that they do in our culture, in our day. Still, the feeling of inescapable doom must have been profound. A man's reputation was everything in George Washington's Virginia. Losing his reputation would be like you losing your girlfriend, along with your house, your health, and your bank account. And your car. Multiplied by a hundred.

George saw a horrible abyss opening before him.

However, on the night that everything changed, he celebrated his appointment as commander and chief at a dinner with a few good friends.

On the evening of June 15, 1775, after Congress (the Second Continental Congress, that is) elected my great-uncle "to command all the Continental forces raised or to be raised for the defense of American

Liberty," Benjamin Franklin, Thomas Jefferson, Benjamin Rush, and fifteen or so others took George Washington to Peggy Mullan's Red Hot Beef Steak Club, just down the road from where Congress had met, and bought him dinner.

The wine had begun to flow long before the sun had set, which may help explain why, after the plates had been cleared away and the first toast was given, to "The Commander in Chief of the American Armies," George Washington sat mute for a moment, apparently waiting for this great commander to rise. When the full weight of the meaning of that phrase finally descended upon George's exhausted head, Benjamin Rush recalled that George "rose from his seat" and began speaking "with some confusion." After George had uncharacteristically mumbled a few words of thanks, the twenty or so people in the room "instantly rose and drank the toast standing. This scene, so unexpected, was a solemn one. A silence followed it, as if every heart was penetrated with the awful but great events which were to follow the use of the sword of liberty which had just been put into General Washington's hands by the unanimous voice of his country."

The cause of George's mumbling trepidation—and of his earlier tears—was more than the exhaustion of the day. It was the result of a realistic appraisal of the situation he now found himself in.

The British Army (and Navy), at the time, were something like the United States armed forces are today—unbeatable. It must have looked like Goliath did from David's vantage point. Except that George, in this analogy, didn't even have a slingshot. Perhaps a pea shooter. There were a few thousand troops currently waiting for him near Boston.

And nothing more.

By any rational measure, George's trepidation was well founded. His conviction that he wasn't prepared or qualified for the post was correct. He did not have the experience of commanding anything remotely as complex as a national army.

He *did* have, though, an unshakable conviction of the justness of the American cause. George had also seen, in the French and Indian conflict, that an intimate knowledge of the home turf, along with a certain amount of cleverness and skillful negotiation with allies, could make a difference.

But a big enough difference?

With these thoughts tumbling around in his head, George looked across the room at Benjamin Franklin, Thomas Jefferson, and the fifteen or so others who had gathered to wish him well, and finished the wine in his glass.

He was, of course, to overcome his fear. Although George's wife, at his request, burnt her correspondence with him upon his death, she overlooked a few letters. Three days after being elected to be "The Commander in Chief of the American Armies" on June 18, 1775, my great-uncle wrote to her, telling the story of his election, at least as he saw it:

> You may believe me my dear Patcy, when I assure you, in the most solemn manner, that, so far from seeking this appointment I have used every endeavour in my power to avoid it, not only from my unwillingness to part with you and the Family, but from a consciousness of its being a trust too great for my Capacity and that I should enjoy more real happiness and felicity in one month with you, at home, than I have the most distant prospect of reaping abroad, if my stay was to be Seven times Seven years.

George did not see this decision as simply choosing the right thing over the pleasurable thing. It was, after all, pretty clearly treason from the British perspective. Beyond that, was it, even in the loosest sense of the word, sensible? Most rational arguments anyone could have thought of would tell George to stick with what he knew, the British. (The side that actually *had* an army.)

George did not add and subtract to arrive at his choice, though. It was a leap, though not exactly of faith. He trusted something that would get you or me locked in a loony bin if we articulated the same thing today.

You, to the intake nurse at your local mental hospital: Hi! I've just decided to take on the greatest army in the world. You know, the army of the greatest empire since Rome? My own army? Well, it's mostly in the imagination of some of my friends. Like Benjamin Franklin! Yeah, *that* guy—the one who flew that kite in a thunderstorm, hoping to get struck by lightning.

George's faith, though, wasn't in men, even those as great as Benjamin Franklin and Thomas Jefferson. Nor was it in something he believed in without proof. He saw himself as trusting a "destiny" whose wise "design" was backed by a "good purpose." He relied upon it because the evidence of his extraordinary life, including his seemingly miraculous escapes from death, had shown him that it worked.

Perhaps some day a supercomputer will be able to calculate all the variables in a situation such as the one George now found himself in. After all, weather predictions, based on known unknowns—if not unknown unknowns—are becoming more reliable. Perhaps a computer will one day be able to rationally balance the mental health (or lack thereof) of King George (who talked to trees and is now thought to have suffered from the mental disease called porphyria), alongside the weather patterns a couple of years hence (in Valley Forge, for example), alongside the likelihood of French assistance. Et cetera. Then again, perhaps there are more things in heaven and earth, or in America's history, than can be dreamt of in a silicon chip.

In any event, George's intuition and faith in his "destiny" was, if not the only thing he had to rely on, certainly the deciding factor in choosing to lead the Revolutionary struggle. As he wrote to his wife, "But, as it has been a kind of destiny that has thrown me upon this Service, I shall hope that my undertaking of it, is designed to answer some good purpose...."

George had been aiming for nothing beyond simply enjoying himself at Mount Vernon, the farm and home he had worked so hard to create. Yet he felt something both larger and more mysterious than anything he could fully grasp or understand guiding him towards the decision he took, in direct opposition both to his personal desires and to anything he could have rationally concluded would be a prudent path: "I shall rely therefore, confidently, on that Providence which has heretofore preserved, & been bountiful to me," he wrote to Martha, "not doubting but that I shall return safe to you in the fall...."

George's decision to submit to his "destiny" as a result of his reliance on "Providence" was to consume most of the rest of his life—while making all of our lives, at least as we live them today, possible.

Here, finally, is how he was to summarize the situation, looking back on it, later:

> It was known that the resources of Britain were, in a manner, inexhaustible, that her fleets covered the Ocean, and that her troops had harvested laurels in every quarter of the globe. Not then organized as a nation, or known as a people upon the earth, we had no preparation. Money, the nerve of War, was wanting. The Sword was to be forged on the Anvil of necessity: the treasury to be created from nothing. If we had

a secret resource of a nature unknown to our enemy, it was in the unconquerable resolution of our Citizens, the conscious rectitude of our cause, and a confident trust that we should not be forsaken by Heaven.

The one thing missing from the list George made of the colonies' resources—"unconquerable resolution," "rectitude," and a "confident trust" in "Heaven"—was his own name. "His Name," the *Panegyrick* had said of the Duke of Schonberg, "alone was an Army."

This had now become true of George Washington's name, too.

Chapter Ten

From the Siege of Boston to the Crossing of the Delaware: George Washington's Fabian Strategy Keeps the American Cause Alive

"He was of…an incredible Patience…."
—H. de Luzancy, *A Panegyrick to the Memory of His Grace Frederick, Late Duke of Schonberg*

Patience can cause miracles.

Lack of patience can cause disaster.

Do you recall that time in Great Meadow, when George ignored the Half King's advice and instead scrambled to get his third-rate fort built in double time? Granted, he had first procrastinated, before rushing the job in the end, but the point is this—he lacked the patience to listen to the Half King, and also lacked the patience to slowly and steadily build a fort the right way. Then there was that other time, when George leapt to the conclusion that the French soldiers who were camped in "Jumonville Glen" were an attack party, not an embassy—and thus went ahead with the ambush that many said started a world war. George's lack of patience, if it didn't cause the war, certainly caused him to be blamed for it. (Possibly, though, it saved his life, if we assume that Jumonville really was out to get George Washington.)

Anyway, I'm impatient right now, sitting around in George Washington's past. Let's fly forward to his present, shall we?

We'll leave the smoking DeLorean in the swamp behind us and take a look at the infant Continental Army. At this point it was nothing but the combined militias of the various New England colonies, which had been transformed into "the Continental Army," in name only, by a vote in the Continental Congress the day before George Washington was elected as their commander in chief. These were the "troops encamped at Roxbury," awaiting George Washington's arrival while they conducted "the Siege of Boston."

To understand how the entire city could be subject to a siege, you have to realize that Boston at the time of the Revolution looked more like an island than part of the mainland. Most of what we think of as Boston today was man-made in the nineteenth century from swamps and sea filled with dirt, sand, and rocks. In the eighteenth century just one thin strip of land in the south—"Roxbury Neck"—connected Boston to the mainland.

Now, in the aftermath of the first battles of the American Revolution, under a land siege by the colonists (which was easy to carry off with only one thin strip of land to guard), the British were finding their position in Boston increasingly tough. The British were stuck on an almost-island, with food supplies dwindling.

Just before George's arrival, the Battles of Lexington and Concord had got the war off to a bang with the shot "heard 'round the world." To this day, no one is certain who fired the initial shot. At the time, some said it was an American militiaman, others said it was a British soldier. Some thought that first shot was accidental; others, on purpose. Many thought it was bystanders shooting from behind—well, if not a grassy knoll, then a wall—or perhaps it came from the window of a tavern. In any case, the initial shot was a spark that lit the kindling that just had been waiting to burn—that almost certainly would have been lit, if not on that day, then another day.

In any event, the war had finally started.

Orders and strategy during these battles, before George's arrival, came from the militias' more experienced officers. When they came at all, that is. The Americans acted in a federal manner, which is to say, different local towns' militias formed alliances for a few hours or a few shots, harassed and fought the British Army as opportunities presented themselves, then went their own ways.

To a certain extent it was beneficial that the colonists didn't know what they were doing. They broke the conventional rules of war without knowing what they didn't know, leaving the educated and experienced British officers flummoxed, often helpless. For example, during what was, in any event, already a British retreat from Concord back to Boston, the British soldiers marched in strict formation along a road, as professional soldiers do. A few colonists, vastly outnumbered by the mass of marching redcoats, hit upon the notion of shooting at British soldiers from the road ahead, at the outer edge of musket range.

Muskets at that time had a range of fifty yards or so, with aim being more a matter of luck than skill. The colonists, though, had a whole army to aim at, which gave them the odds. When the British tried to fire back, they only had a few scrawny colonists scrambling about as targets, who, moments later, were on their horses riding away towards their next position. For several hours this harassment went on, with the Americans shooting from almost out of range, hitting, but not being hit, then riding away to do it again.

A bit later, during the Battle of Bunker Hill—by this point George was en route to Massachusetts—there was disorder again in the American forces. Orders were, at certain crucial junctures, viewed as suggestions and ignored at will.

This led, variously, to gains and losses for the Americans. In the end, though, the British won the Battle of Bunker Hill. It was very much a Pyrrhic victory, however, as there was little strategic advantage to controlling those hills (Breed's Hill and Bunker Hill), while the British had suffered enormous losses—about a third of their troops.

"I wish we could sell them another hill at the same price," said Nathanael Greene, major general of the Rhode Island forces. In fact, the initial reports coming back to George seemed to indicate that Bunker Hill was an American victory. The fact that it was a close call showed George that the American soldiers he was going to command were capable and willing to put up a good fight.

It troubled the surviving British officers that their losses included an unusually high number of their fellow officers. The New Englanders, unencumbered by the domination in their own ranks of officers of a distinct upper class, seem to have been motivated by class grudges alongside anti-British grudges. The evidence shows they aimed disproportionately at officers, often from hidden spots behind trees and rocks and walls.

The Americans seem to have had no respect for the way gentlemen fought wars.

This was the scrappy bunch of untrained colonials that George Washington would lead to victory against the greatest military force in the history of the world.

How did he do it?

How did George even keep these thousands of troops, an army cobbled together from a hodgepodge of different colonial militias, badly supplied, with short and perpetually expiring enlistments, in good enough shape to wage any kind of war at all?

For starters, he had the patience to take advantage of the Americans' home field advantage and deploy a classic Fabian strategy against the invading army.

Fabian strategy? Do you know Fabius? Even if you do, I want to hop in the DeLorean again, so let's take one more trip in time. Grab that broken musket, would you? Thanks, just stick it in there. Yeah, that's the fusion power generator for the time flux–generating module. Cool. Okay, here goes—watch out for the elephants!

Fabius was someone everyone in George Washington's day knew about. Why? He had been selected as the only man in Rome tough enough to take on the invading elephants.

Yes, THOSE elephants. Watch out—No!!!!!!!!!!!!!!!!!!

Okay, open your eyes.

Here we are in the Third Century (B.C.).

Tuscany.

See those elephants poking their long trunks into the smoking remains of the DeLorean? They're part of the invading army threatening Rome.

We're back in the time of Hannibal, who has brought these elephants over the Alps to invade Rome. This has worked, so far, because the Romans didn't bother defending the Alps, as no reasonable person would climb over towering snow-covered mountains, especially with an army of forty thousand and, of course, never with elephants.

Hannibal was not reasonable.

This is why he almost won this war.

"This war" was the Second Punic War, between Rome and Carthage. This is the war Hannibal *would* have won if it hadn't been for a Roman named Quintus Fabius Maximus—nicknamed "Cunctator," the Delayer. (Remember, we're talking about patience here. We will get back to George, if you just have the…um…patience …)

Fabius was a more typical kind of guy than Hannibal.

A regular Roman, really.

Certainly not a macho kind of general. He had been, at least as a child, kind of a nerd. He was slow. But steady. He was even thought stupid, at least in his youth.

He was clearly the tortoise, not the hare.

He grew to be a tall, handsome man with a kind of calm wisdom. His hot-headed compatriots and countrymen wanted glory. He wanted victory. His strategy certainly did not appeal to Romans with WWE testosterone levels (who tended to think Fabius was a coward, and thus gave him what they thought of as the insulting nickname, "the Delayer").

Fabius's strategy did not appeal to those who wanted a quick fix. It required one of the most difficult qualities George learned from the *Panegyrick*, "incredible Patience."

It worked.

Thus the term "Fabian strategy."

Basically, it's what you do when elephants, or British, or mean Earth people (in *Avatar*), outnumber, outgun, out-experience, or out-weapon you. Fabian strategy is the secret that small armies have in their back pocket; it's what gives them a fighting chance against more powerful armies. The strategy involves, in essence, conserving your own resources by avoiding full-on fighting, while doing what you can around the edges to weaken the more powerful enemy army.

Fabius did a nimble boxer's bob and weave against Hannibal's clearly overwhelming force, taking small pieces out of Hannibal's army when he could, avoiding the elephants when possible, ducking direct counter-attacks, avoiding pitched battles. It was a strategy of attrition:

Wear Hannibal's army out.

Deny them access to food.

Fabius and his Romans were fighting on their own home territory, after all. Fabian strategy is, in fact, tailor-made for defending your own country from an invading army. It makes the best use of the home field advantage.

Think of the Russians picking off the frostbitten stragglers from Napoleon's army. Or of the blue people in *Avatar* fighting against the horrible earthlings. Or of the advantage the Viet Cong had—or the Taliban have today—fighting against us on their own home turf.

But to take *advantage* of your advantage, you have to have patience. You can't insist on winning right away, in one big battle that will crown your head with glory.

Most Romans, lacking patience, soon got sick of waiting for Fabius's strategy to work. So they replaced Fabius with a man's man kind of general (well, two, actually, adding to the confusion). The new generals planned one gigantic pitched battle to decisively defeat Hannibal and crown themselves in glory.

Only, Hannibal defeated them.

The Romans were thoroughly trounced at the disastrous Battle of Cannae. With their tails between their legs and the elephants on their heels, the Romans begged Fabius, yet again, to defend Rome.

⁓

Fabius, taking up where he had left off, avoided direct conflict. He retreated at times. He poked and prodded, cutting Hannibal's lines of support, always avoiding full-on battles. Fabius bled the life out of Hannibal's army through pinpricks and attrition.

This boring, plodding strategy eventually led to a Roman victory.

Rome stayed Rome.

Patience.

Far better to be a Roman in Rome than a statue of a brave but fallen Roman soldier, gathering dust on a side street of a largely forgotten territory (Rome) at the edge of Hannibal's Carthaginian Empire.

⁓

George did not adopt Fabian strategy out of military genius, really—at least not at first—but from necessity, and a humble sense of his own limitations. He had told Congress that he didn't feel worthy of the job of commander in chief. They believed him. ("Hey," they may have thought, "George Washington never tells a lie.") So they set up a war council to advise George. At first, it was this war council that insisted on caution.

⁓

Early on in the war, just after American defeat at Bunker Hill, when the British were hunkered down in Boston and George was encamped nearby with nineteen thousand soldiers whose enlistments were going to run out in a few months, George kept trying to think of ways to use his soldiers and attack the British while he still had them. His big plan, at this time, was to attack Boston, first ferrying his army to Boston in boats.

It seemed obvious to him, at least at first, that not to attack the British before it got too cold for battle would be a tremendous waste of resources and opportunity. (Wars had seasons then, just as sports do now.) If they waited 'til it got cold, his army would need nineteen thousand coats. At the end of the calendar year, months before the spring fighting season would begin, his soldiers' enlistments would run out.

It was time to strike.

An American attack, however, was precisely what General Howe, George's counterpart in the British Army, hunkered down in well-fortified Boston, wanted. He knew that an attack on the secure British position in Boston would put the Americans at an extreme disadvantage.

George, despite his eagerness to strike a blow for the American cause, listened to the officers in his war council, who accurately inferred what General Howe was thinking. George's idea for a water crossing—the first of several George would propose—was shot down by George's war council.

Once he would have been too impatient to wait—as he had famously been when the Half King had offered to advise a less experienced version of George during the Battle of Fort Necessity. George now had enough experience—and Duke of Schonberg–like patience—to rely upon the experience of others. He deferred to the collective wisdom of the council of war, which he himself had fought to have created as a check against, in essence, himself. Rather than rushing headlong into a battle for which he was not prepared, George took advice and waited.

The war council, in the end, turned out to be right.

George had nineteen thousand soldiers, a not inconsiderable force. But losing many of them in a pointless battle so early in the war could have led to America's defeat in the first months of the war. At the very least it would have been a pointless, bloody setback.

As it happened, therefore, the first real progress against the British had nothing to do with George, who spent the autumn of 1775 playing a waiting game with the British, as advised by his war council. As the snow started to fall, however, the American can-do, do-it-yourself attitude had started to help the Americans beat the seemingly unbeatable British Navy—without any real navy of their own. (The American "Navy" did have a few boats, but compared to the British Navy, it was like a rubber duckie in a battle with a great white shark.)

How did the Americans do it?

The Americans privatized naval warfare. They gave any captain of any boat the legal right to take any British ship he wanted—well, the legal right from America's perspective, at least—and allowed the boat's captain and financiers to keep the major part of whatever they could get their hands on, including the ships themselves.

This was proving far more successful than America's anemic attempt at an actual navy.

While things were progressing on the water, George was still sitting outside Boston in a kind of stalemate. The supply of gunpowder was so low that George actually gave spears to his soldiers, in case they were attacked and ran out of ammunition. Despite this paucity of powder, in February 1776, George, for a second time, suggested a run across the water—now ice—separating Roxbury from Boston Common. Again, George's plan was rejected by his war council.

George, for the second time, agreed to wait.

He then began following, in full, the strategy that Fabius had made famous. George cut off the British lines of supply. When the British attempted a few foraging parties outside of Boston—taking boats across the water to avoid the siege in Boston's south—they were harassed by the Americans. Things got so bad in Boston that winter that they chopped down the main meeting house, burning it for fuel.

About the time George's war council turned down his second water-crossing idea, Henry Knox returned from Canada—a few weeks later than expected.

George had first taken note of Knox when he saw the ingenious fortifications that Knox had constructed, pre-George, for the Battle of Bunker Hill. One of the first things George did when he arrived in Boston was ask to meet the man who had made them. George and the Bostonian bookselling autodidact became friends; thus, George had Knox in mind when he needed someone to bring back recently captured cannons from Canada.

Knox's heroic transporting of those enormously heavy cannons over three hundred miles of ice, snow, rivers, and mountains is thought by many to be the most amazing technical feat of the war.

It was more than just technically magnificent, however.

A few times the cannons crushed through the ice, sinking to the bottoms of rivers. Every time this happened, Knox's men managed to muscle the multi-ton weapons out of the water, never losing either a cannon or a man. Step by step, mile by mile, more than three hundred miles over mountains and rivers, barely even seeing a road, Knox patiently pulled the cannons until, finally, they were on a hill overlooking Boston.

It was the sight of these cannons—and their effect, blasting down from the hills overlooking Boston, out of range of similar cannons firing up from Boston, below—that finally, in March of 1776, convinced Howe to hightail it out of Boston, up to Halifax.

George's patience had paid off. He had managed to drive the British out of Boston, with no battle, and no loss of life.

Getting the British out of Boston was not a permanent victory for the Americans, however.

It was only a temporary setback for the British.

More troops arrived from Britain a bit later that year.

With these additional troops, the British pushed George's army to the edge of the East River in the Battle of Brooklyn on August 27, 1776. But then suddenly, General Howe unexpectedly called off what could have been an American rout that would very possibly have resolved the Revolution in favor of the redcoats that very night.

He said that his troops had done enough fighting for the day. Why not wait 'til the morning?

It would seem that patience and procrastination are two different things.

General Howe is still criticized to this day for his decision to delay his attack. Which doesn't mean that what George was about to do was easy to pull off.

George was in an almost impossible position.

At this point he had nine thousand troops who seemed doomed to defeat, even annihilation—surrounded on three sides by a vastly superiour force, with his back against an uncrossable river—controlled by the Royal Navy.

No escape.

Throughout the night of August 29, a few of George's soldiers and officers kept campfires burning—but the bulk of the army was freezing, far from the fires. They were walking as silently as they could, group by group, through the mud to the river's edge.

George was finally attempting his first water crossing, although not as he had imagined, when he dreamt of daring raids on Boston.

George's idea of a nocturnal escape across the water seemed on the verge of saving things. Yet the retreat took longer than planned, and at what should have been sunrise, many of his soldiers were still on the island. But early that morning, as the stars blinked out and the dawn almost showed its face, Mother Nature saved the day by extending the night. The Providential fog that rolled in with the dawn provided just enough time for the remaining soldiers to make their escape. George was the last man on the last boat. Nine thousand soldiers got over the river without the British seeing a thing.

Take that, Penn and Teller!

As the sun finally burned through the fog the next morning, Howe's troops had finished their breakfasts and were now suited up in their red coats, ready to put the American rebels to rout. But in the place by the river where they expected to find nine thousand Americans, they found nothing but the charred remains of abandoned campfires and footprints of soldiers left in the mud.

Three and a half months later, two weeks before Christmas 1776, the struggle that George had supposed would be over before the prior Christmas clearly wasn't going as he had hoped. By this point the British had pushed the American army back to the falls of the Delaware River, where George was biding time until, as he hoped, General Lee's troops would arrive.

In the meantime, he whiled away the hours writing letters. In one, to his cousin Lund Washington, who was managing his farm at Mount Vernon, we can see how things looked from George's perspective in the weeks before, arguably, the most famous incident of the Revolution.

Before we look at the letter, though, try for a moment to get that image of George Washington standing on the front of that boat, crossing the Delaware, out of your mind.

Instead, realize this—it might never have happened.

The United States might never have existed.

If you were a gambler in 1776, and you wanted to win, you would have bet that our land would end up like Canada. Canada, whose greatest contribution to the world is maple syrup, a land that has now descended to a point where it lacks even the most fundamental right of free speech. A land whose proudest citizens are toothless men chasing small black rubber disks on ice, forbidden to speak their minds, forced to come to our country if they even want to see a competent doctor.

(We, on the other hand, have been to the moon. Can't argue with the facts…)

We *would* have ended up as a warmer, warmed-over Canada, lacking the freedoms that have made us great, had it not been for the patient perseverance of my great-uncle. He was already fighting a much longer war than he had expected, one that had been composed mostly of defeats and retreats.

Though George didn't know it yet, he was finally on the verge of an actual victory—a defeat of the British Army and their Hessian mercenaries that would astound the British and put hope and new energy into the American cause. But it was the long, patient months of Fabian strategy leading up to this triumph that had made the difference, not the stirring moments picturesquely standing up in the front of a boat crossing a river with the flag rippling in the wind behind him. (Or whatever really happened. The evidence shows it was the boatmen who did the standing, not their soldier-passengers.)

Two weeks before Washington crossed the Delaware, this is how impossible the war seemed from the George's perspective:

> I wish to Heaven it was in my power to give you a more favorable account of our situation than it is. Our numbers, quite inadequate to the task of opposing that part of the army under the command of General Howe, being reduced by sickness desertion... [we] were obliged to retire before the enemy, who were perfectly well informed of our situation, till we came to this place ["Falls of Delaware So. Side"], where I have no idea of being able to make a stand, as my numbers, till joined by the Philadelphia militia, did not exceed three thousand men fit for duty. Now we may be about five thousand to oppose Howe's whole army.... Nothing, in my opinion, but Gen. Lee's speedy arrival, who has been long expected, though still at a distance (with about three thousand men), can save it. We have brought over and destroyed all the boats we could lay our hands on upon the Jersey shore for many miles above and below this place; but it is next to impossible to guard a shore for sixty miles, with less than half the enemy's numbers; when by force or strategem they may suddenly attempt a passage in many different places. At present they are encamped or quartered along the other shore above and below us (rather this place, for we are obliged to keep a face towards them) for fifteen miles.

George sounded even more discouraged a week later, when he wrote to Lund again, referring to "the shattered remains" of militia "reduced to nothing" "by fatigue, want of clothes, etc." concluding that he feared "the downfall of our cause."

George, at this point, was not yet contemplating attacking. He was outnumbered and outgunned, after all. The only thing he could do, as far as he could see, was to make sure he wasn't out-boated, by destroying any boats the British might use. The idea that he might acquire his own boats, to enable *his* army to cross the Delaware, didn't seem to occur to him—he simply wanted to keep the enemy from getting any boats.

More patient waiting was all he had in mind.

After all, once across—or, much more likely, even before they were across, during any attempt his army might make to cross the Delaware—his army would be destroyed. You couldn't very well take an army across a river and not be seen, after all. Howe had troops stationed up and down the Delaware River, just as George did on his side. There was, it seemed clear, no way around this.

George's idea, instead, was to destroy any boat his army could find, to prevent Howe from attempting a crossing of the Delaware towards him. Had the British got most of their troops across, they would have routed George and very possibly annihilated his army, ending the war.

So George still abided by Fabian strategy, avoiding a full-on battle he could not imagine winning. As for the other half of Fabian strategy—an indirect attack to weaken the British? At the time there seemed no way.

But patience is a virtue. George had come up with river-crossing attack plans several times over the past year. None had seemed workable to his war council.

This time, things would be different.

It is easy to imagine an iconic painting of *Howe Crossing the Delaware*. This might be remembered every year on a "George Washington

Day," perhaps even in song. "How Howe crossed the Delaware, and found old George in his underwear, and shot him dead, with tons of lead, and saved our glorious kingdom."

Or whatever.

This might be sung as the fireworks of Guy Fawkes Day exploded overhead, in a combined annual celebration.

Howe had, at the time, the same opportunity George had, with certain outsized advantages. First, despite George's boat-destroying program, Howe could still have crossed the Delaware by boat. George didn't destroy *all* of the boats (after all, George was soon to find enough to cross the Delaware himself).

The British had more troops and were better equipped overall than George's bedraggled army (an imbalance that remained pretty consistent throughout the war).

In fact, there is no easily quantifiable reason that the famous image should not be Howe crossing the Delaware, towards George. There was something less quantifiable, though, that clearly mattered more—George Washington had different ideals in his head than Howe had in his.

Howe, frankly, didn't care as much as George did.

Howe was there to do a job. He had a grudging respect for the Americans and a genuine sympathy for the American cause. He was doing his duty, but not with his heart. (Both his reticence to strike boldly at any time after Bunker Hill, even when obvious opportunities lay in front of him, along with his avowed support of the Americans' rights during his time in Parliament, make his ambivalence unquestionable.)

George, on the other hand was following his principles, for which he felt it was worth risking everything.

He wanted to win more than Howe did.

His patience, in service of this passion, was finally going to pay off. George had finally figured out a way to make his idea work, to lead his army to a victory that would revive the American cause.

Although he had written Lund that without new enlistments "I think the game will be pretty well up," he had finally figured out a way to achieve a decisive victory that would also bring in a new wave of recruits to the American cause.

His course was clear.

⟨ ⟩

Well, not literally clear. There was fog, hail, and snow to get through. And a few other seemingly impossible obstacles.

Such as...remember how George had been waiting for General Lee's troops ("with about three thousand men")? Well, it turned out there was a slight problem. No one had thought to reenlist them. When they arrived, weeks later than George had hoped, Lee's soldiers basically had their bags packed and were waiting to go home on New Year's Day.

All of George's boat-destroying would then have been in vain, as in a few more weeks the river would be frozen solid, and Howe's army would be able to cross the Delaware in nothing more buoyant than their boots.

George knew that the Delaware River would probably freeze solid some time in early January. By then, George's army would have been reduced to next to nothing unless the several thousand soldiers whose enlistments ended could be persuaded to stay—doubtful, in the middle of winter, especially with no good reason for them to believe that the Americans could win the war, or even fight much longer.

George, as strong a believer in Providence as any man ever was, now had to make his own luck. He was stuck, with no good choices—he could either wait to be attacked by a powerful army that would soon be able to walk across a river and demolish his inferior forces or make yet another retreat. Either choice might well end the war in a final American defeat.

With patience, though, George finally found his third option.

On Christmas afternoon, when the army assembled for their daily drill, George had a surprise for them.

He announced that twenty-four hundred soldiers were going on a secret mission with him to attack the British troops in Trenton, which at this time was composed mainly of the notoriously fierce Hessian mercenaries. Other soldiers would be left behind to protect his position by the Delaware falls, with yet others sent on subordinate missions, to cross the Delaware on their own, eventually meeting up with George on the other side.

George asked his soldiers to quickly gather a three-day supply of food.

Soon they were marching upriver. Their destination was a point far enough away from the main camp that the detachments Howe had placed directly across the river from George's position could not see them. George gauged that the next group of Howe's outlooks were slightly too far upriver to see the point George had chosen.

However, George also knew that sound travels far, especially at night. Still, from what George's lookouts had told him, this was as safe a spot as any. George reasoned that at least the element of surprise was on his side—if there was one day of the year when the Hessians would be careless, it would be Christmas Day.

George and his troops were about ninety minutes late for their rendezvous at the river's edge. They had planned to meet just after nightfall, at four-thirty, but arrived at six o'clock. The boats were waiting for them.

No one spoke.

The soldiers boarded the boats, as quietly as they could. The boats were strange to most of the soldiers, looking like giant canoes. They were, in fact, a kind of barge that did resemble giant canoes, designed to take cargo across the river. The army had borrowed them from the nearby Durham Iron Works.

George went across on the first wave of boats.

It was cold, but not too cold, and damp, but not too damp. By the time the boats went back for the second contingent, though, the temperature had dropped. One person reported turning around and seeing one foot less of flowing water, with one more foot of ice crust taking its place, in the space of one minute. When the boats arrived to pick up the second contingent of soldiers, they crunched rather than floated in to the shore. The soldiers crunched their way out to the boats through the fast-forming ice. Their uniforms and capes became solid with ice as the water they had splashed through froze their clothes.

The stars and the moon were gone, hidden above the fog and clouds. The boatmen could barely make out the mini torpedoes of ice, sharp and fast, which approached as silently, and with as much potential danger, as small icebergs. Some continued to peer into the darkness, pushing these missiles away, while other boatmen poled the long boats across the river.

"Durham boats" were forty to sixty feet long but only eight feet wide, giant canoes with no oars. They were propelled by pushing against the river bottom with a long pole while standing near the back of the boat. You then walked the length of the boat along special platforms on the boat's side, pushing the pole hand over hand until it was at about a thirty-degree angle above the water's surface, with your hands almost at the top. At the last moment you unstuck your pole from the mud at the river's bottom, walked to the back of the boat again, and repeated.

The boatmen thought it safe to fill the boats to capacity, with the platforms along which they walked barely above the water's surface. The soldiers shivered and the wind rocked the boats, while every gust of wind or wave made the horses dance like drunken ice skaters, trying to retain their balance. Snow and hail that would continue throughout the day started pelting their freezing faces, sticking to their already icy clothes.

At midnight, when all the soldiers and cannons should have been across, fewer than half had made it. It was not 'til three in the morning that everyone and everything was on the New Jersey side of the river.

It was four in the morning when George finally had his army lined up, ready to march the nine miles to Trenton.

George's original plan had been to attack at five in the morning, when everyone in the Hessian camp would presumably still be asleep. As it happened, the American soldiers didn't reach Trenton till eight o'clock. Fortunately, the Hessians were still recovering from their Christmas feast the night before—in worse shape to meet an attack than they would have been any other day of the year, exactly as George had hoped.

Even tired, sleepy, groggy, confused, and panicked, they were still Hessians, though. George, on the other hand, was surrounded by his largely untrained and mostly unprofessional friends and neighbors.

George's troops first fired at the "out guards" beyond the perimeter of Trenton. The Hessians manning their posts returned fire, continuing to do so as they retreated, firing and retreating behind houses in town, then firing more and retreating again. Meanwhile, the Hessians who were still inside the houses—and mostly still in bed—scrambled to get up and get dressed as they shook the effects of the Christmas feast from their heads.

George couldn't help admiring the out guards—a few dozen soldiers doing their duty in the face of the blaze from the guns of over two thousand American soldiers—saying, "they behaved very well." Now the newly awakened Hessian soldiers, roused from their beds and houses by sharp sounds and sharp jolts of adrenaline, managed to act their professional, trained best, too, composing themselves in a formation in the middle of town from which they began to fight.

They were, though, still dazed and bleary eyed. George reported that in their confusion "they seemed undetermined how to act."

A moment later, though, determination finally found them.

Organized and professional under pressure, they attempted to march out of town via a side road. George inferred their intention, immediately sending soldiers to stop them.

A few moments after the Hessians were surrounded, they surrendered. They were professionals, but no fools.

It was all over in less than fifteen minutes.

Descendants of the Hessian mercenaries live in that area, to this day.

George had waited, and retreated, patiently—Fabian-style—until he found himself in a place where he could see an opportunity to strike an effective blow.

Then (and only then) he seized it.

Final victory would not come for five long years. Yet the course was set when George crossed the Delaware, his own Rubicon. George was successful because he and his soldiers patiently pushed a bit more, tried a little harder.

General Howe, on the other hand, was visiting his mistress and gambling in New York when George Washington was crossing the Delaware. The simple act of wanting something more than someone else wants it, and being willing to do more than they are willing to do, was in George's case—and that of his American soldiers, too—made easier because they had something great and magnificent to work for. Not just the victory of their side in a military engagement, or the potential career advancement or personal glory, but liberty.

George's incredible patience finally paid off when, a year after two river-crossing plans had been shot down by his advisors, and after a third relatively ignominious river crossing achieved only escape from seemingly certain defeat, he finally had his day in the fog. All of those prior events had prepared George for the most iconic moment of the American Revolution. It was a stunning if imperfect success that proved to the world that the Americans had a chance. Without this victory, the American army might simply have melted away, as the short militia enlistments came to their ends and a losing cause failed to attract more volunteers. Without Trenton, the French would never have come to our assistance, either—a deciding factor in the war.

Darker days were still ahead.

Chapter Eleven

Valley Forge

"The study of Military Discipline."
—H. de Luzancy, *A Panegyrick to the Memory of
His Grace Frederick, Late Duke of Schonberg*

If the winter of 1776 seemed tough, it was nothing compared to Valley Forge.

Perhaps we've heard that story before. But what is often overlooked, what is really shocking, is what happened *after* the long, hard winter at Valley Forge, in the spring. What our post-Puritan culture celebrates is the suffering; it doesn't celebrate how an eccentric German with a disingenuous résumé, a fake title, and Michael Jackson's fashion sense saved our country.

Hey, this ain't your grandma's American Revolution.

When George arrived outside Boston to take command of the Continental Army, he took an initial tour of the tents. A visual cacophony is the best way to describe what he saw.

He found some tents made from canvas, obviously put up in a great rush, other "tents" carefully made from mud and rocks, some "tents" of sticks, and a few even made of bricks. An observer reported that some of these "tents" were wrapped in "withes, in the manner of a basket," often "curiously wrought" with doors and windows.

Like giant hobbit homes.

The jarring point to George was that each structure was a "portraiture of the temper and taste" of the individual man who had created that particular "tent."

George was a big fan of discipline—particularly for armies. As he had written to the captains serving under him in the French and Indian War, "Discipline is the soul of an army. It makes small numbers formidable, procures success to the weak, and esteem to all."

In this he was, once again, following the example of the Duke of Schoenberg, who, the *Panegyrick* said, "gave himself wholly to the study of Military Discipline" and was such "an Excellent Commander" that to his men, "No attempt seem'd difficult, if but done by his Command."

Unfortunately, the army George took in hand outside Boston had very little that resembled "Military Discipline." It was, in his own words, "a mixed multitude of people under very little discipline, order, or government."

This lack of order had something to do with the fact that the Americans were trying to put together an army on the fly, to defend their country before it really existed. But it had, perhaps, more to do with the character of New England and Yankee individualism.

The most important influence behind this was religion.

The New England colonies had been founded, after all, for religious reasons. Some of the sects created in the generations following the initial waves of pilgrims and Puritans strayed far, superficially, from the staid images we have of the original New England settlers. All of them retained, though, at their core, the most basic Puritan idea of a personal relationship with God, rather than following God's—or anyone's—rules.

This made New England a very strange place, as George was about to learn, a place where the main rule was that the only rule which matters is your own.

The pilgrims and Puritans who founded Massachusetts had left England to worship God in their own way rather than be forced to conform to the rules and rituals of the Church of England. When they set themselves up in New England, it turned out, perhaps not surprisingly, that some nonconformists didn't want to conform to nonconformism, either. Beyond the Baptists and Quakers who were in constant conflict with the Puritan authorities, there were freethinkers such as Thomas Morton, who set up an eighty-foot maypole and a "barrell of excellent beare" and managed to get himself kicked out of Massachusetts on three different occasions—and Roger Williams and Anne Hutchinson, whose "antinomian" ideas made them so unwelcome in the Bay Colony that they ended up founding Rhode Island, as a place where they wouldn't have to conform to the nonconformists.

In one of the more extreme religious groups that sprang up around this time, adherents danced naked in the moonlight, wailing and howling, not at the moon but at the God beyond it (although those within earshot might complain that this was a distinction without a difference). In all of these sects, though, was one constant. Even in the more staid religious factions in New England, such as those that claimed a Harvard degree was necessary to preach the words of Jesus, there remained the pietistic notion that every person had to know God personally, although these more staid sects accomplished this through introspection, not naked nocturnal wailing.

When you talk to God (either by howling at the moon or sitting in silent contemplation), you don't take kindly to mere mortals bossing you around. Not even six-foot-three heroes.

Was George going to change this undisciplined Yankee individualism overnight?

Don't bet your curiously wrought withes on it.

George, in fact, was sensible enough not to try to change things overnight.

Incrementally, however, he changed the disorder he initially found into an army with enough order to win a war, while still retaining enough individualism to be American. These two attributes were both vital to America's success, as the relative order George imposed never turned his soldiers into obedient automatons, as European soldiers tended to be.

Some degree of liberty amongst soldiers fighting for liberty was going to be necessary. It was a volunteer army, after all. The overriding reason everyone in the American army had joined, including George, along with the French who would join later, was at one level the same: the quest for liberty (even if, in the French case, it was the idea of liberty in the abstract, for others).

Some liberty-loving New Englanders clung to an antinomian independence that simply wasn't compatible with the discipline necessary for any army, though. When, after his initial shock at seeing the Tolkienesque tents, George walked up to sentries during the first days after he arrived, the sentry would often refuse to let him pass to see his officers.

An officer, to be fair, might be currently engaged. A barber/officer might be shaving one of his soldiers, for example.

George was a class-conscious Virginian who believed that officers and soldiers were as distinct as cream and cats. The very different New England outlook was hard for him to fathom.

One thing he must have found most difficult to accept, though, was this: that he—George Washington—was not believed when he said he was George Washington.

"George Washington? No, mate. You don't look a thing like him." (Or words to that effect.)

George's scrupulous bookkeeping, something he maintained his whole life, tells us the price of George's first step towards solving this problem: for three shillings and four pence, George bought "a ribbon to distinguish myself."

This was a small first step towards the creation of the disciplined world-class army that George would eventually lead. A ribbon so that people would recognize him.

Most of us have heard about the hard, cold winter at Valley Forge. The bloody feet in the snow and all the rest.

For those of you who for whom the details are a bit hazy, war was a summer thing in those days. No major battles were expected to be fought in the off season. Both armies would hunker down for the winter. Valley Forge, Pennsylvania, was selected as the winter home for the twelve thousand or so soldiers directly under George's control in the fall of 1777, a year after the crossing of the Delaware had given the Americans their first unambiguous victory.

Although the first months at Valley Forge were a hellish struggle—if hell can be freezing, that is—there are no contemporary images of the cadaverous survivors to remind us of the horror.

The most famous image, which is both fictional and trite, is a painting made 198 years after the (non) incident, depicting George Washington, fully clothed and shod (as he of course would have been), praying alone in the snow (as he never did). For those of a less Norman Rockwellesque frame of mind—it was actually a guy named Friberg who made that particular falsely iconic, Rockwellesque image—Valley Forge is seen most often as a metaphor for the entire revolutionary struggle: against impossible odds, impossibly undersupplied troops suffered and sacrificed with no realistic hope in sight.

But they soldiered on.

Without any evocative images to remind us, though, the true horror is often forgotten. As fall turned into winter in 1777, two-thirds of the twelve thousand soldiers camped in Valley Forge still had no shoes. No shoes! At one point, a third were listed as unfit for duty—well, four thousand or so, which was more than a third once you subtract the twenty-five hundred who had died by the spring from the horrific diseases that sliced through the camp, all of them untreatable at the time and most of them contagious.

Dysentery, typhoid, consumption, pneumonia, jaundice, etc., all had their way with the troops. It didn't help that the conditions were horrifyingly unsanitary by modern standards (and by contemporaneous Prussian standards, but we'll get to that in a minute). Nor, of course, did the freezing cold offer any comfort.

In short, George Washington's army was in desperate conditions—even more desperate than the circumstances of the Duke of Schonberg's army that, as George had read in the *Panegyrick*, once suffered "an incredible scarcity of all things; and the rage of Hunger, more cruel than that of the Sword...weaken'd below by Mortal Diseases; consum'd from within with want; and fac'd without, with a numerous Army...." This was warfare in the era before modern technology, when the difference between defeat and victory wasn't who had stealth fighters and bunker-busting bombs, but who was best able to rise above hunger and disease to fight on.

Lack of adequate shelter, at least at first, contributed to the misery, suffering, and disease of George's men. Hobbit homes would have been a step up from the accommodations originally available at Valley Forge. Malnutrition didn't help. The soldiers survived, at times, on nothing but "fire bread," made from flour, melted snow, and nothing else. Occasionally their diet would be supplemented by fallen animals, which were butchered where they fell. They would let what little might remain rot, although the rotting was, as some small consolation, limited by the cold.

They relieved themselves where they were, the germ theory of disease being a century in the future. The cold therefore prevented at least some incidents of illness by freezing things that might otherwise putrefy.

But the cold also killed throughout that winter.

This suffering, epitomized by shoeless soldiers' bloody footprints in the snow, is the darkest image that comes to us from that winter at Valley Forge, Pennsylvania.

What most people don't see is why and how the American soldiers—those who survived, that is—overcame all of this. They emerged tougher, stronger, and better, rather than weaker, crippled, and dispirited, as would surely have been the case without the entrance, towards the end of that winter, of someone almost more prototypically American—or at least more self-made—than George Washington.

Lieutenant General Friedrich Wilhelm Rudolf Gerhard Augustin Baron von Steuben—Baron von Steuben for short—was little of what his name would suggest. For one, he seems to have been a self-appointed baron. Then again, Michael Jackson was a self-anointed King (of Pop). Self-anointing, rather than inheriting titles, seems to be the American fashion, so von Steuben fit right in.

Nor, going a little deeper, had he been a lieutenant general in the Prussian army, as the Americans believed. He had risen to the rank of major there and later been given the honorary title of lieutenant general in a prince's court, after he had been downsized out of the Prussian army. Von Steuben *was*, though, indisputably a Friedrich, a Wilhelm, a Rudolf, and a Gerhard, all at once, which is more than most people can say for themselves.

Von Steuben is often given short shrift for his inflated credentials, but as he was to make his biggest mark in a land in which no one of importance had any credentials—the most notable of all, such as Washington and Benjamin Franklin, lacking even university degrees—an observer might ask a big, historical so what? Okay, he was a captain and then major, never a general in the Prussian army, but it *was* the *Prussian* army, widely considered the best in Europe. And he wasn't just any staff officer, he had been aide-de-camp to the King of Prussia. The King!

Von Steuben was even one of thirteen officers selected for a *Spezialklasse der Kriegskunst*, a kind of warfare class conducted by the King. Presumably the baron—or whatever he was—was chosen for that class by the King himself. As von Steuben didn't speak English very well, the whole "lieutenant general in the Prussian army" thing was very possibly a misunderstanding. Meanwhile the title, if incorrect, did arguably convey his background and skill in a kind of shorthand.

Anyway, the somewhat inflated background is what Benjamin Franklin conveyed in a letter he wrote to George Washington (who was later to repeat the characterization), when Franklin was in Europe scouting out potential officers.

If the inflated military rank was of the same provenance as the "baron" title—which might, to be fair, have been the fault of faulty genealogical work by his father, not deliberate mendacity on the part of either von Steuben fils or père—or if they were both puffery, we still won the war, which we might not have done otherwise.

Von Steuben proved himself by his actions, just as George Washington and Benjamin Franklin (and all great Americans since) have done.

Von Steuben, after all, started his life in a land where a "baron" title would open up vistas—promotions, positions at court—that would be otherwise closed to him. He then came to a land where a convenient conflation of ranks advanced his career to the level where his skills and talents naturally should have placed him. We are here today, most would agree, because von Steuben overcame the limitations of his birth by the only means reasonably available, puffery. It sounds unpleasant. But it worked.

Von Steuben, who loved the pomp of the army as much as anything else, traveled to America, somewhat exotically, not with a wife but with a greyhound. Von Steuben's dog, whether by nature or nurture, had learned to howl when someone sang out of tune (but to wag his tail when the singing was in tune). The dog's short-legged, jowly master wore "a splendid medal of gold and diamonds" on his chest, which was the outward sign of an honorary knighthood. How could he be ignored?

George Washington rode out especially to meet him, and was, if not instantly taken, then very soon impressed. The "baron" may have been eccentric, but then geniuses often are, aren't they? He was, as George was soon to see, exactly the man George needed to supply the order and discipline the American army so desperately needed.

Possibly von Steuben's most important contribution to the American army—don't laugh, it saved countless lives—was putting the latrines *down*hill from where the soldiers lived. Sounds obvious, doesn't it? The Americans hadn't thought of it.

Oh, and he also came up with the idea of the latrines themselves. *Some*one had to suggest them, and that someone was the little "baron" himself. He had picked up his ideas in Germany, where latrines were standard issue. The Germans, for all their faults, are good at a few things.

Despite his Prussian background, von Steuben was American enough to particularly point out what he found a refreshing—if at first infuriating—difference between American soldiers and their European counterparts. Ultimately, the difference in American soldiers was the spirit of the Revolution itself, its *raison d'être*. Or, as Von Steuben put it, "The genius"—that is, the inherent spirit—"of this nation is not in the least to be compared with the Prussians, the Austrians, or French." While you could say to a European soldier, "'Do this,' and he doeth it," in America, von Steuben discovered, "I am obliged to say, 'This is the reason why you ought to do that,' and then he does it."

In other words, Americans thought for themselves. Even the common soldiers didn't let themselves be pushed around.

If only Americans still had this spirit today, we might still be a great country. Instead, we meekly submit to authority, we show our ID to get on even a domestic plane, we are stopped at internal checkpoints a hundred miles from any border and asked to prove our citizenship, we have arguments about what "rights" certain amendments "give" us. (The Bill of Rights does not *give* us rights; we give the government certain powers and retain all other rights. The Bill of Rights was meant to be no more than a small reminder of a few of our limitless rights—thus the Ninth and Tenth Amendments, to remind us of that. No one seems willing to even tar and feather a politician over these outrages, much less take up arms against the thugs who do far worse than impose a three-penny-a-pound tax on tea.)

A war was fought, ultimately, over the unfairness of a three-penny-a-pound tax on tea and what that represented—by men who would die rather than be pushed around, even symbolically. Even during that war, as von Steuben said, no soldier would do anything without first being convinced it was the right thing to do. They surely hoped that we, their progeny, would also know the freedom they fought for.

Today it all seems like a lost cause. Maybe, though, it's not too late.

as von Steuben is best known for something most people would argue is more significant than latrines and camp layout: organizing the troops, drilling them, and training them, thus turning them from ragamuffin nobodies into an armed force that would go on to blow away the greatest army on Earth.

He's remembered for that, but none of that would have been possible without the fundamentals he taught the Americans even before the actual training.

Von Steuben turned Valley Forge from a disorganized hodgepodge of housing, surrounded by frozen half-rotting animal carcasses and human defecation, into neatly ordered rows of soldiers' accommodations, neatly ordered rows of officers' accommodations, and neatly ordered everything else, leaving everything in its place and a place for everything, including the new latrines which were now, logically, downhill from everything else.

Von Steuben then organized the troops to fight in a Prussian way, modified for America by streamlining some procedures down to their essentials.

The most important thing to be able to do in a battle, at a time when guns were inherently grossly inaccurate, was to load and reload as quickly as possible. Any particular shot was probably going to miss, so it was important to get off as many shots as possible. Von Steuben trained and drilled the formerly ragtag troops 'til they could fire faster than they had thought possible.

Staying in formation, moving as a unit, was something the Greeks first discovered enabled them to beat less organized foes. Von Steuben got the troops to do the modern version of this.

Although his ideas were propagated to the entire army, both by speech and in writing, the soldiers under his direct command, who trained directly with him, often proved the most effective, demonstrating von Steuben's talent as well as his knowledge. One notable time, for example, his division stopped a retreat by acting in accordance with their disciplined training while all the other troops continued to run in panic.

Over time his work would, more and more, affect all of the army.

This training soon turned into the greatest amusement at Valley Forge (not that there was much else available in the way of amusement). Contests between officers and their units fired up the men's competitive instincts, turning the training into a sport. Von Steuben's eccentricities—especially from an American perspective—kept things lively. "Over here! Swear at him for me!" he'd yell to his translator when upset, other times expressing his energy in "whirlwinds of passion" as he rode about the field.

Von Steuben pulled victory out of the chattering cold and almost limitless depression of that dark winter at Valley Forge. Under George Washington's guidance, he gave the American army a form in which the soldiers' natural desires and talents could flourish.

What von Steuben started would never turn George's army into slaves, nor automatons. Instead, von Steuben's training created that quintessentially American phenomenon, the citizen soldier. The Americans were now disciplined enough to fight as a unit, to shoot, reload, and shoot again, with the speed that was needed to win. It is unlikely our army would ever have won the war without this disciplined precision.

The discipline learned from von Steuben, coupled with the innate "genius" of the American character, created a disciplined army of individuals, motivated by a mutual love of liberty.

⁓

America has fallen hard and fast since the days of von Steuben and George Washington. Today, we have ravaged the spirit of virtually limitless freedom that we fought for. The conditions we're living under today would make what happened at Valley Forge impossible.

First, von Steuben never would have made it to America—or at least not into our bureaucratized army—at all. He'd have had a background check, and if the faux baronetcy didn't stop him, surely the inflated military résumé would have. Von Steuben's eccentricities and evidence of his résumé-padding would have been easy to find in the NSA's complete collection of data from his phone calls and his baronvonsteuben-rocks@gmail.com account. (Not that federal officials would ever, ever actually read the emails or listen in to the phone calls of anybody but terrorists. Just ask General Petraeus. Or the American soldiers in Iraq who learned that the intimate details of their private phone calls with their wives back home made such great morale boosters when details were swapped among the personnel at the "NSA listening facility" at Fort Gordon, Georgia.)

The fact is, if eighteenth-century America had been the kind of surveillance state we live in now, von Steuben would never have got the security clearance he needed to train George Washington's army. Even if you believed the lie that they only look at the pattern of phone calls, what would the pattern of communication between Jefferson, Washington, Franklin, et al., have looked like? The rationale for a drone strike aimed at Monticello's cupola, that's what.

More to the point, the corporate media that controls most of the nation's minds, if not yours, would never have allowed the groundswell of support for the Revolution in the first place. Therefore, the Continental Congresses never could have happened. Therefore, George would not have been offered the post of commander in chief of so much as an army of wishing wells.

Beyond this, the ideas of freedom in opposition to the government expressed by our Founding Fathers would surely have been brought to the attention of "Homeland Security." A modern Thomas Jefferson, discoursing on the subject of "the blood of patriots and tyrants," would find himself locked in a mental hospital for his own "protection," like Brandon Raub, or in prison without bail or trial, like Justin Carter. Any "revolution" he wrote a "declaration" for would be destroyed by a SWAT team in an afternoon.

Think a bit further about the world we've created for ourselves. Destiny or no, George Washington could never be so much as a lieutenant in any army today, as he didn't have a certificate attesting that he had dutifully submitted to the bureaucratic notion of what education is. Had he submitted to such a thing, or the equivalent in his day—had he, in fact, gone to Appleby School, as he almost did—he would not have led the life he led, nor become the man he became.

The George Washington, therefore, who might have been "qualified" to be an officer by today's standards would not, in fact, be George Washington. I have that lock of his hair, remember. Let's clone him, send the clone to one of our nation's "educational" institutions, and see what we come up with.

Not George Washington.

George Washington, Thomas Jefferson, and the other American revolutionaries realized that no law, rule, regulation, nor custom that violated the rights endowed in Americans by their Creator had any validity. George's passion in fighting against oppression came from that revolutionary realization. With the help of von Steuben, Jefferson, and the rest of the Revolutionary crew, George coordinated the army, the government, and the society at large to help win the struggle.

The right to ignore unjust laws, rules, orders, and regulations is "endowed" in us by our Creator (and affirmed by the Supreme Court in the early 1800s, not to mention at the Nuremberg trials of the Nazi war criminals). It is vital to think for yourself, as von Steuben pointed out the first American soldiers were already doing, in a way European soldiers never would (and, incidentally, in a way that would get an American soldier court-martialed today).

If you fail to do what George Washington did—fight to change any law that infringes upon your freedom and bring to that fight the discipline that you need to win—you will be less than George Washington was.

Chapter Twelve

George Washington, Cincinnatus, and Bozo the Clown

"But how unprofitable is the happiest Nature, if it be not sec-
onded by a Generous Education? And what does it signifie to be
descended from Heroic Ancestours, if we are not made capable of
treading in their steps?"
—H. de Luzancy, *A Panegyrick to the Memory of*
His Grace Frederick, Late Duke of Schonberg

This chapter tells the story of George Washington, Cincinnatus, and Bozo the Clown.

Also, at one point—spoiler alert!—Michael Jackson moonwalks through the room. (This happens very quickly, so keep your eyes open).

I assume that a colorful image of Bozo the Clown popped into your head the moment you read that beloved name, that a hazy but not entirely unclear image of George Washington emerged in your mind's eye when that familiar name struck your consciousness, but that the name Cincinnatus, at best, evoked an image no more clear or evocative than a stone statue in the basement of a museum, lit by fluorescent lights and covered in cobwebs.

If that assumption is wrong, my sincerest apologies.

This chapter won't attempt to compress the story of George Washington's actions at the end of the Revolution into the few pages allotted to it, as these things are well known, related in countless books, films, television shows, magazine articles, museum exhibits, and, for all I know, greeting cards.

These stories are well known, but apparently to no effect, as our society, our politicians, and even our military officers continue to become more venal as the decades roll on, as our once-great American republic descends into the cesspool of an unexceptional democracy.

Well, at least we can laugh. Here comes Bozo the Clown.

Instead of repeating the well-known yet apparently useless stories of the most famous episodes of George Washington's life, albeit possibly told with my inimitable charm and *je ne sais quoi*—this chapter will instead give the backstory. It will tell you why George Washington did what he did.

I might point out that I am not acting on my own, but in league and in concert with the people who founded our country. I mean this in a more direct way that you might initially assume, as I shall explain.

One of the most venerated things about George Washington, in most places around the world, barely registers on U.S. radar. Just as fish don't notice water. For us, it's just there.

Americans assume that presidents—and other heads of government around the world (with a few notable exceptions)—act within certain boundaries, such as walking away from power at the end of their terms. We also take for granted that generals and other military officers never question that they are subservient to civil authority. We don't think this is worth thinking about—perhaps forgetting that, without George Washington's precedent, this sort of thing couldn't be imagined.

Originally, there weren't any laws limiting the term of the presidency in the United States. There didn't need to be. Why?

Because of George.

The tradition of stepping down after no more than two terms was a reflection of the actions and character of George Washington, retained in the American psyche and spread around the world by the power of his reputation.

A lot of people don't realize that the Twenty-Second Amendment to the U.S. Constitution, which limits the term of president to a maximum two elected terms, was only needed after a left-wing "progressive" Democrat, Franklin Roosevelt, tried to stay in power for four terms in order to continue inflicting his will and political philosophy on a country that had been founded on very different principles (those of liberty and limited government). Roosevelt only failed to reach the full sixteen years that he was trying for—or, who knows, maybe he was planning to run for a fifth term—when he died near the start of his fourth term.

It was after this episode that the Twenty-Second Amendment was thought needed. Unfortunately, although the Twenty-Second Amendment limited the term of the president, it did nothing to check other expressions of the authoritarian impulse that continues to expand the powers of the presidency far beyond the original bounds set out for it in the Constitution. The president's job, you know—the executive branch—is primarily to execute the will of Congress. George Washington believed it was one of the worst breaches of duty possible for a president to publicly express an opinion, one way or another, about a law. Much less promote laws or legislation. Much less ... well, much less.

Although presidents in our day cannot be elected to office more than twice, they can, and do, regularly act in the sort of dictatorial manner that would have appalled any of the men who fought to found our country.

It is important to remember, however, that George Washington and the other men who helped found our country weren't born with halos around their heads, nor immunity from the impulse to impose their wills and values on others. Nor were they born knowing the right thing to do, nor why the right thing is the right thing. Which is to say, George Washington didn't emerge from the Potomac River fully formed, with a shiny silver dollar in one hand and the sword of freedom raised above his head in the other.

The genesis of his character, and of the generation of people who helped found our country, was something much simpler: they weren't complete morons, and in fact knew a thing or two about history. Like the Duke of Schonberg, they had "a Generous Education" that had made them capable of "Treading in the Steps" of the heroes of old—even if those heroes weren't literally their ancestors.

Education is a relative thing, of course.

George, after all, considered himself to be uneducated. He had missed out on the English education that his father and older half-brothers had gotten at Appleby. Yet he lived at a time when supposedly "uneducated" people had far more knowledge about the history of Western civilization than most university graduates do today. Kids in George Washington's day knew the heroes of classical antiquity as well as kids today know Disney characters. Almost anyone in George Washington's time, from the designers of household objects (which reflected, more often than not, Greek and Roman themes), on up to, well, to the president, were as aware of the history of classical Greece and Rome as we are aware of the breasts of—well, name your favorite movie star or pop singer.

Pause to think of breasts. Sigh. Continue writing.

This is how the legendary Roman hero Cincinnatus came to be vital in the creation of the United States.

It started with people's knowing who he was.

Today, people know more about Britney Spears than Roman spears, and the city of Cincinnati than Cincinnatus. (Actually, I don't know anything about Cincinnati. Except I imagine it's boring—sorry, Cincinnati.)

George took his inspiration on the particular point of giving up power (rather than clinging to it until he died, as Roosevelt would) from Cincinnatus. George brought the lesson of Cincinnatus, along with other ideas, assumptions, and expectations learned from the ancient world, forward to his own day, and beyond.

These ideas and ideals are barely thought of anymore. The men who fought the Revolution did their best to let us know why they risked their lives and fortunes for something as insubstantial as the ideal of liberty and limited government. It would seem from a cursory glance around us, though, that they were not entirely successful.

However, one way they tried to bring this message to us has been successful. The proof? You are reading these words. Here, then, is a personal message from George Washington and the founders of our country, delivered exactly as they wanted:

At the end of our Revolution, the officers of the Continental Army, from both sides of the Atlantic (there is a French society, along with the American one), started a society named after the legendary Roman hero Cincinnatus. Although George at first objected to the Society of the Cincinnati (the plural of Cincinnatus), feeling it smacked of the creation of a kind of hereditary aristocracy, he eventually relented, joining as its first president.

The society limits its membership to one descendant for each of the officers who served in the American Revolution. The purpose of the society is to maintain true American ideals. It is questionable how much a society that preaches most often to the converted can help America as a whole, but it tries. I am doing my own small part even as I write these words.

By your reading these words, you are helping make the effort successful.

So, if you'd be so kind, read on.

Cincinnatus had it going on. He was a Roman senator, back when being a senator meant you were badass and dope.

Speaking of "badass" and "dope"…those people (to use the term loosely) of whom we are aware, in our society, through the media—the people, for example, who have made "badass" and "dope" part of our language—are, almost exclusively, narcissistic, cultureless cretins, rabble-rousing ragamuffins, solipsistic sociopaths whose mere existence makes it seem likely, even (especially?) to an atheist, that the "end times" are near. From politicians to pop stars, comedians to journalists, talk show hosts to professional athletes, there is no one in this group who, if you were a space alien constructing an intergalactic throughway that would necessitate the destruction of our solar system (as the building of an ordinary terrestrial highway might necessitate the destruction of a hill)—if you were such an intergalactic construction foreman, none of the people whom the media venerates would cause you a moment's pause before you detonated the sun.

We live in a society, after all, in which Bozo the Clown has more fans than Cincinnatus.

Despite this, they *are* here with us—those people who might cause the intergalactic foreman a moment's pause before he detonated the sun. They are everywhere. Look, you yourself might be one of them. It's just that in the way we have our society constructed—upside down—no truly great man will ever become as well known in our society as Cincinnatus was in his society, nor as—temporarily—powerful as Cincinnatus once was. (The "temporarily" part being the important part.)

This is because the Roman Republic was right side up.

You, likely, are at least partly brainwashed by the same element in our society that, in other societies, elected Hitler, or caused the seventy-five-year terror of the Soviet Union, or for that matter has turned much of the Western world into fascist nanny states—those possibly well-meaning but ignorant, stupid, and misguided people who believe that the rule of the demos, the mob, is somehow noble and good.

They didn't think this in Rome, nor even pretend to think it.

The degradation of a society ruled by the mob would not have surprised George and his friends. "Hence it is," opined James Madison, "that such democracies have ever been spectacles of turbulence and contention; have ever been found incompatible with personal security or the rights of property; and have in general been as short in their lives as they have been violent in their deaths." This is why we (Americans) started out referring to ourselves as a "republic," not a democracy. The Constitution guarantees every state "a Republican Form of Government," not the tyranny of the majority.

(Aside from that guarantee in the Constitution, the United States—or, as it used to be commonly referred, *these* United States—were regularly referred to as a "republic" as recently as World War II, and even into the 1950s. I recently came across John Wayne using that term in a propaganda film from World War II that I saw on AMC. It *was* momentarily disconcerting to hear "the American Republic," rather than read those words in a dusty book. However, it wasn't just that word—republic—that was different. When John Wayne talked about what Americans were defending, he talked about freedom and liberty, something you don't hear too much about any more. Especially tellingly, he conflated "freedom" and "liberty" with the totality of the "rights" America was fighting for. This was before "rights" became hopelessly conflated with "entitlements.")

Democracy—the rule of the demos, the mob—doesn't work, and never has. The "Arab Spring" devolved into riots and the rule of delusional religious fanatics in the wake of amnesia about what happens when mobs rule. It wasn't any kind of aristocracy that picked Hitler or Stalin, after all. Nor, for that matter, Obama or Bush. In non-political realms, mobs pick Michael Jackson over Bach, and *Jersey Shore* over *The Tempest*. Mobs don't have a good track record.

Cincinnatus was poor when he did the thing that has us, today, still talking about him. He was poor because of his son, Caeso, who had been accused of murder, skipped bail, and thus left his father destitute. Cincinnatus *had* been wealthy, but no more; now he scraped by on a small farm. Although Cincinnatus was poor, he was still a member of Rome's upper class—the patrician rather than the plebeian class. Class was, at this time, a result of breeding and family history, which was associated with education, culture, values, honor, and dignity. Patricians like Cincinnatus were expected to know certain things and live up to certain ideals.

Nothing is ever perfect—if it were, Cincinnatus would not be an exception, even among the members of his class. Still, Rome had ideals that were vastly different from anything commonly believed today, although those ideals *are* closely in line with the principles that abounded when our country was founded and were reflected in the actions and assumptions of virtually everyone alive at the time.

In Rome, a society that saw itself as ruled by the best sort of people (even if the "best" sort of people weren't always *truly* great), the men in charge at least had a clear idea of what values were ideal. Personal ambition, which we venerate, was anathema to them. Selfless service, they venerated.

Classical Rome didn't have a purely hereditary aristocracy like England. The purely hereditary English aristocracy had, inevitably, devolved by the time of our Revolution into a bunch of useless, drunken, uneducated, arrogant twats (that's the cliché, but there was a great deal of truth to it, as George learned through his encounters with Lord Fairfax). The genius of the Roman Republic was that positions of power weren't purely hereditary. From within the hereditary ruling class, merit—or, realistically, because no system lives up to its ideals perfectly, sometimes things less noble than merit—allowed men to rise to positions of power, positions that were always temporary.

It's that last point—that these positions were *always* temporary—that is most important.

You couldn't sit around drunk and just be a "lord," as in England (or, in Lord Fairfax's case, Virginia). Yet also, in Rome, there wasn't much worry about falling too far outside of your class. That class security limited the kind of pathological ambition that characterises the political class in our own country. The Roman Republic was a kind of middle way, between misrule by toff aristocrats and the clamour of the mob. It worked beautifully, until…well, that's another story.

The thing to remember about Cincinnatus is that he, exceptionally, *had* fallen very low for a patrician, into something close to poverty. Despite this, he retained the noble ideals of his class. His story is almost always told in shorthand as if it were only about the nobility of resigning from power. But the details are important. We're not just talking about some ancient Roman version of George Bush Sr. retiring to Kennebunk-port.

That wouldn't be extraordinary.

Caeso, Cincinnatus's son, had been overly keen, in his youth, to keep the lower classes at bay. Caeso was a big teenager and a petty bully. He bullied for a reason, though: in order to keep Rome civilized, with the upper class unquestionably on top, where both he and his father felt it belonged. The consent of the people was important. That was one thing. But you wouldn't let the mob rule. That would have been truly unthinkable.

The actions Caeso took that got him in trouble had been done in pursuit of these ideals. He just wasn't quite as good, politically, as his father, so the rabble grew to hate him. He had, to be frank, done some pretty undignified things, such as throwing representatives of the plebeians out of meetings that they had a right to attend. Still, the rabble overreacted, abusing the limited power they had, by bringing what seems to have been trumped-up charges against Caeso.

Caeso was accused of murder, in the sort of farcical tabloid kind of murder case that still appeals to our mob instincts and, in our day, sends TV ratings skyrocketing. Someone claimed that years earlier Caeso had punched his relative during, as it happened, the tail end of a plague. Later on, the guy who had been punched died. He had the plague when he was punched, he had the plague when he died, and people rarely die from being punched, whereas they quite regularly die of the plague. (That's why it's called a "plague," not "a mass bout of the sniffles.")

Now, years later, when there was a political witch hunt against Caeso, someone thought to bring up this (seemingly non) incident, for the first time.

Realizing that the deck was stacked against him in a rather pressing way—after all, Caeso faced losing his life—he left Rome. He had left a bail of ten thousand asses as a surety that he'd show up for the show trial that seems to have been preplanned to find him guilty.

Caeso's father, Cincinnatus, had to pay the bail when his son didn't show up. As a result of the loss of the value of ten thousand asses, along with, possibly, unrelated financial difficulties, Cincinnatus lost most of his land, property, and wealth.

Even so, a few years later, when a leader was needed to help save Rome, no one went running to a member of the rabble in search of greatness.

The Senate had decided that Rome needed a dictator, for a limited six-month term, to rally both the city and the army in order to fend off an attack. Invaders had got as close as the land directly outside Rome's walls. It was a dire situation, raising the justifiable fear that Rome itself was about to be snuffed out, as happened regularly to other societies at that time.

The situation was a little more complicated than that, actually. The reason Rome was in such trouble was that—in the midst of a war, no less—the lower-class portion of the army had gone on a kind of strike.

When the several senators who had come to collect Cincinnatus found him, he was tilling his own field, something most gentleman farmers wouldn't even know how to do.

Cincinnatus was made dictator for six months, yet in just sixteen days he had the situation entirely under control. He defeated the enemy, resigned his post, and immediately went back to his farm.

None of us would be here today, civilization as we know it would not exist, but for both halves of this heroic act—winning the war and immediately returning Rome to its republican form of government, rather than retaining power for himself, as, arguably, most men would do (at least for the full six months).

Without this act, Rome wouldn't have been the Rome we know, nor would George Washington have known how to be the George Washington we know.

He would not have had the model that he had. Our history would be entirely different.

The ripple effect.

It can be powerful.

⁂

The ripple effect, of course, depends on people in the present knowing and understanding the past—an idea that, itself, is fading into the past. In the more recent past—that is, George Washington's present— even moderately educated people such as George knew the stories of the West's first attempts at civilization.

⁂

Not to belabor the point, but remember—Cincinnatus wasn't just some guy who had been thrust into power. His son's life and his family's fortune had been almost completely demolished by a portion of Roman society—the rabble.

Now, he had all of society under his ultimate control, along with an excuse to go after the rabble. After all, they were responsible not just for his own problems but, because of their strike, for Rome's dire military situation.

With his job done and Rome secure, Cincinnatus had five and a half months left to exact revenge, to seek compensation—to demand it—

and to punish those who had unjustly destroyed his family, which he could have done with the justification that their strike had almost destroyed Rome.

He had impunity.

He could do anything he wanted to do.

Wouldn't you take advantage of this opportunity? Most people would think about it, at least, I think. It must have been a very hard thing to resist.

Yet resist he did.

Cincinnatus did not go back to the immense farm and property that was, by the right of natural justice, his. He did not go back to his former life, with his family's property restored by a stroke of his own pen.

Cincinnatus realized that would be wrong, in the bigger picture.

Maybe he would be right, in the short term, to get back what was rightfully his. But in the long term? What kind of precedent would this set? Someone in charge of Rome— put in office in order to save Rome— would serve himself? He would benefit from this awesome responsibility, personally?

This was unimaginable to a Roman of the upper class, or at least ideally unimaginable. The reason Cincinnatus is remembered to this day is that, tragically, most men don't live up to ideals. Cincinnatus did. Just as George Washington did.

The Romans were fully aware of the sorts of things kings did—monarchy and similar kinds of dictatorships being just about the only other form of government man had ever known. The Romans knew that their society was different from other societies because they were different (or at least aspired to be different) from other people.

Nothing as small and inconsequential as one man's personal ambition, not even his own, would allow Cincinnatus—if he acted as a true Roman—to do anything but what he, in fact, did do.

George Washington never learned how to operate a plow, himself, but in many ways his story was right in line with the story of Cincinnatus. Although not a recluse at a poor farm when he was chosen to lead the Continental Army, as Cincinnatus had been when he was tapped to rule Rome, George had been ensconced, quite happily, on his farm. He was, like Cincinnatus, impelled to serve his country by a sense of duty. Along these same lines, by the Revolution's end George *had* lost most of his wealth, as Cincinnatus had lost his wealth earlier in his life. George's farm had all but been ruined by mismanagement during his long absence.

Beyond this, there is a persistent myth that at the end of the Revolution, George Washington turned down an offer to become king of America.

There *was* talk, it is true, among some of the officers of the Continental Army, about making George Washington a king, at least a modified, non-hereditary king. The story that he was "offered" the position of king is a hyperbolic exaggeration, though.

George's nobility, therefore, in "turning down" this offer down is also somewhat overstated. For one thing, as George was clearly aware, regardless of the few people who liked the idea of his becoming king, there were surely many more who would hate the idea and even consider it as treasonous as George did (if you can be treasonous to an ideal that has not yet formed itself into a country).

If you think, "Oh, *anyone* would do what George did," consider an historical parallel happening at almost exactly the same time. The French Revolution revved itself up a lucky thirteen years after the American Revolution. A victorious and much-admired general eventually emerged from the French Revolution, too. There was only one small problem (literally). Rather than having the ideals of George Washington, this general had a bit of a Napoleon complex.

Or just think of the position George was actually in.

Floating on a sea of uncertainty, with no mooring, no stability, and nothing to look back on in living memory, nor in the memory of anyone he knew, nor in the memory of any relative or ancestor he could think of, but one single thing that provided stability, one word that was synonymous with "government"—a king. The examples he knew of government without a king weren't from his experience—or the experience of his ancestors for eons. They were from ancient Greece and Rome.

Rome was an almost mythical past, as far away from George as dragons seem to us. The history of the ancient world had only recently been rediscovered, almost by accident, in books and documents that, before their rediscovery, had been mostly ignored for a thousand years.

The ideals and lessons of the ancient world had, almost by a fluke, made it through, past what was once called the Dark Ages to the enlightened times George and his compatriots saw themselves as living in.

It was not, therefore, only George's character that made him reject the idea of becoming king. For it is entirely possible to imagine someone becoming a king for selfless reasons, if he truly believed monarchy would offer stability and solidify a new political order. It was also the ideals of Rome, and in particular the legend of Cincinnatus, along with the character of the Duke in the *Panegyrick*, that made George react as he did to the suggestion that he be king.

The somewhat undramatic story of the "offer" George had to be king went like this:

An officer in the Continental Army wrote to George shortly after the conclusion of the war, telling George something he had already heard rumors of, that the idea of making George the king of America was gaining more and more traction amongst the officers of the Continental Army.

George responded quickly, decisively, and hotly:

> Sir: With a mixture of great surprise and astonishment I have read with attention the Sentiments you have submitted to my perusal. Be assured Sir, no occurrence in the course of the War, has given me more painful sensations than your information of there being such ideas existing in the Army as you have expressed, and I must view with abohorrence, and reprehend with severety.... Let me conjure you then, if you have any regard for your Country, concern for yourself or posterity, or respect for me, to banish these thoughts from your Mind, and never communicate, as from yourself, or any one else, a sentiment of the like Nature.

Around this time King George said that George Washington would be the greatest man in history if he walked away from power and went back to his farm. King George couldn't imagine it. Yet George Washington did do just that, twice, first after the Revolution was won; and second, at the completion of his second term as president.

The story of Cincinnatus was part of George's "Generous Education," just by virtue of the fabric of the society in which he and the Duke of Schonberg lived. George and his compatriots knew enough history to know what to avoid, as well as what to strive for. The Duke's character and the story of Cincinnatus were a big part of what made George Washington great. George's own character and story, one hopes, can be a similarly important lesson for us.

Chapter Thirteen

George Leaves the Presidency—and the Republic—on a Firm Footing

"To be as intent to overcome our Selves, as our Enemies, is the highest improvement of Vertue."
—H. de Luzancy, *A Panegyrick to the Memory of His Grace Frederick, Late Duke of Schonberg*

In a time before television or photography, people such as George Washington and Benjamin Franklin, the most famous men in America at the time, existed in a kind of mental space, in the minds of most Americans, that no human being can occupy today.

With Twitter and YouTube and Google Image search, you can learn of someone, admire his accomplishments, and find a picture of him scratching himself in an indecorous way, all in forty-five seconds. From admiration to familiarity to disgust, in the time it takes an egg to go from raw to runny.

The only way you can imagine what most people thought about George Washington in his day is to believe for a moment in Mount Olympus and its inhabitants. Then try to picture—not Zeus, nor even his parents—but Gaia and Uranus, Zeus's grandparents.

So, so far away, so unimaginably different from yourself.

With that idea in mind, now try to understand how it felt to be in those United States, at that time, a society without a king in a world in which kings were thought indispensable. Start by thinking of yourself waking up tomorrow with no car, no gasoline, and no banks or credit cards …

In that situation, it is easy to imagine how people's minds focused on George Washington *as* the government.

No buildings, no symbols, no monuments—those would come later. At first there was only George Washington, whom most people had never even seen. In this context the true miracle of what George Washington did can be most fully understood. As he could have done whatever he wanted to do. He could have got away with basically anything. Who would have stopped him?

He was, after all, George Washington.

He *didn't* try to get away with anything, of course. Instead he gave something—something extraordinary. George Washington gave the United States a government grounded in the virtues that had made him great. Under George's influence, shaped by the precedents he established, the new American nation started out with a government that had the same integrity, faith, strength, forthrightness, dependability, balance, modesty, resolve, courtesy, patience, and discipline that George himself had.

Yet George knew from personal experience that it is even more difficult to conquer yourself than it is to conquer your enemies.

So George put his countrymen on the path to the self-mastery that he had struggled for and achieved under the influence of the *Panegyrick*—knowing that it could make America great, too.

Like George Washington, the American people had a temper that was naturally "hot and strong." If that wasn't clear from the Revolution itself, it became obvious in the years immediately after the Revolution was won.

The Americans had won their independence, but they didn't seem to be able to settle down to enjoy it in tranquil harmony. Disputes and even violence—over soldiers' back pay, over trade and tariffs, over the federal debt, over inflation and the money supply—erupted all over America.

Shays' Rebellion is perhaps the best known of these eruptions, not least because of George Washington's personal involvement.

By 1786, Daniel Shays was leading a protest by men in western Massachusetts who felt exactly the same way towards the eastern establishment as people such as George Washington had felt towards England, before the Revolution. Some argue that there was a great deal of hypocrisy in George's opposition to Shays' Rebellion—a rebellion of powerless people in America, against an entrenched power—simply, it would seem, because now George was on the side of the powerful.

But George Washington knew that if this sort of thing were allowed to go unchecked, it would lead to anarchy—thereafter, any time any group of people got upset with those in power, they could start their own mini-revolution.

Thomas Jefferson, on the other hand, didn't see this as a problem. Shays' Rebellion was the catalyst for his oft-quoted line, "The tree of liberty must be refreshed from time to time with the blood of patriots and tyrants. It is its natural manure."

Logically, it is hard not to side with Jefferson on this one; there would seem to be no consistent set of moral values that would make a revolution a great and noble cause when you were being oppressed, and criminal when you are one of the ones in power. Then again, look what happened in France. There were revolutions within revolutions, one subgroup after another revolting against their former comrades—devolving, in short order, into a bloodbath from which a tyranny emerged far worse than the one that had caused the whole thing. Which is perhaps why we should recall that Jefferson, though he'd disagreed with George on this point, also said that George Washington made the best real-world decisions in the country.

George's Shays' Rebellion quote wasn't as memorable as Jefferson's. (Then again, "Pass the salt" is not as memorable as "I am the eggman, goo goo ga joob.") But, in the right circumstance, less memorable is more useful.

George said, regarding Shays' Rebellion, "Let us have a government by which our lives, liberties, and properties will be secured, or let us know the worst at once." The kind of government George was insisting on required everybody to conquer themselves, recognize other people's rights, and, at least first, try to work out disputes via a political process, instead of starting a new rebellion whenever the urge struck.

The new American establishment tended to see Shays' Rebellion as group of ne'er-do-wells in the western hinterlands who wanted to shut down courts to prevent judgments against them for money they owed. The rebels themselves pointed out that the people they owed the money to were largely wealthy establishment people in the East, who had rigged the system to their own advantage, and the disadvantage of the farmers in the West.

Shays' supporters weren't unique.

There were veterans and small farmers throughout the new American states complaining about unpaid war salaries, outrageous and unfair taxes, and—do times ever change?—pushy know-it-alls from the East, inflicting their will on less corrupt westerners.

In Massachusetts judges from the East Coast would ride into towns in the west and charge exorbitant fees to hear a case, often more than the judgment under dispute. A nearly universal demand of people in places and social conditions like western Massachusetts was for lawyers to be outlawed. Of course, it would have been a marvelous improvement for civilization had this demand succeeded. This call reflects the timeless outrage of uncorrupt, honest, hardworking people at the trickery and dishonesty of people corrupted by life in the city—arrogant "city slickers" with no "real world" experience, of all stripes.

Elsewhere in the country, legislatures were busy passing laws to, more cleverly, accomplish the same goals the farmers in western Massachusetts were striving for. They passed laws voiding contracts and thereby voiding debts. In Rhode Island, they were a bit more clever still—in fact, almost as devious as the Fed is today. The Rhode Island Country Party got itself elected, then pulled off a trick combining the values of Robin Hood with the cunning of Goldman Sachs.

They printed paper money not backed by anything tangible. Sound familiar? Then they forced creditors to accept this worthless paper. The legislature thereby wiped out the debts of the small farmers through inflation, while on paper—with nothing but paper—the debts had been paid. Of course, the other side of the coin—well, the other side of the worthless paper—was that for every debtor that was helped, there was someone who had loaned money that was hurt.

In any event, the same issues that had led to outright rebellion in Massachusetts were threatening the rule of law and the security of property all over the newly independent United States.

Therefore George opposed not only Shays' Rebellion, but also creating money out of thin air.

Then as now, printing vast quantities of "money"—or, in modern parlance, doing QE or "quantitative easing"—makes everyone, especially those who owe money, happy in the short term. Unfortunately, the short term is as far as the hotheaded people who support such things seem willing to see.

They're carried along on the immediate whims of their passions.

But maturity—or "Vertue," as the *Panegyrick* called it—means conquering your impulses and putting off short-term pleasure for long-term happiness. Printing money didn't work in the long run then, any more than QE works now.

At least that's what George thought.

In addition to being unfair in the short run—printing money is in essence stealing from a large swath of society, redistributing wealth by affecting the relative value of property versus money—George pointed out, "An evil equally great is the door it immediately opens for speculation, by which the least designing, and perhaps most valuable, part of the community are preyed upon by the more knowing and crafty speculators."

George was right, you know. Wouldn't our country be better if the obvious path to riches was making something, or doing something? Yet because of fiat currency, and all that results from it, a large majority of graduates from the best universities, who presumably have the most opportunities, go into banking, a field in which they engage in "speculation" while preying on the "most valuable ... part of the community." This artificial economy affects everyone, though. Why do we hope that home prices go up? Shouldn't we hope they go down, so more people can afford homes?

Through the nineteenth century and up until the creation of the Federal Reserve in 1913, there was, overall, very little if any inflation (and some deflation). Back then, the greatest minds went into inventing the light bulb and the airplane and doing all the other things that made our country great.

Where are the Thomas Edisons today?

They're all Warren Buffetts. (And please don't tell me the invention of the iPhone is in the same league as the invention of the airplane. Although both, admittedly, led to angry birds—or Angry Birds.)

Which is to say, printing money leads, if not in the short term, then shortly thereafter, to people who actually do something productive being screwed over by people who do nothing but play games with money. In our times QE is sold as a helpful kind of "stimulus" for the economy, and thus relief for the people who are suffering the most from the recession— but somehow the bankers always seem to do better out of it than the unemployed. There's a short-term benefit for some debtors, and speculators get rich, but that's not worth the long-term relative impoverishment of the "perhaps most valuable ... part of the community," at least as George Washington saw it.

George's point of view—at least in the short term—won.

In 1787, George put the full weight of his name and his reputation behind the Constitutional Convention in Philadelphia. If he hadn't supported it, the convention might never have happened, and almost certainly it never would have produced a Constitution that could be ratified by the states.

The new Constitution would give the new federal government power enough to resolve many of the issues threatening the new country. More important to most people at the time, it put definite limits on the federal government's power.

In fact, the U.S. Constitution, repeats, and repeats again, that the federal government may do nothing—but nothing—not specifically and clearly stated in it.

The worst elements of city slicker lawyers, combined with the most venal of those spineless creatures known as politicians, have destroyed the Constitution, in all but name, giving us in our day a totalitarian nanny state of the sort that no one in George Washington's day could conceivably have dreamt of in his worst nightmare (if not quite as bad—yet—as the rest of the Western world).

The Constitution is a recipe for self-control and "Vertue" in government. That's our legacy from George—and James, and Ben, and the rest of them.

So what happened? How did we end up with the government we've got today? The honest and simple answer is that very few people know our history all that well, and therefore very few people know why our government was set up as it was. Most people have never lived in another culture where they could see, today, the direction we are heading in, if looking at history books is too much trouble.

Combine this utter ignorance, a lack of morality, and the self-dealing skills of a rapacious political class, stir in two-hundred plus years of venality, and—voilà!

Take money-printing, and specifically the issuance of fiat currency—i.e., money based on nothing but hope and dreams. In fact, any kind of paper money is specifically, clearly, deliberately, and consciously banned by the Constitution, as they'd just got over the debacle of the "Continental" dollars.

The Constitution allows the federal government only to "coin Money"—that is, to make it out of gold and silver. Article 1, Section 8.

Fiat currency finally exploded in the period following the Civil War. The Supreme Court had ruled that it was illegal—the Constitution did not authorize it (and, remember, the only things the federal government may do are those things specifically spelled out in the Constitution. The federal government may not even breathe if it is not mentioned in the Constitution, and then only the specific number of breaths mentioned and only the prescribed manner).

But then the former slave owner President Grant, fresh from leading an army responsible for killing half a million Americans, "packed" the Supreme Court with two more judges than it had ever had before and retried the issue. This time, whaddaya know? The Supreme Court agreed to a Grant-o-centric misreading of the Constitution, allowing the enormous debt incurred by the federal government during the Civil War to be ameliorated by a one-time printing of a limited amount of worthless paper money.

"One-time"? Is that what you said? Sorry, I can't hear you—this printing press just makes too much noise!

Lying next to the Constitution on the trash heap of history we find integrity. What is it about our society that makes even the word sound so uncool and naive?

The best way to see what integrity looked like in George Washington's day is the brightest place of all—lighthouses. Lighthouse keepers were one of the appointments George got to make.

What. A. Cool. Job.

You get a free house, and, in many cases, you get to build it (the new nation needed lots of new lighthouses). You get to hire people to build your lighthouse if one's not already there, you get to design it as you like, you get to live there, and you get paid for, kind of, hanging out.

I mean, it's not for everyone, maybe, but, hey …

There were thousands and thousands of new jobs, of all sorts, that George got to fill as the first president, yet he, by and large, refused to give *any* of them to people he knew or had a personal connection with. He was as scrupulous as the best kind of school principal might be in selecting a student for an award. He tried to get objective information, and he actually put the best man for the job *in* the job.

Which would seem normal, except…I mean, think about the clowns, the buffoons that get put in actual positions of importance in our day—ambassadors to the best countries, for example. Some mosquito-infested backwater or dangerous war zone gets a career diplomat, but the cushy posts, where you get to spend most of your day throwing parties on our tax dollars, are given to people who have, in essence, paid for the posts by arranging large campaign contributions.

There is no other honest word for it than bribery.

When it's not monetary bribery, appointments to posts in the government are payback for political favors. Republicans and Democrats are equally guilty, the ubiquity of this kind of behavior having made it seem so ordinary that the word "guilt" almost seems too strong.

The politicians who act this way are guilty of failing to even try to emulate George Washington. They're all cowards and disgraces in a country founded by, among others, George Washington.

Your gut is where you process your feces. It is not a place from which a president should make decisions. Nor is "feeling the pain" of the population a way to think things through. Nor is an arrogance that you are so cool you can do whatever you want.

George Washington had opinions, just as you and I do. He had things he wanted done, just as you and I do. But he didn't do them. Just because he was president, it didn't mean that he did whatever he wanted to do.

He made it an almost unbreakable rule never to interfere with the legislature. He refused to get on one side of a bill or the other. Legislation was not what *his* branch of the government did. He had a veto, but he would never interfere in the legislature.

He did have a duty to make suggestions to Congress, such as his call for the use of armed forces to protect the Western frontier from the Wabash Indians. But he would not have dreamt of interfering with the legislative process, much less ordering the armed forces to do something without a declaration from Congress. He was establishing a pattern for future presidents, a series of precedents that would keep, he hoped, any of his successors from going outside the limited powers the Constitution had given them and doing some completely crazy thing like, say—let's really go out on a limb here—starting a couple of decade-long undeclared wars, or monitoring the phones of everyone in the United States, or declaring unilateral and secret power to murder anyone he wanted to, anywhere in the world, whenever the whim struck him.

Can you imagine George Washington claiming the right to do that? Can you imagine?

George Washington was single-handedly carving out the groove for the brand-new United States government to roll in. George said, "Few who are not philosophical speculators can realize the difficult and delicate part which a man in my situation had to act.... I walk on untrodden ground. There is scarcely any part of my conduct which may not hereafter be drawn into precedent."

Why, and how, have we descended so far from this?

George's hope that his actions would be a precedent followed by future presidents was the vainest and most unrealistic hope of his life.

The destruction of all that the founders of this country fought for and hoped for is most clearly the result of the utter and frightening ignorance on the part of most people alive today, voters and politicians alike, of the values and ideas upon which our country was founded. The most nauseating thing to me is hearing politicians cite my great-uncle as a symbol, while their actions demonstrate their utter ignorance of his character and political precedent. While George's "Vertue" may be beyond their ability to even aspire to, the fact that they literally don't understand that they must aspire to it would be the most distressing of all to any member of George's generation.

Charles-Louis de Secondat, Baron de la Brède et de Montesquieu, had something to say on this subject. When James Madison was writing the first draft of the Constitution, he got the basics—separation of powers; executive, legislative, and judicial branches of government; and checks and balances—all straight from eighteenth-century French historian and political philosopher Montesquieu, who had also noted that, to succeed, different sorts of governments require different characteristics in their people. Despotic regimes require fear. Monarchies require honor. And republics require *vertu* in their citizens.

No wonder today isn't the heyday of the American republic.

By the time George was wrapping up the second term of his presidency and packing to head back to Mount Vernon, he was already worried about what would happen to our country if the people ever stopped having virtue. He, in fact, put a lot of thought into where the virtue necessary for sustainable republican government might come from.

So just once more before he steps off the national stage and heads home to Mount Vernon, let's listen to George. Because, you never know, if enough of us start listening to him again, there's a remote chance we might be able to pull our republic out of the swamp into which it's sinking.

It seems, from its name, as if George Washington's Farewell Address would have been delivered somewhere—in Congress, from a mountain top, or maybe even in a church or theater.

But it wasn't.

The Farewell Address was actually a letter George wrote in conjunction with Madison and Hamilton, over the course of four years. It was finally published in a newspaper just before his resignation from the presidency.

The only thing anybody remembers from George's Farewell Address seems to be the quote about avoiding "foreign entanglements." As with most things in the popular imagination, that isn't exactly right. George's exact words were to advise his countrymen "to steer clear of permanent alliances with any portion of the foreign world."

Why?

> Nothing is more essential, than that permanent, inveterate antipathies against particular Nations, and passionate attachments for others, should be excluded; and that, in place of them, just and amicable feelings towards all should be cultivated. The Nation, which indulges towards another an habitual hatred, or an habitual fondness, is in some degree a slave. It is a slave to its animosity or to its affection, either of which is sufficient to lead it astray from its duty and its interest.

There he is again, telling us not to let our passions control us, but to conquer ourselves instead.

In league with Montesquieu, George was so sure that virtue was absolutely necessary for his country that he recommended not only morality, but religion as a necessary support to back it up:

> Of all the dispositions and habits which lead to political prosperity, religion and morality are indispensable supports.... The mere politician, equally with the pious man, ought to respect and to cherish them. A volume could not trace all their connections with private and public felicity.... let us with caution indulge the supposition that morality can be maintained without religion. Whatever may be conceded to the influence of refined education on minds of peculiar structure, reason and experience both forbid us to expect that national morality can prevail in exclusion of religious principle.

This was a pretty common idea at the time, derived, in a large part, through observation—therefore, somewhat scientifically. The people who had created our constitution looked at societies that had attempted similar forms of government to the one we were trying, and saw that virtue seemed the key to the survival, and success, of republics.

Then they noticed that virtue wasn't so easy to keep up without religion.

As even the cynical Voltaire had noted, "I want my lawyer, my tailor, my servants, even my wife, to believe in God. And I suspect that I shall thus be less robbed and less cuckolded." In the same vein, John Adams asked Thomas Jefferson how long he thought the nascent French Republic could last, ruled by "twenty million atheists." (As was to become clear, eleven and a half years. Not old even for a cat.)

John Adams, therefore, seems to have been right to question the ability of people without "religious morality" to rule themselves. The call for liberty, equality, and fraternity in the nascent atheist Republic of France was followed by the invention of the guillotine and the wholesale murder of the aristocracy, along with the murder of just about anyone else who displeased those at the French Republic's helm. Other highlights included such spurts of deluded genius as replacing the seven-day week with a ten-day week, along with a host of other no less crazy, but far less funny "reforms," all coming from people whose "refined education" had clearly lacked sufficient measures of "vertu" and religious principles.

A little over a century later, the Communist and Fascist countries that destroyed their churches did even worse.

Perhaps George had a point. Historical precedent does seem to back him up and suggest that men without the specific virtue of religious morality can never rule themselves.

Still it may seem odd that George Washington would be the one to say that "national morality" won't exist without "religious principle." George Washington *did* keep a Bible by his bed, along with a copy of Addison's *Cato*. However, George himself was not a strong believer in religion *per se*. He was a strong believer in Providence, but as for the rituals and specific doctrines of church, he avoided them.

George still believed that the morality of a nation is supported, fundamentally, by "the pious man," in whose hands, George understood, the country's fate is held. George believed that even if the politicians became corrupt and venal, as he fully expected some to be, the people (that means you) would be a check on the government.

Part of the explanation may be that the "religious principle" taught in colonial churches might surprise you.

It's not your mother's morality (unless she's really cool).

***

The "morality" promulgated by churches in colonial America during George Washington's lifetime might, literally, blow you away.

Sermons before and during the Revolution urged Americans to recognize their "right, by the law of God, of nature and of nations" to rise up and "suspend, alter or abrogate...laws, and punish the unfaithful and corrupt" government officials who were imposing King George's tyranny on them. Preachers told Americans it was the "duty" of "every member" of the community "to concur in advancing those glorious designs"—nor did they shrink from articulating the method necessary: "blood for blood."

That's the kind of morality that the rigorously churchgoing people of Massachusetts were following even before George arrived to lead them as the commander in chief of America's armed forces. Its echo can be heard in the vigilant self-government George urged on his countrymen in his Farewell Address.

These same ideas were the essence of the Declaration of Independence: "When a long train of abuses and usurpations pursuing invariably the same Object evinces a design to reduce them to absolute Despotism, it is their right, it is their duty, to throw off such Government, and to provide new Guards for their future security.—Such has been the patient sufferance of these Colonies; and such is now the necessity which constrains them to alter their former Systems of Government."

Everyone understood what that meant. No one expected the world to change through a game of Tiddlywinks, or mere words alone.

So find yourself someone who preaches the morality of the Revolution, and remember, each day, that it is your duty to keep in check the scoundrels and oppressors who claim to be following George Washington's precedents—but are really busy trashing them.

Tar and feathers, anyone?

Chapter Fourteen

George Washington's Fame

"He was the only person who did not praise his actions."
—H. de Luzancy, *A Panegyrick to the Memory of*
His Grace Frederick, Late Duke of Schonberg

When I first read the phrase from the *Panegyrick* that now sits atop this page, it seemed to say "don't praise yourself." But that's not what it says. If someone is the "only person who did not praise his actions"…c'mon, logic, logic…everyone else must praise his actions.

So, what does that mean for George Washington? Simple. If he was really going to follow the example of the Duke of Schonberg, he would,

281

of course, not praise his actions. But he would also make sure everyone else did.

Which is exactly what he did do.

Did it work? Look around you …

We don't tend to admire people who set out to be admired.

But in George Washington's day, your reputation was like capital. So you collected as much admiration as you could.

The first half of George's life, devoted to winning his reputation and increasing his wealth, was more selfish—not *selfish*, but *more* selfish—than the second half, when George Washington scrupulously reinvested the capital he had gained during the first half of his life, to help us all.

Although some of the things George had done to burnish his reputation might appear cynical, they weren't done for cynical motives. He spent his youth in a quest for honor and glory. But during the second half of his life, he spent it all.

For you and me.

Seeing backstage, behind the scenes, how George's reputation was polished to shine so brilliantly that we can hardly see him through the glare, doesn't take away from the substance at the story's core: that is, George's character. George managed to be honorable, and virtuous, and also to let us all know about it. The reputation he gained was then used to provide him the opportunity for further sacrifice towards the realization of principles he believed in.

For you. For me.

For the world.

All this despite the fact that all he ever wanted during the second half of his life, personally, was to enjoy his home at Mount Vernon, something he almost never got to do.

❦

How do we get to see backstage?

George's authorized biographer broke his word to George, and left a document un-burnt that George had told him to burn. This un-burnt paper contains George's notes on the biography his friend was writing about him.

How did this come about? And why?

Before George's friend got on the case, and started his biography of George Washington, George was already fantasizing about how it would go. Writing to his close friend Lafayette, George mused about the benefits of a first-class "Bard," who might "hold the keys of the gate by which Patriots, Sages and Heroes are admitted to immortality."

"Acting reciprocally," he contemplated, "heroes have made poets, and poets heroes":

> Such are your Antient Bards who are both the priest and doorkeepers to the temple of fame.... Alexander the Great is said to have been enraptured with the Poems of Homer and to have lamented that he had not a rival muse to celebrate his actions. Julius Cæsar is well known to have been a man of a highly cultivated understanding and taste. Augustus was the professed and magnificent rewarder of poetical merit, nor did he lose the return of having his atcheivments immortalized in song.

At about this time, David Humphreys, George's friend and former aide-de-camp in the war, had been in Paris as part of a delegation negotiating commercial treaties. He was also was hanging around town, drinking wine, and, whenever the subject came up, talking about his friend, George Washington.

Wouldn't you, if you knew George?

He soon started writing letters to George, working up to the idea of a biography. First he suggested that "some writer"—not *him*, aw shucks, geez, just "some writer"—should "assume the pen, who is capable of placing your actions in the true point of light in which posterity ought to view them." Humphreys even suggested an outline for the proposed work focusing on George's role as an officer, while continuing to pretend he was not offering himself as the author. Just the guy who makes the outline. The pre-author.

At first, George didn't even answer his letter.

In his second letter from Paris, Humphreys told George that he thought it was important that someone should write "a good history of the Revolution, or of those scenes in which you have been principally concerned," and summarized his proposed role in the project: "I shall be strongly tempted to enter on it, more with the design of rescuing the materials from improper hands or from Oblivion, than from an idea of being able to execute it in the manner it ought to be done."

This second offer still didn't inspire a response from George. The third time, though, was the charm.

This time, Humphreys wrote, "I have become acquainted with a circle of noble & literary Characters who are passionate admirers of your glory...."

Ah, "glory." Go on …

"… and since my last letter to you I have been strongly urged by some of them to undertake to write either your life at large, or if I had not leisure and materials for that work, at least a sketch of your life & character."

Bingo.

"Sketch of your life and character."

In those pre-photographic days, of course, art always improved on the subject—or the artist wouldn't be paid. Perfect.

This would of course be a literary sketch, not a painting, but the principle still applied. Even better for George, he only had to pay with access to his papers and a bed.

George replied, "The sentiments of your last letter on this subject gave me great pleasure; I should be pleased indeed to see you undertake this business." He didn't just offer the self-appointed representative of "passionate admirers of your glory" the chance to write about his "life & character," he invited him to stay at Mount Vernon while he created his masterwork. George had just acquired an authorized biographer. Whether or not he would live up to the standards of "Antient Bards" remained to be seen.

With George's assistance Humphreys was to begin writing the proposed biography, submitting parts as he proceeded, for George's approval. Before George gave Humphreys any thoughts, though, he swore him to more than just secrecy. George was worried about having "vanity or ostentation imputed to me," so he stipulated that "after Colonel Humphreys has extracted what he shall judge necessary, and give it in his own language, that the *whole* of what is here contained may be returned to George Washington, or committed to the flames."

George referred to himself in the third person throughout his work on the biography. That is not as strange as it may at first seem, as it would have made it much easier for Humphreys to incorporate George's thoughts as his own.

Just copy them, word for word.

It is through Humphreys's disobedience of George's instructions that we now have a unique opportunity to see the way George's mind really worked, unencumbered even by the strictures of style necessary when writing to your closest friends.

⁂

Who is more inspiring? Batman or Superman? George wanted you to think he was Superman (a faultless hero), but he really was Batman (a hero propelled, in part, by imperfections).

This is good. Because who can relate to Superman?

George's preference to be seen more as a Superman sort of hero was largely a function of the times he lived in. People wanted Supermen, and George, pretty nearly, fill the bill.

For our times, though, that doesn't work. The shiny, perfect heroes that people in the eighteenth century wanted to lead them don't inspire us. How can you emulate someone blindingly perfect? Their perfection seems unattainable.

George was, in fact, not nearly as perfect as his reputation. He had a temper he had to struggle to control. He made some really stupid mistakes, sometimes ignoring wiser and more experienced men, and, it has been argued—not by me, but by a lot of people, at the time, especially—he single-handedly started a world war.

If you were a pretty great guy, but, gosh, geez, you had once inadvertently started a world war (or if people *said* you had), would *you* feel good about yourself? "I got straight As in school, once won a spelling bee, and—oh, yeah, there was that one world war I started." How would you feel about yourself? Good?

Yet George *did* manage to feel good about himself, which in itself is a miracle. George's psychological buoyancy was one of the causes of his success.

Positive mental attitudes may be overrated, but they are not irrelevant. One way to achieve the confidence George seems to have had is by selective forgetting and remembering. Studies show that any mentally healthy and reasonably optimistic person casts a glowing haze over his past. This is human nature, at least for successful people. And George was a very successful person.

Some of the things George wanted included in the biography seem vain and possibly trivial to us—his stone-throwing prowess in his youth, for example, and the fact that he became a major when he was still in his teens. Other things George wanted known to us, even if they may have been ego boosts for George, are anything but trivial. One note George wrote to Humphreys said, "Whether it be necessary to mention that my time & Services were given to the public without compensation, and that every direct and indirect attempt afterwards, to reward them I would refuse anything that should carry with it the appearance of reward—you can best judge."

Okay, so that makes George look pretty good. But it has also helped countless other Americans *be* good by following his lead and giving without asking for anything in return.

Today, there is a strange idea of "fame" that no one would have understood in George Washington's day. People want to be well known, today, just as they did in George's day. But today, it doesn't seem to matter what they are known for. George wanted to be great, like the Duke in the *Panegyrick*—loved and admired for his hard work, his heroism, his contributions to his countrymen.

Compare that with people on the television talent shows that have dominated the media for the past few years. What does this kind of "fame" mean, what does it consist of?

This has been articulated by the judges, who say things like, "Everyone in America will be talking about you tomorrow." This is said, perhaps, in to an old lady with a very talented squirrel that figure skates on a tiny, frozen lake.

Then consider America in her more glorious days. Even long after George Washington's day, fame was bestowed on people such as Wilbur and Orville Wright, who followed their true passions, which were not, fundamentally, about what other people thought of them—or at least they were not simply that other people should think *some*thing of them, and that they would do whatever it took to make that happen.

The Wright brothers didn't dress in clown suits and sing arias while balancing plates on their noses, for example. They invented the airplane.

The simple fact of other people knowing who you were wasn't the point. To do something truly great was the point. For the Wright brothers, it was flying. For George Washington, it was winning a Revolution and becoming the father of a new nation.

For you…?

Our age is so reflexively cynical, so unconsciously skeptical, that the many heroic histories associated with George Washington are more often than not dismissed without reflection or thought.

Although it is fun, I think, to see the truth behind these legends, the more fundamental lesson is that George really did figure out how to be a hero. Not just to be notorious, but famous for being great.

George Washington was born with a seed of greatness. It was the work of at least half his life to nurture that seed until it bore fruit. He believed that Providence helped guide him, along with the *Panegyrick*.

Now, you have that guide, too.

If you really see what made George great, there is no reason you can't be great, too.

The good news is, you don't even need a figure-skating squirrel. Nor do you need to be president.

The way to be like George Washington is not to do what George Washington did, on the surface. He shot redcoats, for example. Well, hey, maybe that's your thing. But probably not.

The way to be like George Washington is to do what he did on the inside, which may mean doing something that no one has ever done before, and no one else but you could conceivably do.

At its core, the way to be like George Washington is to follow your own destiny, while learning from and bearing in mind the best ideals of the past. These were conveyed to George through the *Panegyrick*, by his family, and through his education, limited though it may have been, which instructed him in the failures and successes of previous men and their civilizations.

If you trust in Providence, follow your conscience, and keep an eye on the past to guide you, while you keep another eye on your goals, then you, too, can be good and great, just like George Washington.

Appendix

A

PANEGYRICK

TO THE

MEMORY

OF

HIS GRACE

Frederick

Late DUKE of

SCHONBERG,

Marquefs of *Harwich*, Earl of *Brentford*, Count of the
Holy Empire, State-Holder of *Pruffia*, Grandee of
Spain,&c. General of all His Majefties Land Forces,
and Knight of the Moft Noble Order of the Garter.

By *H. de Luzancy*, Minifter of *Harwich*, Chaplain to the
late Duke, and to his prefent Grace of *Schonberg*.

LONDON,
Printed for *R. Bentley*, in *Ruffel-ftreet* in *Covent-
Garden*, 1690.

ADVERTISEMENT.

I*T will not be amiſs to tell the Reader, that there having been a Deſign, to give ſome preſent Account of the Life of* His Grace the late Duke of Schonberg, *at laſt, it was thought fitter to write a Panegyrick, than a Hiſtory. Several Memoirs are now wanting to perfect the one, and there is Matter enough to fill up the other: Both agreeing in this, that nothing is omitted in a Panegyrick, that is great or conſiderable in Hiſtory.*

It may be Objected, that it is a way of writing ſomewhat ſtrange and extraordinary to us: That there is very few pieces of that ſort extant in Engliſh *; and that nothing ſatisfies and inſtructs ſo much, as a Critical and Exact Calculation of times and places, as being that which gives not only a general proſpect, but alſo a particular account of Mens Lives.*

But this is eaſily anſwer'd, if we conſider, that tho' the Pens of this Nation, ſo admirably
                                                exercis'd

Advertisement.

exercis'd in all other kinds of Writing, have in a great measure neglected this; yet it is excellent in it self, and much admir'd by Ancient *and* Modern *Authors.*

The best of the Greek *and* Roman *Writers, have not only left us several Pieces that are Originals in that way of Writing; but even prescrib'd a Method to attain to its Perfection.* Longinus *and* Pliny *have far outdone the Histories of their times:* Gregory *the* Nazianzene, *and* St. Ambrose *of* Milan, *tho' in a less Polite Age, and a courser Stile, have excell'd in it. The* French *have rais'd it of late to a great height, and their* Oraisons Funebres, *particularly that of* Mareschal de Turenne, *the* Prince of Condé, *and* Madam de Longueville, *might pass for Models to future Ages, if they had not too much the Air of Sermons.*

This is ventur'd amongst the rest, by way of Essay, and if not accepted, will only serve as a Preface to the Duke of Schonberg's *History.*

A

(7)

A

Panegyrick to the Memory, &c.

THE Lofs of *His Grace the Duke of SCHONBERG* has fill'd *Europe* both with Grief and Amazement. So great a Perfon grown old in the Commands of Armies, might have promis'd himfelf a better Fate, and died in the Arms of his Friends. Hero's feem to have a title to Life ; and tho' they have run a long courfe of years, their Death is always furprifing and untimely. The end of this Noble Duke was fo to us; but the Blow would have fmarted much more, had it not been in a manner fwallow'd up with the News of the great Victory

in

(8)

in *Ireland*, and the loud acclamations of joy to *W I L L I A M the Third* fuppreft all other Paffions whatfoever. Happy then to fee before he was taken away, the fuccefs of his Royal Mafter, and to have been an Inftrument of that Victory which fettles him in his Kingdoms.

Let us pay him after his death that admiration which us'd to attend all the Actions of his Life. It is a Theam on which may be fpent all the Beauties of Eloquence, and a Subject worthy the beft Pens; in which the Orator has this advantage, That what he has to fay is above the improvements of Art, and the mean affiftance of Flattery.

The true Reprefentation of that Noble Perfon is of it felf a Panegyrick; and only this is to be faid of him, *That Greatnefs and Goodnefs, fo feldom united in others, have been in him infeparably linkt; That he has been confpicuous to the World by good Actions, as well as famous Exploits;*

(9)

Exploits ; That he has not only been a Great, but also an Excellent Man.

The real Greatneſs of Men is chiefly deriv'd from the Nobility of their Birth, the ſplendour of their Employments, and the reputation of their Performances: The one is a kind of Capacity for the greateſt Truſts ; the other an Argument of their Worth and Abilities ; and the laſt a ſplendid diſtinction from the Herd of Mortals, who act within a narrow Sphere, and are forgotten in the Crowd.

The DUKE had the advantage of the Firſt, by a long and uninterrupted deſcent of Noble Anceſtours In the *Palatinate* : That Country gave him to the World, as a new Ornament to a Family already honour'd with the greateſt Civil and Military Offices, both at home and abroad. He had in his Veins the Blood of Princes of the Empire, of Statholders, and of *Mareſchaux de France* : He brought their inclinations into the

B   World,

(10)

World, and 'made fince a vaft addition to their Stock of Fame and Honour.

But how unprofitable is the happieft Nature, if it be not feconded by a Generous Education? And what does it fignifie to be defcended from Heroick Anceftours, if we are not made capable of treading in their fteps? Education makes us truly what we are; and if Nature prepares Men to, it is that that lays the Foundation of Great Actions.

The DUKE was brought up by thofe Mafters who took care to perfect in him the Chriftian and the Gentleman; two Qualifications fo far from being inconfiftent, that the one infinitely helps the other; the Service of God fitting us for that of the Prince; Fenc'd then with Principles of Honour and Vertue at home, he was ventur'd abroad; *Germany, England, France* and *Holland* fpent his younger years. The three firft, the greateft Courts; the laft, the plaineft; but perhaps the

wifeft

(11)

wifeft part of *Europe*. Travelling was
not then, what the monftrous Corruption
and Degeneracy of this Age has made it
fince. It is now refolv'd into fmattering
of *French*, and a perfect Syfteme of all
manner of Vices: Men of Quality then
did not only learn Languages, a fine fort
of Accomplifhment; but did endeavour
to penetrate into the Interefts, Defigns,
and Inclinations of other Countries; and
came home Wifer, Better, and fitter to
Govern themfelves and others.

The D U K E became fo abfolute a
Mafter of thofe Languages, that it was
hard to difcern which was moft Natural
to him: And tho' he had not been here
of many years, yet he had preferv'd the
Beauty and Purity of the *Englifh* Tongue,
to a great degree. But he had fo acquainted himfelf with the Secrets of *Europe*, as
to underftand the management of all
Courts, and be as fit for the Cabinet, as
he prov'd afterwards for the Camp.

B 2   His

(12)

His Genius leading him to Martial
Affairs, He gave himself wholy to the
study of Military Discipline : Nature had
fitted him, for what *Europe* admir'd him
afterwards; that is, for an Excellent Commander. And really, this is the Scene of
that Great Man's-Life. It is the Theater,
where his Actions have replenish'd the
world with astonishment; and made him,
if not Superior, at least Equal, to the
MONTECUCULIS, the *TURENNES*, the
CONDES, that is, the *CÆSARS* of our
Age.

He had a Robust, and Strong Body,
capable of the greatest Hardships. He
was Naturally Active, a great lover of
Exercise, Healthful and Temperate to
Admiration. He neither Courted, nor
Fear'd Danger; ever Himself, ever Fortunate, ever preventing the worst,
and Surmounting the greatest Difficulties.

He

(13)

He would not prefume to Command, before he knew perfectly how to Obey. He began by the fmalleft charge of the Army; and ow'd his Advancement, neither to the advantage of his Quality, being then Count of the *Holy Empire*, or to the Credit of his Friends ; but to his own Perfonal Merit : He did not Court, but Command his Advancement; and fo diftinguifh'd himfelf, as to fix the eyes of *Europe* upon him, and perfwade the World, that he had no Obftacle, but his Religion, to the greateft Honour that *France* could give him.

But omitting the particular account of what he did in an Inferiour Station, as that that would change a Panegyrick into Hiftory, and fwell a Difcourfe into a Volume: we fhall only praife what feems moft confiderable. Thus laying afide *Bourbourg*, then a moft important place to the *French*, defended by the D U K E againft two powerful Armies, which he
forc'd

(14)

forc'd by his Conduct to Raife the Siege; and the tedious Wars of *Roufillon*; What more Glorious or Succefsful ? What more Wife and Fortunate, than the bufinefs of *Portugal*? That Kingdom had fallen into the hands, and remain'd fome years under the Command of *Spain*. A happy Confpiracy, if that Name can be given to the Afferting the Liberties, and fecuring the Throne of a Nation, broke at laft the fatal Yoke. But the grief of lofing the Fruit of an Ufuipation, to which time had given the face of a good Title, rais'd the Fury, and ftirr'd up the whole Power of the *Spaniards*: Befides the Natural Strength of that People, who are generally Brave and Great; they had Peace with *France*: They were eafily perfwaded, that their united Forces, would quickly oblige their Enemy to return to their Obedience. Thus they pour'd their vaft Armies into the very Bowels of *Portugal*; and had almoft put a period to the War,

(15)

War, and to that ftrange Revolution. It was then, and not before, that the *Duke* was fent to Command what Forces the Diftreffed *Portuguefes* could make. His Name rais'd their drooping Spirits: His Valour made 'em Brave, and his Conduct Wife: He retook their Towns, and beat their Enemies in all the Rencounters he had with them:He overcame them in feveral Battels. But in the laft, wherein *Don Juan* of *Auftria* had receiv'd vaft Reinforcements from *Spain*, and was refolved either to perifh, or fecure that Country to his King, who had been at fo vaft an Expence of Blood and Treafure to preferve it; He Defeated him fo abfolutely, that he never appear'd more.

The *Spaniard* was forc'd to accept of a Peace, which before the *Duke's* coming, he could not be prevail'd upon to grant; to Treat with thofe he had call'd Rebels, as with his Equals; and to acknowledge *Portugal* a Free and an Independent King-dom.　　　　　　　　　　　　　　　All

(16)

All *Europe* was amaz'd at this: The Poets and Orators fill'd the World with his Praises. *France* who is equitable to none, but those whom they think will advance their Interests, was just to him in that point: *Lewis the Invincible*, who shall be so, till *William* the Third can meet him in the Field, sent to offer him *the Baston of Marefchal de France*; a Dignity, which is to this day the greatest Reward of Merit in Chriftendom; as Ancient as that Monarchy, and never paid but to Eminent Services. But indeed, it was offer'd on a Condition, which the *Duke* rather than accept, would have forfeited all the Glory of his past Life. It was defir'd of him, that he would leave the Religion of his Ancestors, and be of that of the Prince who employ'd him. This was urg'd with all the earnestness imaginable, and such Infinuations added to it, as would have shaken the conftanteft Man. But oh, the Power of Honour and Religion! oh, the
Refolution

Refolution of a fetled Mind *!* The *Duke*
anfwer'd the King, *That he thought himfelf*
extremely unhappy, that his Majefty fhould have
fo ill an Opinion of him, as to think that all that
is Great in the World, could make him change
his Religion. That if, upon fuch low Mo-
tives, he abandon'd the Service of the God
of his Fathers, he fhould deferve the fcorn
of all Men, and in particular of his Majefty :
And that he who was not true to God,
could never be faithful to his Prince. Thus
he declin'd the Splendid Offer ; and fhew'd
a Soul that was proof againft the moft
prefling Temptations of Mankind.

But his Merit, a fhort time after forc't
that Dignity from their hands. The vaft
Defigns of *France*, made them difpence
with their Bigottry : They were fenfible,
that thofe Men carry'd Succefs and Victory at their heels : That King then fent him
the *BASTON*, without any other condition than that of ferving his Prince ; and
could but admire his Generofity, equal to

C   a

(18)

a Great Man of the same time, in all other parts; but much greater in this, that the other was overcome; loſt firſt his Religion, and ſhortly after his Fortune with his Life.

CATALONIA and *FLANDERS* ſaw him with this increaſe of Honour. In the one, he repreſt the Inſolence of the *Spaniard*. In the other, he laid the foundation of thoſe Conqueſts, which like a rapid ſtream did ſince overrun the *Spaniſh Netherlands*. He oblig'd the Heroe of this Age to raiſe the Siege of *Maeſtrick*, when nothing but a Surrender was expected.

His vaſt Skill in Military Affairs, made the Souldier bold and ſecure under him. No attempt ſeem'd difficult, if but done by his Command. He was the Love as well as the Terror of his Enemies. For no General was ever ſo averſe from Violence, even againſt thoſe he had vanquiſht. The War was never with him, what it is

now

(19)

now with some Generals the other side of the Sea, where burning of Towns, laying a whole Country in Ashes, and sparing neither Age nor Sex, is lookt on as a great commendation to Posterity.

The furious Zeal of the common Disturbers of Mankind, I mean the *Jesuits*, having rais'd a violent Persecution against the *French* Protestants; The *Duke* was involv'd in their Fate; and forc'd to leave a Service so highly Honour'd, Advanc'd, and Oblig'd by him. His Great Soul, would not suffer him so much as to complain. He was mov'd with every bodies loss, but his own; and pity'd those unfortunate Counsels, which depriv'd a Prince of so many of his best Subjects.

His Imperial Majesty had some thoughts to offer him the Command of his Armies. But this was soon obstructed by the *Jesuits*' Faction; a sort of Men, whom it is even dangerous for Crown'd Heads

(20)

to difoblige. Several other Princes courted him to their Dominions: His Duty carry'd him to the late Elector of *BRANDENBOURGH*, a Wife, a Religious, a Brave, and a Fortunate Prince.

ENGLAND then began to be diftracted, not with Fears and Jealoufies, but real Terrours. It had no more the looks of that happy Ifland; where Peace and Plenty, Honour and Security, feem'd to have feated themfelves for ever. King *JAMES* declaring himfelf for a Religion fo inconfiftent with the Laws, Interefts, and Inclinations of the People, banifht every thing that could be call'd Joy. But his endeavouring to fupplant the Ancient Religion; to fubvert the Laws; and affume to himfelf a Power, deftructive of the very Conftitution of this Government, fill'd all Men with an incredible Sorrow. The Confternation was much increaft by that Declaration, which put no bounds to any fort of Profanenefs. The Imprifoning

(21)

prifoning the Reverend Prelates of this Church, made them think it high time to look to themfelves. The Eyes, the Hearts, the Prayers of the Nation, were all directed to him who has undertaken and perform'd our Deliverance.

His Majefty Came, Saw, and Conquer'd King *JAMES*: But did not think the Enterprife eafie or likely to fucceed, without a General of Reputation. *SCHON-BERG*, the Famous'ſt Captain of this Age, was the King's choice; and this I take to be the higheſt Commendation can be given him, and the fineſt part of that Picture which is now drawing. That the Croud ſhould ſpend themfelves in loud Acclamations : That *Orators*, *Poets*, and *Gazetteers*, ſhould noife it all the world over, is indeed confiderable. But that King *WILLIAM*, who has fo great an infight in Men; who is himfelf for Wifdom and Valour, for Conduct and Courage, the admiration of all People, ſhould truſt
him

(22)

mind with *LEWIS* of *France*, the Glory
of extirpating the *Northern* Herefie.

But oh the Vanity of Men, whofe Defigns fight againft God, and are not mo-
dell'd by the Rules of Juftice and Equi-
ty ! His now Majefty Lands, and God
who takes away the Spirit of Princes,
left King *JAMES* no Refolution. But
this may be affur'd with Truth, that the
Duke's coming over, helpt as much as
any thing to diftract his Councils. The
King's Forces were far from being numerous; but the Name of *SCHONBERG*
alone was an Army. His Age, his Reputation, his Fortune, gave a quick motion
to the undertaking : The old General had
croft the Sea with chearfulnefs, and a certain alacrity, which is an undoubted fign
of Victory. But the Almighty would
have the fuccefs wholy due to himfelf.
The Kingdom call'd in a Conqueror, but
was not Conquer'd; or if it can be call'd
a Conqueft, it was only of the Hearts
of

(23)

him with the Undertaking, fpeaks the whole Character of the *Duke*, better than any thing that can be faid of him.

Heaven feem'd to have prepar'd a concourfe of Caufes, to work and haften that aftonifhing Revolution which we have feen, and Pofterity will fcarce believe. Such were the Religion of King *JAMES*; The rafhnefs of his Counfels; The laying afide his Fathers and Brothers Friends; The contriving to Ridicule and Ruine a Church, which is the beft Support to the Crown; and above all things, the falfe Glory of imitating *LEWIS* the 14*th*, in being confin'd by no Law, and proceeding by Arbitrary Methods: All thefe things made way for this wonderful change. He had a numerous and fine Army. He was made to believe that his Subjects would tamely yield to any thing. He could not be perfwaded, that *Englifhmen* would roufe at laft, and fecure themfelves and their Laws. He fhar'd already in his

mind

(24)

of the Nation, who Confpir'd to make themfelves happy, by declaring *WILLIAM* and *MARY* King and Queen.

But *Ireland* alter'd the Face of Affairs, and prov'd the Seat of that War which we had fo happily avoided. There King *JAMES* found not only a retreat, but alfo a numerous Army. He overrun that Kingdom with an incredible celerity; and found no refiftance but in *LONDON-DERRY*; a place, where the Courage of of the Inhabitants, and the Zeal of an honeft Clergy man fupply'd the want of Walls, of Guns, and all other things neceffary for the maintenance of a long Siege.

The *Duke* was fent thither with Forces highly magnify'd to us, or to Foreign Nations; but inconfiderable in themfelves. Yet he undertook the charge; and let the *Irifh* know of his Arrival, by the taking of *Carrick-fergus, Belfaft*, and fecuring to his Royal Mafter the *North* of *Ireland.*

He

(25)

He met there with Enemies unknown to him before, and which would have daunted any but an Invincible Courage; and tho' the rest of that Campaign, be not famous by the taking of Towns, giving of Battels, and other Events of noise in the world; yet Envy it self must confess, that to consider the thing in it self, none but *SCHONBERG* could have done what was done the last Winter. Mortality rag'd then to that degree, that the greatest Defeat could not have consum'd more of his Men. The Army was reduc'd to one half, and that half afflicted with infinite distempers. There was scarce two thousand in the whole, that did not share the common Calamity: Add to this an incredible scarcity of all things; and the rage of Hunger, more cruel than that of the Sword. Attackt from above by continual Rains; weakn'd below by Mortal Diseases; consum'd within with want; and fac'd without, with a numerous

D   Army,

(26)

Army, yet he fecur'd the *North* of *Ireland*; grew upon his Enemies, and made way for that abfolute Conqueft, referv'd to our Great Deliverer.

He liv'd to fee it, and helpt to reap thofe Laurels, which Crown'd the Sacred Head of *WILLIAM* the Third: The River *Boyn* faw the Conqueror lead a Victorious Army; and decide at one ftroke the Fortune of that Kingdom: Unhappy only in this, that there the Great *SCHONBERG* was loft: An Unknown and Inglorious hand gave him the fatal blow; and depriv'd the World of one of its greateft Ornaments. And this fets off the Vanity of Humane Things, beyond the improvements of Eloquence: No Greatnefs fecures from the Grave; and He, who had run through fo many dangers, and left nothing to Fortune in any of the Actions of his Life; is involv'd in the common Fate, and dies the Death of a Private Souldier.

Thus

(27)

Thus, Falls *Frederick Duke of Schon-berg, Marquefs of Harwich; Count of the Holy Empire, State-Holder of Pruffia, Grandee of Spain, Marefchal de France, General of the Forces of* England, France, Portugal,*&c.* Who for Valour, Honour, and all the Accomplifhments of a Great Captain, if we except King *WILLIAM*, to whofe Blood all thefe things are Hereditary, has not left his Equal behind him.

But all that has been faid here, is but one part of his Character. He is as admirable in his Private, as in his Publick Capacities; and there is as ample a Catalogue of his Vertues, as of his Exploits. To be Great and Good is extraordinary and difficult. To live in the Noife and Violence of Wars, and yet preferve a Religious Temper, and a Confcience tender of the leaft Evil, is infinitely rare.

(28)

To be as intent to overcome our Selves, as our Enemies, is the higheſt improve- ment of Vertue; all this was in the *Duke* to an eminent degree. He was of an Affable, Candid, and Obliging Nature. It was harder to him to deny a Favour, than to another to be deny'd. He ne- ver ſuffer'd himſelf to be askt, when he ſaw a real Merit; and refus'd with an extream Civility, what he could not grant.

Temperance, which in moſt Men is an acquir'd Habit, and the reward of re- peated Endeavours, was in him only the reſult of a happy Nature. *LUCAN* ſaid of *CATO*, in a lofty way of Expreſſion, par- donable to none but a Stoïck, *That the Illuſtrious Roman rather ſuffer'd than enjoy'd any Pleaſure.* As if Paſſion could raiſe us above Paſſion, and Senſe make us in- ſenſible. But it muſt truly be ſaid of the *Duke,* that thoſe Luſts never maſter'd him; which if they were not ſo general- ly indulg'd, would look ſtrangely to Men of

(29)

of Honour. His Duty was his greateſt Paſſion; and the diſcharge of the Noble Truſts put into his hands, his only pleaſure. And beſides the Infinite Bleſſings which Temperance heaps on its Admirers; to this may be attributed that ſtrength; that vivacity, that ſoundneſs of mind and body, which he preſerv'd to a vaſt Age; and might have done many years longer, had not the Unfortunate Blow prevented it.

He was of a Frugal, and yet a magnificent Diſpoſition. Nothing ſo Noble as his Houſhold, his Equipage, his way of Living : And yet nothing of Luxury, Pride, Oſtentation, and a certain deſire to look Great by Colour and Noiſe.

He was in his different Employments, the only Perſon who did not praiſe his own Actions; as ſilent, as if he had not been concern'd in the things that were ſaid of him: and in this, truly Great, to be above the mean Inſinuations of Flatterers.

(30)

Flatterers. A Famous Wit in *France*, was commanded to Compliment him at his return from *Portugal*; and to make his Atchievements in that Country, the chief Theam of his Harangue. He did it to the Admiration of all who heard him, but the *Duke's*. His Modefty was more troubl'd at his Praifes, than ever his Courage at the fight of the *Spanifh* Battalions. He told plainly the Orator, *That he had done nothing to deferve that large Encomium ; but only endeavour'd, to be as inftrumental as he could to the Glory of his Prince.*

What fhall I fay of the Noblenefs of his Mind; and of that Character of Honour, Truth, and Juftice, which was fo Natural to him: Exact to the Rules of Civility, Breeding, and all the Accomplifhments of Men of Quality; things that feem'd to be born with him; and yet incapable of the Diffimulation, and other fordid Arts of Court. He could

not

(3ɪ)

not promise, what he did not intend to
perform. All his Offers of Service, were
Realities. Free from that duplicity and
emptinefs, which with fome Affectation of
Mode and Gallantry, make up now the
Gentleman.

And as for the evennefs of his Temper, which in a hot and ftrong Conftitution is the more to be admir'd, it can
fcarcely be expreft. He was of an eafie
Accefs, and an incredible Patience. Never Angry, never Diftafted, but alwaies
the fame, willing to oblige, and averfe
from difpleafing even the moft ordinary
People. The moft furprifing dangers,
never betray'd in him any fear. The
moft Glorious Succeffes never fhew'd in
him any Pride. Mafter of himfelf in an
Adverfe Fortune: But that that is much
rarer, Mafter of himfelf in a profperous
State.

These Accomplifhments flow'd from a
Religious Temper. Piety that admirable

(32)

ble Difcipline, which Divinifes Man, and raifes him above himfelf, was his continual Application. The Softnefs of the Court; the Violence of Wars, and the diftraction of Great Employments, could not bear down in him that ftanding Principle of his Life. He fear'd him who is worthy to be fear'd; and lookt upon Atheifm and Profanenefs, as Enormities to be detefted by all Men; but wholy inconfiftent with the Temper of Perfons of Honour.

He was Bred in the Proteftant Religion: But did not owe the Zeal he had for it, to the firft Impreffions of Education, or the Examples of his Anceftors, but to the inward Conviction of his Mind. One of the ftrongeft Arguments to embrace it, is, that it is highly Rational in it felf, and free from thofe Impofitions, which other Opinions force on our Reafon. It protefts not only againft the ill waies of propagating Religion, such

such as Cruelty and Violence; Hypo-crifie and Unfaithfulnefs: But againft thofe defigns alfo, that are irreconcilable to the innate Notions, and Apprehenfions of Mankind.

The *Duke* was not then a Proteftant, be-caufe it was the Religion of his Country, or the Stream of the Times. He did not per-fevere in it, as Men do in thofe ways, which once efpous'd, they cannot be perfwaded to abandon. He was perfectly acquainted with thofe Arguments, which evince the Truth of what we believe. This made him inacceffible to the repeated Endeavours of a fort of Men, whofe chief care is to creep into Noble Families: And under pretence of winning their Souls to God, get their Eftates to themfelves: Attempting to cor-rupt thofe Confciences which they cannot inform: working upon the Senfes and Lufts of Men: And by the imaginary Hopes of this, making them forfeit thofe of the next World.

E   The

(34)

The fureft Argument that we are perfwaded of the Truth, being to practice what we believe; the *DUKE* had always a fincere Attachment to any thing that was a part of Religion. He was free from Affectation, Biggottry, and a fort of intemperate Zeal, which is rather a Scandal than a furtherance to Chriftianity. But of the other fide, as exact to the Publick and Private Duties of Piety; as if his Life had not been taken up with Military Troubles, but confecrated to Heavenly Cares. It was faid of *Theodofius*, by the Eloquent Bifhop of *Milan*, *That his Houfehold had in the Royal Palace of a Prince, the Devotion of a Monaftery.* Really, the *DUKE* of *SCHONBERG* fufferd no Vice in his Family; and his way of living, was the beft Pattern that could be given his Servants. And as for thofe Magnificent Offers, which the Court of *France* made him fo often, of Honour and Advancement, if he would be perfwaded to Change his Religion: How could he catch at thofe Baits, who was ready to venture all that he had

in

(35)

in the World, rather than be guilty of fo odious a Sin?

It is an eafie thing to talk Eloquently, and even Zealoufly of Religion. The World is full of Perfons who can do it to admiration. But to lofe for it Honours, Eftates, Dignities; and readily to forfake all that can make our Life pleafing and happy, is given but to few. It is a Vertue of the Primitive times, which ours are feldom capable of. And whether it comes from the ftupendious degeneracy of Mankind; or God's anger to us, who gives us over to our Paffions; that Heroick temper of Chriftianity, is almoft worn out of the World.

We faw it reviv'd in this admirable perfon; who when it came to the point, either to Worfhip with his Prince in the Temple of *Rimmon*; or lofe not only his Favour, but with it a fplendid Fortune; *chofe rather to fuffer affliction with the People of God, than to enjoy the pleafure of Sin for a Seafon, and efteem'd the Reproach of Chrift, greater Riches than the Treafures of* Egypt.

E 2

When

(36)

When rageing Popery, not satisfied with the havock it had made of the Lives and Fortunes of ordinary Men, durſt even attempt Perſons of the firſt Rank; it fixt on the *Duke* as the grand Object of its Hatred. He was one who could never be brought to humour their Superſtitious Follies; or give any hopes of reconciliation to the pretended Infallible See. The natural Character of his Mind, rais'd him above the Frowns and Careſſes of the then Miniſters, and as his advancement was not influenc'd by their Friendſhip, ſo he would not owe his preſervation to their Pity.

Nor did ever the Spirit of Jeſuitiſm appear more in its true Colours, than in the *Duke's* Caſe; that is, ill natur'd, hard hearted, and inflexible.

The remembrance of ſo many important Services done to *France*: His indefatigable Zeal in proſecuting the Intereſts of that Crown: His ſo often try'd Loyalty to their preſent King in times of diſtreſs: The unparallel'd Modeſty and Wiſdom of his Carriage

riage to them of that Religion, could not
secure him from their Fury. He muſt not
only ceaſe to live glorious, but even to live
at all, except he is Proſelyted to the Church
of *ROME.* And the mildeſt temper that
this Charitable Church could find, was, that
by a voluntary, he ſhould prevent a forc'd
Baniſhment.

Thou didſt receive the Blow with intre-
pidity; and gav'ſt to all the Members
of a Purer Religion, an Example fitter for
the Primitive times of the Church, than
thoſe laſt days of ours. Thou could'ſt pre-
ſerve thy Duty to God in the Engagements
of a ſecular Life; and ſacrifice the Intereſts
of thy Fortune, the Felicity of this World,
and the Advantages of thy Family, to the
Obligations of thy Conſcience. Like Holy
Eleazar, no Oppreſſion, no Violence, no
Rage of a furious *Antiochus,*could make thee
abjure the Laws of thy Fathers; the Pious
Cuſtoms of thy Anceſtors; or the Love of
thy People. Thy old Age would not be
ſtain'd with ſo foul an Infamy; and give
ground

(38)

ground to Pofterity, to fay, that the *GREAT SCHONBERG*, blemifh'd the Glory and Innocency of his Life, by yielding fhamefully to the Promifes or Threatnings of the Enemies of his God.

At paft feventy years old, *THE DUKE* faw himfelf ftrip'd of all that he had in *France*; and as much as lay in his Enemies *Power*, expos'd to the wide World. Yet he did not fo much as complain of a Government, in which it is hard to fay, which is moft Eminent, Cruelty, or Treachery ? He did not exclaim againft the Ingratitude of a Country, which his Valour had render'd both Safe and Glorious. Nor fo much as wifh'd the Powers above to punifh the extream injuftice of thofe left in truft below.

He had fcaice left that Kingdom, and thought himfelf fecure from that Barbarous Oppreffion which leaves nothing unattempted to carry on its Defigns; but he fell into a new fort of danger. He was overtaken at Sea by a Storm, which, contrary to the nature of things extreamly violent,

(39)

lent, prov'd tedious and lasting. Two days
and two Nights that Element was in a rage,
and mock'd both the Pilots skill and the
Sea-mens endeavours. There was no calm
but in the *DUKE*'s Looks, who knowing
whence the Blow came, apply'd himself to
divert it. He caus'd continual Prayers in
the Ship, to be made to him who Commands the Waves to be still. That Piety
which had supported him in so many dangers, was their Preservation. God seem'd to
have given him the Souls of these Men.
There is none of them that perish'd, or suffer'd Injury.

He is now himself in the Port; free from
the Troubles and Agitations of this Life. He
has chang'd the Glories of this World, into the solid Blessings of the other. Whatsoever he did in this, was only in order to
that. He has obtain'd it, and finish'd a long
course of Vertue and Honour. He lives to
Posterity, by the large share he has secur'd
to himself of the History of this Age; and
his Name cannot be forgotten, so long
as

(40)

as Men are capable of admiring great Actions.

But he has taken a furer way to perpetuate his Memory; and that is by leaving two Sons behind him, who are two exact Copies of that excellent Original. *HIS GRACE, CHARLES,* now *DUKE of SCHONBERG;* and the Right Honourable *MENAR, Count of SCHONBERG;* Persons of that Noblenefs of Mind, Reputation in the World, Capacity for Military Affairs, Religion, Conduct, Wifdom, Courage, Sincerity, Candor, and all the Vertues of Men of great Quality, as have already, and will in few Years more, find ample matter for the largeft Panegyrick.

FINIS.

Acknowledgments

I want to thank, first and foremost, all of you who support Mount Vernon. This book would not exist without Mount Vernon, and therefore, without you. All the people who work there—from the onsite firemen to the Ladies' Association which runs the whole show—to the people who support it by visiting it, and donating to it, all help keep the memory of George Washington alive.

Everyone who loves Mount Vernon would agree with me in giving special mention to James Rees, Mount Vernon's president from 1994 to 2012. As long as I can remember, Jim has encouraged me to help spread the word about George Washington, my great uncle, and his house, Mount Vernon. By building the multimedia Education Center at Mount Vernon, Jim brilliantly turned what could have become an old-fashioned memorial into a fully immersive experience. I enjoy it more than most museums, and even more than Disney World. It is the perfect twenty-first-century way to understand much about my great-uncle's life.

Still, a vital part of understanding anyone, especially George Washington, is understanding his character and values, internal things that can only be conveyed in a book. Thus Jim Rees asked his friends at

Regnery to help me create *The Education of George Washington*, to carry on a tradition I've taken part in every several years since I was a small child, usually at some special event at Mount Vernon, or a holiday such as the Fourth of July. Early on, I learned to make television and radio interviewers happy with childish jokes about cherry trees. Later, I worked at taking more important ideas from George Washington's life and compressing them into sound bites. Finally, when I was earning my graduate degrees, the penultimate eye-opener was being immersed in the world that shaped George Washington—colonial America as it intersected with the ideas and ideals of the Enlightenment, and everything else that helped shape our country.

Perfect timing.

Dr. Crackel, the editor of the George Washington Papers Project at the University of Virginia, joined Jim Rees in encouraging me to write not just any book, but an eye-opening book about the little-known formative years of George Washington's life, including a new discovery. This new discovery, we felt, would help you understand the qualities that enabled George Washington to turn himself from an uneducated, impoverished boy with limited prospects into one of the greatest people the world has ever known—successful, but also noble and good.

Beyond the helpful people at Regnery and those mentioned above, without my friends and relatives this book could not exist. I'm thinking of you as I write these words. Thank you for being as great and good as you are, and encouraging me through example as well as active encouragement, to write a book that will, I hope, help make the plan George Washington used for his success available to us mere mortals.

Austin Washington
January 1, 2014

Bibliography

Manuscript and Archival Sources:
George Washington Papers at the Library of Congress, 1741–1799.
Library of Congress website.

Printed Primary Sources:
Abbot, W. W., ed. *The Papers of George Washington*. Charlottesville:
University of Virginia Press, 1983–1995.

Fithian, P. V. *Journal and Letters of Philip Vickers Fithian*. Charlottesville:
University of Virginia Press, 1968.

Fitzpatrick, J. C., ed. *The Writings of George Washington from the Original
Manuscript Sources, 1745–1799*. George Washington Papers at the
Library of Congress, 1741–1799. Library of Congress website.

Hamilton, S. M., ed. *Letters to Washington and Accompanying Papers*.
George Washington Papers at the Library of Congress, 1741–1799.
Library of Congress website.

Humphreys, D. *The Life of General Washington*. Athens: University of
Georgia Press, 1991.

Jackson, D., ed. *The Diaries of George Washington.* George Washington Papers at the Library of Congress, 1741–1799. Library of Congress website.

Merril, D., ed. *Jefferson: Writings.* New York: Peterson, 1984.

Ramsay, D. *The Life of George Washington.* New York: 1807.

Rhodehamel, J., ed. *Washington's Writings.* New York: Library of New York, 1997.

Weems, M. L. *The Life of Washington.* New York: M. E. Sharpe, 1996.

Printed Secondary Works:

Adams, C. F., and J. Adams. *The Works of John Adams, Second President of the United States: With a Life of the Author, Notes and Illustrations, vol. 2.* Boston: Little, Brown, 1850.

Anderson, D. R. "Chancellor Wythe and Parson Weems." *William and Mary College Quarterly Historical Magazine* 25, no. 1 (1916).

Appleby, J. "Republicanism in Old and New Contexts." *William and Mary Quarterly* 43, no. 1 (January 1986): 20–34.

Ariès, P. *Centuries of Childhood.* New York: Vintage Books, 1962.

Bailyn, B. *Education in the Forming of American Society.* New York: Norton, 1960. Rpt. 1972.

Billias, G. A. *The Massachusetts Land Bankers of 1740.* Orono, ME: University of Maine, 1959.

Bonomi, P., and P. Eisenstadt. "Church Aderence in the Eighteenth-Century British American Colonies." *William and Mary Quarterly* 39 (1982).

Boorstin, D. J. *The Colonial Experience.* London: Phoenix Press, 2000.

Brown, R. D. *The Strength of a People: The Ideal of an Informed Citizenry in America, 1650–1870.* Chapel Hill: University of North Carolina at Chapel Hill, 1996.

Butler, J. *Awash in a Sea of Faith.* Cambridge: Harvard University Press, 1990.

Cappon, L. J., ed. *Atlas of Early American History.* Princeton: Princeton University Press, 1976.

Clark, H. *All Cloudless Glory.* 2 vols. Washington, D.C.: Regnery, 1995–96.

Cohen, P. C. *A Calculating People: The Spread of Numeracy in Early America.* New York: Routledge, 1982. Rpt. 1999.

Cooper, J. F. *Tenacious of Their Liberties: The Congregationalists in Colonial Massachusetts.* New York: Oxford University Press, 1999.

Earle, A. M. *Child Life in Colonial Days.* Stockbridge, MA: Berkshire House, 1993. Originally published in 1899.

Fink, R., and R. Stark. *The Churching of America.* New Brunswick: Rutgers University Press, 1992.

Ford, P. L. *Washington and the Theater.* New York: 1967.

Franklin, B. *The Autobiography and Other Writings.* New York: Penguin, 1986.

———. *The Autobiography and Other Writings.* Gutenberg online edition.

Freeman, D. S. *George Washington.* London: Scribner, 1948–57.

Higham, J. "Hanging Together: Divergent Unities in American History." *Journal of American History* 61, no. 1 (June 1974).

Hinchcliffe, E. *Appleby Grammar School: From Chantry to Comprehensive.* Appleby: J. Whitehead and Son, 1974.

Holland, J. G. *History of Western Massachusetts* 1 (Springfield: 1855).

Jefferson, T., *Notes on the State of Virginia.* 1781.

———. *Writings.* The Library of America, 1984.

Kerber, L. K. "The Republican Ideology of the Revolutionary Generation." *American Quarterly* 37, no. 4 (Autumn 1985): 474–95.

Lee, L. *Journal of a Young Lady of Virginia, 1782.* Misprint of 1787. Richmond: 1871.

Lewis, J. *The Pursuit of Happiness: Family and Values in Jefferson's Virginia.* Cambridge: Cambridge University Press, 1983.

Lewis, T. A. *For King and Country: George Washington, the Early Years.* New York: 1993.

Litto, F. M., "Addison's Cato in the Colonies." *William and Mary Quarterly* 23, no. 3 (July 1966): 431–49.

Longmore, P. K., *The Invention of George Washington.* Charlottesville: University of Virginia Press, 1999.

Marini, S. *Radical Sects of Revolutionary New England.* Cambridge: Harvard University Press, 1982.

Marshall, J. *The Life of George Washington.* Philadelphia: C. P. Wayne, 1804–1807.

McConnell, M. W. "Establishment and Disestablishment at the Founding, Part I: Establishment of Religion." *William and Mary Law Review* 44.5 (2003).

McDonald, F. *Novus Ordo Seclorum.* Lawrence: University of Kansas Press, 1985.

McLoughlin, W. *New England Dissent, 1680–1883, Vol. 1.* Cambridge: 1971.

Middlekauff, R. *Ancients and Axioms: Secondary Education in Eighteenth-Century New England.* New Haven: Yale University Press, 1963.

Miller, J. C. *Origins of the American Revolution.* Boston: Little, Brown, 1943.

Morgan, E. S. "The Puritan Ethic and the American Revolution." *William and Mary Quarterly* 24, no. 1 (January 1967): 3–43.

Patterson, S. E. *Political Parties in Revolutionary Massachusetts.* Madison: University of Wisconsin, 1973.

Peterson, M. *Thomas Jefferson and the New Nation: A Biography.* 1st ed. New York: Oxford University Press, 1975.

Pocock, J. G. A. "Between Gog and Magog: The Republican Thesis and the Ideologia Americana." *Journal of the History of Ideas* 48, no. 2 (April–June 1987).

Pryor, E. B. "An Anomalous Person." *Journal of Southern History* 47, no. 3.

Randall, W. S. *George Washington: A Life.* New York: Henry Holt, 1997.

Reed, A. C. *The Life of George Washington Written for the American Sunday School Union.* Philadelphia: 1829.

Richard, C. J. *The Founders and the Classics.* Cambridge, MA: Harvard University Press, 1994.

Rodgers, D. T. "Republicanism: The Career of a Concept." *Journal of American History* 79, no. 1 (June 1992): 11–38.

Schlesinger, A., Jr. "Nationalism and History." *Journal of Negro History* 54, no. 1 (January 1969).

Smith, A. *An Inquiry into the Nature and Causes of the Wealth of Nations* 2. New York: Oxford University Press, 1976.

Smith, D. B. *Inside the Great House: Planter Family Life in Eighteenth-Century Chesapeake Society.* Ithaca: Cornell University Press, c. 1980.

Stout, H. S. "Religion, Communications, and the Ideological Origins of the American Revolution." *William and Mary Quarterly* 34, no. 4 (October 1977).

Szatmary, D. P. *Shays' Rebellion: The Making of an Agrarian Insurrection.* Amherst: University of Massachusetts Press, 1980.

Tagney, R. G. *The World Turned Upside Down: Essex County during America's Turbulent Years, 1763–1790.* West Newbury: Essex County History, 1989.

Taylor, R. J. *Western Massachusetts in the Revolution.* Providence: Brown University Press, 1954.

Washington, G. W. P. C. *Recollections and Private Memoirs of George Washington.* New York: Derby & Jackson, 1860.

Whitefield, G. *George Whitefield's Journals.* London: Banner of Truth Trust, 1960.

Winthrop, J. *City upon a Hill.* 1630. http://www.mtholyoke.edu/acad/intrel/winthrop.htm.

Wood, G. S. *The Radicalism of the American Revolution.* New York: Alfred A. Knopf, 1992.

Zuckerman, M. "William Byrd's Family." *Perspectives in Modern History* 12 (1979): 253–311.

Index